Gavin White is also author of:

Babylonian Star-lore. An Illustrated Guide to the Star-lore and
Constellations of Ancient Babylonia
[To be updated & republished by late 2014]

The Queen of Heaven

The Queen of Heaven

A New Interpretation of the Goddess in Ancient Near Eastern Art

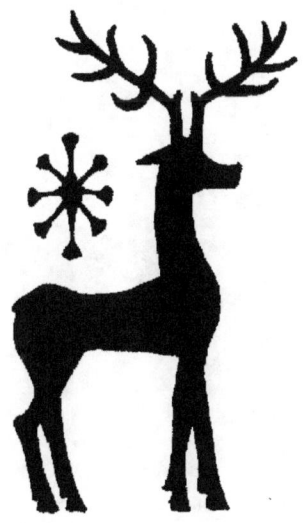

Written & Illustrated by

Gavin White

Solaria Publications
9 Sanford Walk
New Cross
London SE14 6NB

ISBN: 978-0-9559037-1-7
First Published 2013
© 2013 Gavin White

Contents

Foreword & Introduction   9

PART ONE: The Origins of the Child
The Child   13
Metaphors of the Child   17
Animal Metaphors   27
The Seed of Mankind   35
The Symbol System   44

PART TWO: The Goddess of the Skies
The Goddess of Life   53
The Bird Goddess   60
The Storm Goddess   72
The Celestial Goddess   85
The Fertile Skies   97
The Waters of the Sun   105
The Flower of Heaven   116

PART THREE: The Fall of the Goddess
The Battle of the Gods   131
The Sun & the Child   144
Death Enters the World   158

Bibliography   169
Symbol Index   172
Sumerian Signs   183
Word Index   186
Chronological Tables   188

PRONUNCIATION GUIDE

I have followed the common practice of rendering Sumerian terms either in bold or capital letters, and setting Akkadian terms in italics. Modern renditions of Sumerian and Akkadian use a number of alphabetic characters unfamiliar to most western readers; the four special characters below represent the following sounds:

Š – should be pronounced as "sh" as in 'shop'. It is often rendered as 'sh' in modern works.

Ṣ – should be pronounced as "ts" as in 'Tsar'. Some modern works on Assyriology choose to render this character as 'z'.

Ṭ – is a harder sound than ordinary "t".

Ḫ – should be pronounced as "ch" as in Scottish 'loch'.

In addition to these characters, Akkadian recognises three main forms of vowels – short, long and contracted, the last of which is really a combination of two vowel sounds. The respective lengths of the vowels are represented as 'a', '$\bar{a}$' and '$\hat{a}$'.

A NOTE ON CUNEIFORM SIGNS

The sign-forms used in this book are taken from the very earliest tablets so far discovered in Mesopotamia. The reason why I have adopted these early signs is that they are much more differentiated and it is generally easier to see the pictorial basis for the signs.

Foreword

The seed of this book was originally born out of an email correspondence with a fellow enthusiast of the ancient world named Tom van Bakel.[1] Tom was kind enough to share with me some of his ideas about Near Eastern art. Tom's main theory was that a great many symbolic designs found on ancient cylinder seals were specifically about the birth of children. These ideas interested me. They seemed new, and on the evidence Tom produced, they seemed to be worthwhile exploring and discussing further.

For many months we corresponded, Tom pouring forth ideas and endless illustrations of seal designs, myself reacting, criticising and commenting upon various aspects of his ideas. At first, I was pretty sceptical of many aspects of Tom's ideas; indeed, we still disagree in many areas. Nevertheless, Tom's fundamental insight that the child and human fertility were at the heart of so many ancient designs was slowly being absorbed by me and was gradually growing on me.

A year or more later, I came across a Sumerian incantation concerning the safe birth of a child and in the process of reading this I had a flash of intuition. What I could only describe as one of those moments when a whole mass of ideas suddenly come together and make sense.

I realised that the symbolic imagery of the child was fundamental to understanding the nature of the archaic heavens and the animal symbolism found in the constellations. A few days later, I emailed Tom and mapped out a basic scheme of symbolic metaphors that integrated the essential insights of his theory with my own ideas and background knowledge concerning the Ancient Near East.

Everything else followed on from that. The application and exploration of these ideas as an interpretative model led to me to explore anew the annals of Mesopotamian art – a treasure-house of images stretching back into prehistoric times. This book, the first of a projected series, is the end result – the working out of that original moment of insight.

Without Tom's insights, his patient persistence and continuing correspondence, this book would never have been written and for that reason I'd like to dedicate it to Tom van Bakel, of Sint Pancras, the Netherlands.

---

[1] Tom originally studied building engineering and became interested in the sacred architecture of churches, mosques and temples. He developed some new ideas on the as yet undeciphered Indus script before bringing his attention to the seal designs of the Ancient Near East. To access Tom's ideas for yourselves please visit his websites – searching for "Tom van Bakel"

Introduction

Art is as old as humanity. While the languages of prehistory are irretrievably lost, and the material artefacts – chipped stones and carved bones – tell us so little about our forebears, the artworks of prehistory can still speak to us across untold millennia. Even so, isolated carvings of bison or the silhouettes of hands on the walls of a cave, although they may allow us to make an emotional connection with their creators, remain stubbornly silent as to their meanings and the creative impulse that inspired their making.

It is only in the Neolithic period, with the invention of pottery, that the situation improves. Many thousands of fragmented pots, vases and storage jars, unearthed from far-flung sites attest to the emergence of an artistic tradition. Many such shards are decorated with geometric designs, plant-forms and animals. Together, they constitute the first tangible evidence of a symbolic tradition – a basic language of visual forms.

Images and icons have their own unique way of communicating. For the modern world, the 'narrative' that these images speak is another lost language. But like the un-deciphered scripts of extinct cultures their meanings can be recovered if we can ascertain the overall context of the designs and the meanings of the individual signs. The task at hand is rather like breaking a code – if you have sufficient material and variant forms, then you are in with a chance.

The resultant decipherment of the artistic symbols can present a very different picture to that gained from written myths. The same truth is borne out in many other cultures [2] where the icons of native art and the narrative of written myth can be totally mismatched, even contradictory in nature. In this book, we shall always follow the narrative of symbols rather than words.

For these reasons, a formal written introduction to this book, so dedicated to the traditional visual arts, is not at all appropriate. Exploring a symbol system is a bit like learning a new language; it is best to just jump in and start.

---

[2] A very good introduction to the relationship between art and myth in Greek culture is T H Carpenter's *Art and Myth in Ancient Greece*, Thames & Hudson, 1991.

PART ONE:
The Origins of the Child

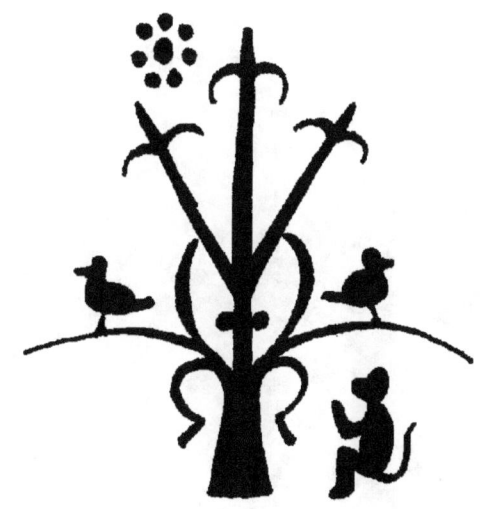

The Child

The nature of the child, and the forces that created him, lie at the very heart of our present study into ancient art and symbolism. Images of children, both boys and girls, appear in many ancient designs, but one particular type of design stands out from the rest. It has a very regular set of characters and is obviously centred upon the child. A very good example is seen below in figure 1:

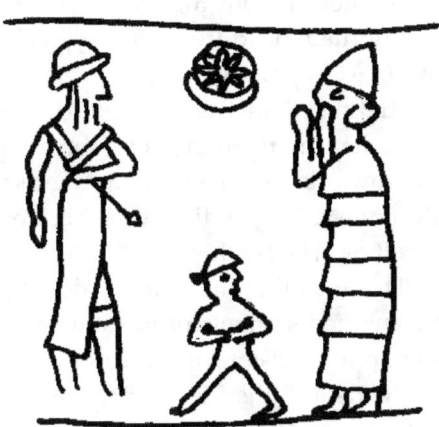

1 A Syrian seal centring upon a child [1]

This simple image will act as a template to start us off on our study of ancient art. We will start by examining its component parts.

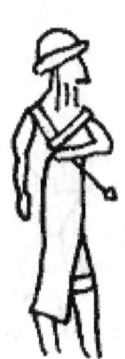

Over on the left-hand side, we see a well-attired male figure. Previous studies have identified him as a high-ranking official or dignitary. In some instances this rather standardised figure can even represent the king.[2] The distinction between noble and king is difficult to pin down as far as these designs are concerned, but for our purposes it is perfectly acceptable to call him 'the Lord' or 'his Lordship'.

His Lordship typically holds some type of weapon in one of his hands, sometimes a spear or a curved scimitar or, as here, a short-handled mace. He is very easy to recognise due to his elaborate fringed dress and his domed hat. Another characteristic feature of the Lord is the way he is always depicted with one leg emerging from his tunic. This combination of elements makes the figure of the Lord very easy to identify, even in badly damaged or fragmentary examples.

---

[1] Syrian seal, 18th century BCE. Collon 1987, fig 183 on page 49.
[2] Collon 1975, page 186-8 under the section 'male figure with high oval headdress'.

The Child

The next major figure is seen over on the right-hand side of the seal. Here we see an elegant female figure wearing a multi-layered or flounced dress. She can be confidently identified as a Lama goddess, a rather generic class of 'minor' goddesses who are very commonly seen in a wide variety of ancient designs. Her generic image may well be based on a class of priestess who are frequently seen introducing worshippers into the presence of the gods. In this particular design, she wears a simple pointed hat but more often than not she is seen wearing a horned headdress, the typical headgear of all divine beings in Mesopotamian art.

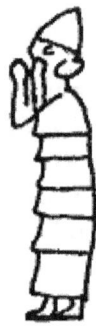

Previous studies have defined Lama as an 'intercessor' between the divine and human worlds.[3] And fulfilling her intermediary role, she often appears in temple scenes leading human worshippers towards the images and inner sanctums of the gods (*see fig 148*). Her function in this design is clearly indicated by her posture – with up-raised arms she prays to the gods on behalf of his Lordship.

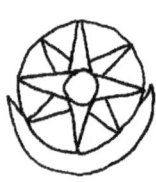

The gods that the Lama goddess prays to are represented by the combined symbols of the sun and moon that are typically set in the upper registers of these designs. In ancient thought the host of the gods and the idea of heaven are so closely inter-connected that they can almost be treated as identical concepts. This close identity is neatly expressed in the Sumerian writing system where both 'god' and 'heaven' are written with one and the same sign (**An**), which is represented as an eight-rayed star (*right*).[4] The role that the gods play in these designs will gradually be revealed in the course of the book. For now we should simply note that the gods and the heavens are an ever-present and integral part of bigger picture.

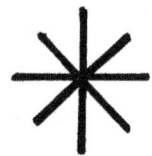

The **An**-sign

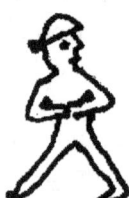

Between the Lord and the Lama-goddess stands the centre of all our attention – the tiny figure of a child. In this example, as in many others, he wears some kind of cap. The other thing that stands out about him is his unusual posture with legs set widely apart. This may well be explained by sets of young boys (*right*),

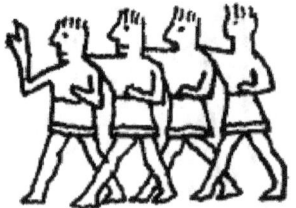

Detail from fig 80

---

[3] Collon 1975, page 181, under the section 'the Babylonian goddess'. This reference indicates that her more precise role is as mediator between human worshippers and their tutelary, or protective, deities.
[4] PSD: DIĜIR [deity] (often written DINGIR in other sources) & AN [sky].

The Child

which show identical children seemingly marching along in unison. In other designs the boys can be intertwined with each other in more complex geometric patterns.

Now that we have looked at the different elements of our template design, we need to start asking how they all fit together and make sense as an integral whole.

The role of the Lama-goddess provides the basic answer to our question as she links all the other elements together. From what we have learnt already, we can be sure that she is praying to the gods on behalf of the Lord. But what is she actually asking of the gods?

Judging by this first design alone, two possible answers come to the fore. One possibility is that this is a quaint family scene in the temple, where the Lama-goddess prays to the gods to protect, or otherwise lend a beneficial influence to, the Lord and his son.

The other possibility is that the Lama-goddess is praying to the gods to grant the Lord a son and heir. In other words, the child is not a material reality as yet but a 'future outcome' that is wished for. You could almost vocalise Lama's prayer as: "May the gods in heaven, grant the Lord a son and heir". As the investigation unfolds it will become apparent that this second interpretation is the only solution that makes any real sense of our material.

Even though the child is widely represented as a boy, there are a number of examples that replace his figure with that of a tiny girl (*below*). From such examples, we can infer that the underlying meaning of these designs is to petition the gods to grant his Lordship the broader boon of healthy children, boys and girls, who will continue his bloodline and family name.

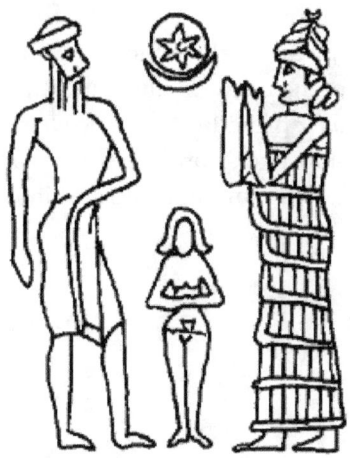

2 Seal design with a girl [5]

---

[5] Detail of an Old Babylonian seal. Frankfort 1939, detail of text fig 40.

The Child

Interpreting these designs within the sphere of human reproduction, brings them to life, even in the modern era, as they touch on such intimately and timeless human concerns. The relentless drive for progeny is the impulse behind these simple images and a whole genre of ancient art we are about to start exploring.

Before that, however, it will be useful to summarise the basic layout of these template designs (*figs 1 & 2*) in a semi-schematic format. This focuses our attention on the central place of the child and the heavens in these designs:

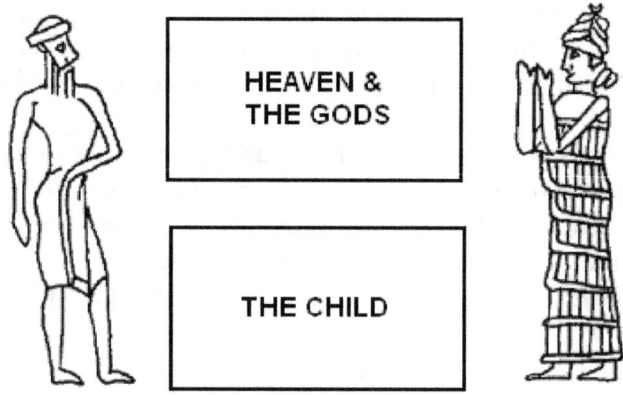

Schematic diagram of the template design

The four basic elements seen in the template – the Lord and Lama-goddess, the heavenly sign and the child – form the essential cast of characters in a multitude of closely related designs. As a general rule, the Lord and Lama-goddess are the unchanging elements. Apart from minor changes like their hats or the weapons carried by the Lord, these two figures appear in almost identical format in dozens of designs. On the other hand, the way that the heavenly realms and the child are portrayed changes. And this is the important part, as it provides the basic elements of a symbolic key.

In the next section, we will start to explore these new variations set upon the theme of the child and, by doing so, we will start our journey into the symbolic dimensions of ancient art.

Metaphors of the Child

From time to time, almost every parent will refer to their children by a variety of affectionate names. At times they can be 'playful cubs' or 'cheeky monkeys' even 'little monsters'; the tiniest of babies can also be referred to as 'ducklings', 'squabs' and 'fish's fry'. Beyond being characterful and emotionally engaging nicknames, these designations are actually a very useful way to approach the principles of visual symbolism.

Of course, a human child isn't really a monkey or a cub. We are using the terms as 'metaphors' – which the dictionary defines as 'figures of speech founded on some kind of resemblance'. This mode of thought, so common and casual in nature, ultimately provides us with a key to understanding how ancient cultures expressed themselves through their artwork. However, the visual metaphors of ancient art are rather different from their literary counterparts as visual metaphors posit a much stronger sense of identity between the symbol and the thing it represents.

One of the commonest and most important such metaphors was to represent the human child by the figure of a bull-calf.

The Bull Calf – the 1st Major Metaphor

The fundamental connection between the calf and child can be surmised from our first design. All the familiar elements of the template design are present and easily recognisable, but the kneeling figure of the child is here joined by the symbolic figure of the calf:

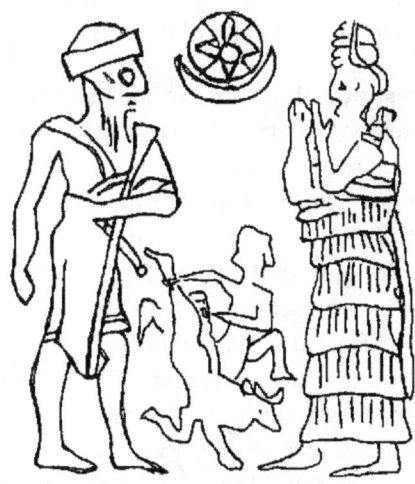

3 The bull-calf metaphor [1]

---

[1] Syrian, early 2nd millennium BCE. Collon 1987, fig 181 on page 48.

Metaphors of the Child

The calf is actually posed in a very specific manner – it is what I call the motif of the 'descending calf'. In folk ritual and magical incantations, the symbol of the descending or falling calf is used to represent the newly born child, whose 'descent' refers to it falling from its mother's womb at birth. One particular incantation, used to aid a mother in the pangs of childbirth, very explicitly describes the newborn baby as a 'calf fell down on the ground like a gazelle's young'.[2]

Another very similar design uses exactly the same symbolism as our previous design but reduces the images of the child and the calf to their heads alone:

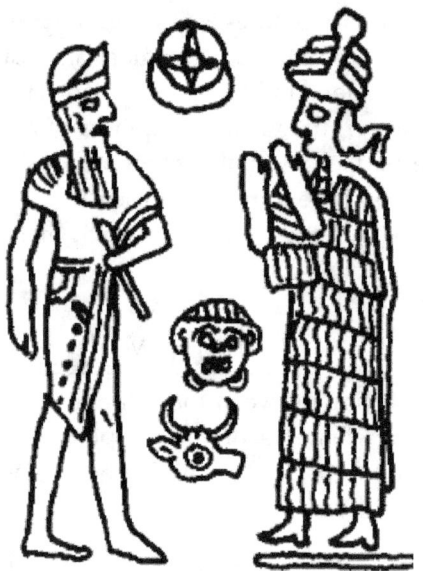

4 The metaphor of the bull-calf [3]

First of all, this design shows that there is consistency in the overall system. But it also very neatly demonstrates one of the few 'laws' of artistic symbolism – that a whole being can be represented by its head alone.

The same principle holds true in the writing system used in the Ancient Near East, where many animals are represented with signs that just depict their heads. One such sign, representing a calf's head (*right*) encapsulates the fundamental identity between the child and calf seen in our illustrations.

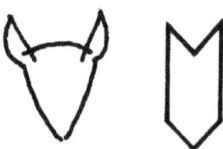

Two versions of the **Amar**-sign

As can be seen, the **Amar**-sign depicts the face of a calf, and its principal meaning is indeed 'calf', but it is also commonly used in the much broader sense to convey the idea of 'young and youngster' as well as the

---

[2] Veldhuis 1991, page 8 & 9, line 31.

[3] Detail from a seal from Alalakh (Turkey), 1500-1000 BCE. Collon 1987, fig 185 on page 49.

Metaphors of the Child

specifically human senses of 'son and descendant'.[4] The term 'calf', in the sense of son, is often used in personal names of the type 'Amar-Sîn' – one of the kings of the Third Dynasty of Ur – whose name literally means 'Calf of the Moon god'.

Far from being a term of mere affection, the appellation of 'calf' given to the child is really part of a broader complex of ideas that links mankind to the heavens. On the one hand, the child, its parents, and indeed the whole of humanity, can be identified with cattle. And on the other hand, cattle are also a fundamental symbol of the heavens in Sumerian thought.

At the most exalted level, the entirety of heaven could be symbolised as the great Bull of Heaven or as a great cow.[5] This mythical lore that connects cattle with the heavenly realms goes some way to explaining why the heavens are always represented in our template designs. The symbol of celestial cattle provides an intrinsic link between the child and the heavens – ultimately the 'calf' born of the great cow of heaven is the human child.

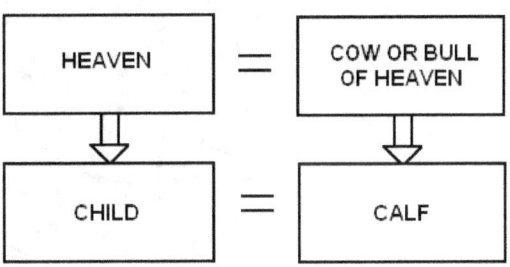

This, I believe, is the inner meaning of the venerable icon known as the 'cow & calf'. Ultimately, I would argue that it is a glyph of the heavenly realms producing the child in its very own image.

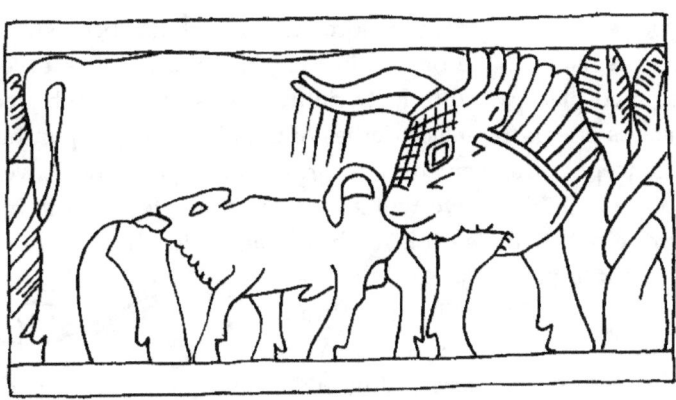

5 The cow and her new-born calf [6]

This is how symbols operate. Through a simple starting metaphor – the child is a calf – they link into the bigger symbolic framework of the celestial cattle, which represent the heavenly realms where the child has its origins.

---

[4] PSD: AMAR [young]. See also CDA: *māru* meaning 6.

[5] Inanna, the 'Queen of Heaven' was frequently described as a divine wild cow in Sumerian mythology. Search the ETCSL website with the term 'cow'.

[6] North Syrian ivory plaque. Louvre AO 11452.

Metaphors of the Child

A Variant Form – the Flying Bird & Calf

The image of the descending kid or calf is often seen in an alternative form where it is carried by a flying bird. This icon is first found in 5th millennium art and it remained a favourite theme of artists until the final demise of traditional Mesopotamian culture.

Our next design is somewhat different to our previous template images as it incorporates the figure of a major goddess, who is widely known as the Syrian goddess.

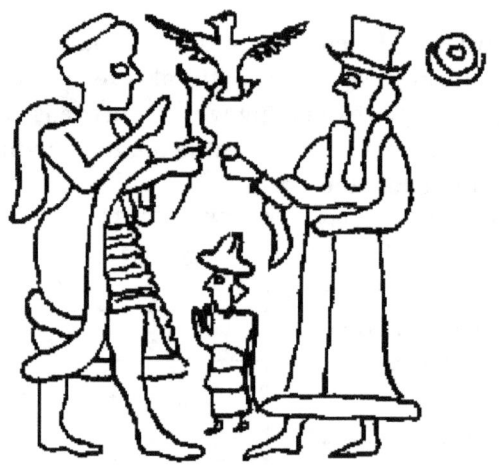

6 The flying bird and calf motif [7]

The Lama goddess still prays for his lordship but she has been shrunk down and is found in the lower register of the design in the place normally reserved for the child. Taking her accustomed place we find the Syrian goddess,[8] who can be recognised by her distinctive top hat. As one of the major deities of the Near Eastern pantheon she must be representing the concept of the heavens, and presumably she is the power that grants his Lordship the boon of a child. As we will see a little later (*fig 24*), the bird is one of the Syrian goddess' principal symbols – it is her bird that carries the calf-child down from the heavens and delivers it to the Lord.

As a basic symbol, the flying bird is naturally associated with the expanse of the skies. When combined with the image of the 'descending calf' it forms a very common icon that expresses the idea that the child starts its life in the heavenly realms and then descends to earth to be born among men. In essence, this icon is identical to the stork of European folklore that delivers newborn babies to their mothers.

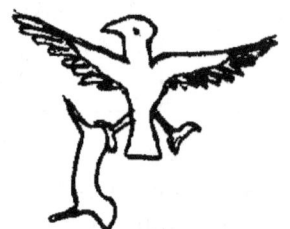

Detail of fig 6

---

[7] Detail from a Syrian seal (2000-1500 BCE). Collon 1975, fig 60.
[8] Collon 1975, pages 180-181 under 'Syrian Goddess'.

Metaphors of the Child

The stork may be thought to deliver the child to its mother at birth, leaving the babe in the proverbial 'cabbage patch' for the mother to discover. However, another very common set of bird icons, like the one below, show another way to depict the same basic story.

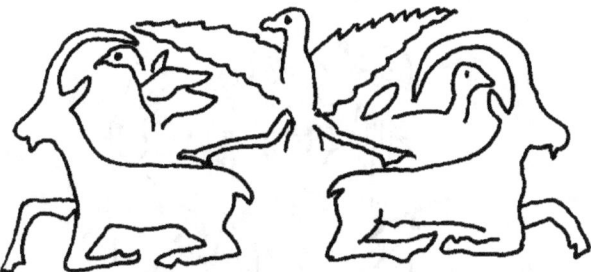

7 The heavenly bird with her chicks [9]

The heavenly bird is still delivering her 'chicks' to their mothers on earth, but now that the whole picture is set out, it is easy to see that there is something else going on here. This image is actually depicting the bird of heaven alighting upon the mother beasts. By doing so, the bird 'touches' the rump of the mothers-to-be and thereby blesses them both with the seed of their child. That the horned goats are the parents rather than kids is proven by our next design, which depicts a pair of goats eating from the seed-bearing plants – this is another metaphor of impregnation that we will explore in more detail a little later.

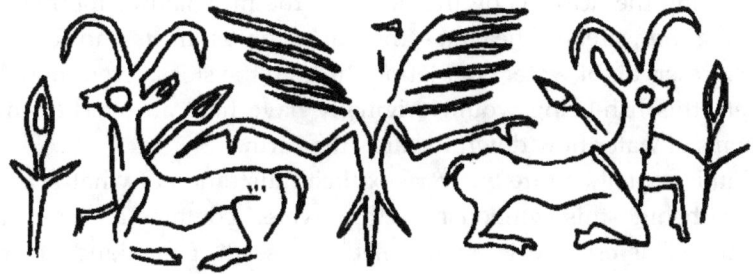

8 Another long-legged bird carries its calves [10]

We are now getting to the crux of how a symbol system actually works. The human mother and child may well be at the very heart of the whole system yet direct depictions of them both are relatively rare. Instead we see them being constantly represented by their symbolic forms – the mother beast and her calf, the bird of heaven and her chicks.

---

[9] Amiet 1961, plate 56, detail of fig 770.
[10] Amiet 1961, plate 55, fig 758.

Metaphors of the Child

The Celestial Waters – the 2nd Major Metaphor

In our next illustration we are presented with a rather bizarre scene. The central portion of the design is given over to a very different metaphor in which a kneeling child appears to emerge from the waters of heaven.

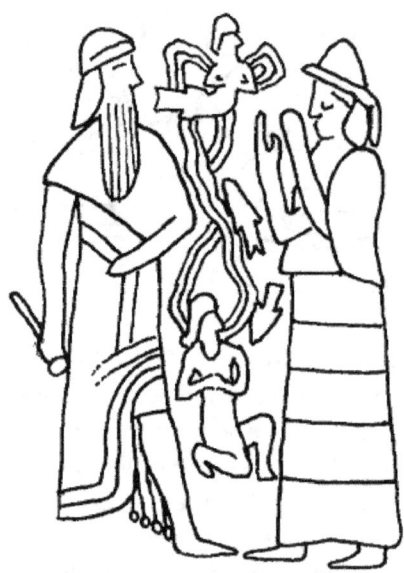

9 The metaphor of the celestial waters [11]

By representing the heavens by the figure of the mermaid or merman, this design must be depicting the waters of heaven – the rains, clouds, mists and fogs that together constitute a vast reservoir of water circulating through the skies. Even though there is no visible trace left, this fish-being would originally have held an overflowing vase from which the streams of water flow down towards the earth.

This design is actually a rare but very explicit illustration of what I call the celestial waters. The idea behind this symbolism is that 'water' contains a secret potency – the germ of the child. This essence is often called the 'seed of mankind' in mythical and magical texts; it can be male or female in nature, partaking of the nature of both sperm and egg. This rather beautiful idea is realised in our design in the way that the two celestial rivers are enlivened with the images of two tiny fish. Together with the child, they represent the indwelling life of the waters.

The cuneiform writing system provides us with another useful parallel, which goes a long way to confirm our theory about the sexually potent waters. In Sumerian the concept of 'water' is denoted by the **A**-sign (*right*), which either depicts

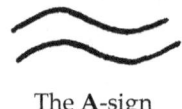

The **A**-sign

---

[11] Babylonian seal, 1500-1000 BCE. Collon 1987, fig 236 on page 59.

Metaphors of the Child

the meandering banks of a river or the wave-like character of moving water. This sign has the primary meaning of 'water', but its secondary meanings are translated into the microcosmic sphere of men, where the sign is commonly used to write human 'semen' and 'progeny'.[12]

As yet the study and understanding of the Sumerian language is still in its early years. On the other hand, the Akkadian language is much better known as it is closely related to modern Semitic languages. And in Akkadian 'water' is known as *mû*, whose meanings extend to 'bodily fluids' and 'secretions' in general, and more importantly for our purposes, it also refers to the 'amniotic fluids' of the woman's womb.[13]

From all this we can infer that the celestial waters can be equated to the reproductive fluids of the male and female, which both contain their own 'seed'. In the context of this design, we could infer that the twin fish swimming in the waters are the separate 'seeds' of the parents, which combine to form the embryonic child.

Imagining that the heavenly waters contain the foetal forms of humanity is tantamount to redefining the heavens as feminine and decidedly womb-like in nature. The seed of the father may be present, but the resultant embryo can only survive and evolve within the body of the mother. It is as if the dome of heaven was being likened to the rounded belly of the mother heavy with child.

The celestial origin of the fish, and of the seed of mankind that it symbolises, is self-evident in the next design, which shows that the fish has its true home in the womb of heaven:

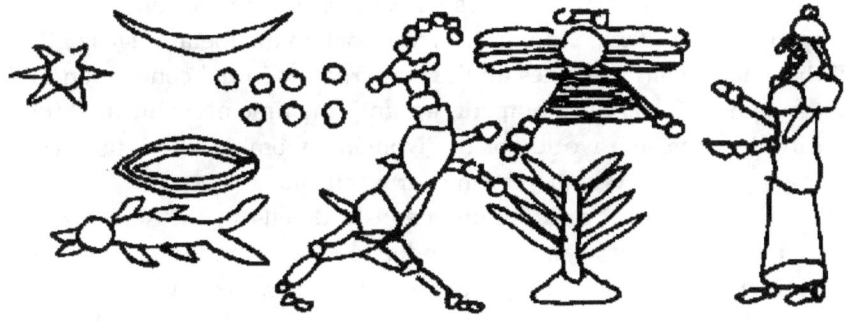

10 The womb of heaven and its fish-like embryo [14]

The arcane idea, that the heavens are distinctly feminine and womblike in nature, is given dramatic confirmation in this design. This rather unattractive image presents us with the grand proposition that the sun, moon and stars together constitute the womb of heaven in which the fishlike human embryo starts its life.

---

[12] PSD: A [water]

[13] CDA: *mû*

[14] Ornan 2005, fig 207.

Metaphors of the Child

Naturally the idea that the heavens are feminine and womblike in nature will conflict with received wisdom that regards the sky as pre-dominantly masculine. In the earliest myths of mankind, the sky-father is widely regarded as the principal representative of heaven. It is he, in the form of rain, who mates with mother earth to produce all life. The sexual polarisation of heaven and earth as male and female is certainly a fundamental pattern in written myth. But that doesn't mean that the idea is eternally valid, nor that it is exclusive of other theories. The Vedic hymns of ancient India are proof of this.

In one famous hymn, the poet speaks of his (and mankind's) heavenly origins: 'The sky is my father, here is the navel that gave me birth. This great earth is my mother, my close kin. The womb for me was between the two bowls stretched apart. [15]

At first reading, this hymn gives us the conventional view that sky-father and earth mother come together in union to create the child. However, the metaphor breaks down when it has to attribute the 'navel' and 'womb' of the sky to the sky-father. Such attributes obviously point to the feminine nature of the skies. The navel of the skies must surely refer back to the umbilical cord of the mother that nourishes the heavenly foetus. The Vedic poet also slips in a new metaphor for heaven and earth – they are two bowls, two daughters, who between them give birth to the sacred child. [16] The 'womb' within which the foetus dwells is located between heaven and earth – in other words, it is placed in the skies. The Vedic poet has given us a significant clue concerning the creation of the child – it is born of two mothers. One mother may be of the earth but the other has her home in the skies.

The symbolism of the fish and celestial waters, first of all, forces us to reconsider and expand our notion of the child. By referring back to the foetal stages of the baby, the concept of the 'child' really stretches all the way from its initial conception in the sexual waters, all through its foetal development, up until the time of its birth. Our designs are really picturing the invisible worlds of the woman's womb, 'where the eye of the sun does not bring light', as an Akkadian birth charm puts it. [17]

The idea that the foetal child simultaneously dwells in the skies proves that the heavens and its life-bearing waters are understood as feminine in nature. The final equation is simple: the fish swimming in the waters of heaven is the foetal child within its mother's womb. The waters of heaven are thereby equated with the life-bearing amniotic waters that nurture the new life within the mother.

While figure 9 seems to imply that the twin fish are the parent's individual seeds it is more common to use the fish as a straightforward symbol of the embryo swimming in the creative waters. Our next image (*overleaf*) follows this pattern.

---

[15] O'Flaherty 1981, pages 79-81, verse 33 (Book 1, hymn 164)

[16] Another Vedic hymn identifies heaven and earth as two goddesses, 'the two bowls that give birth magnificently'. O'Flaherty 1981, page 203, verse 1 (Book 1, hymn 160)

[17] Old Babylonian incantation. Cunningham 1997, page 110.

Metaphors of the Child

Although this design uses a similar set of symbols, they are arrayed somewhat differently and this leads to a slightly different interpretation. Here the waters of heaven are symbolised by the goatfish above, and the child that is granted to the Lord, is represented by the fish, pure and simple. In this case, the single fish must represent the human embryo swimming in the amniotic waters of its mother's womb.

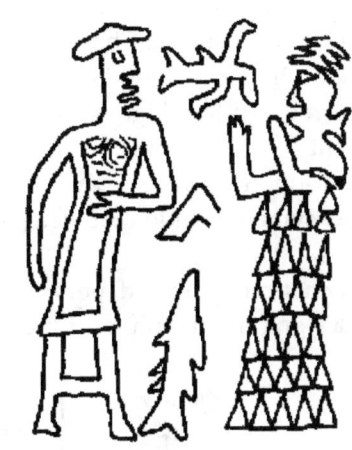

11 The child is symbolised as a fish [18]

Some of the designs seen in this chapter, especially the ones that feature the celestial waters (*below*) help us to refine our understanding of how ancient artists used the design-space available to them on the seals. While the Lord and Lama-goddess generally occupy the full height of the design, the central area between them is divided into two or sometimes three sections. As we have already seen, the upper and lower registers relate to heaven and earth, [19] and the cosmic level in between, although not always utilised, represents the weather-bearing skies with its life-bearing waters.

The celestial waters that fall from the skies provide the material link between heaven and earth. Their presence in our designs prove that the aerial realms of the skies are as much a part of the mystical conception of the child's origins as is heaven and earth. It is through the skies, in the talons of a bird or riding on the celestial torrents, that the child descends from the eternal heavens to be born upon the earth.

So even though we have only looked at a handful of designs, we can already start to see that there are common patterns and themes emerging from our corpus concerning the origins of the child and its descent from the ethereal realms of heaven.

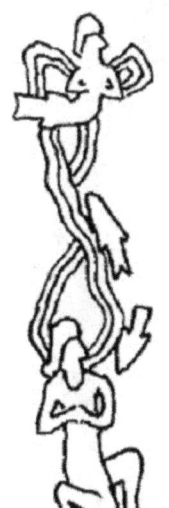

Detail from fig 9

---

[18] Frankfort 1939, detail of text fig 42.

[19] The same holds true in the cuneiform writing system where AN (heaven) can also convey 'upper' and KI (earth) can mean that which is 'down below or lower'. PSD: ANA (upper) & KI (place).

Metaphors of the Child

The material covered in this section has developed our understanding of how the child comes into existence. The ancients viewed the child's formation within the cosmic framework of the Three Worlds. They believed that the original conception of the human child occurred in the highest heavens, and that the foetal stages of the child's development occurred in the weather-laden skies with their ever-flowing waters. At the end of the formative process, the baby was born upon earth, thus completing the final link of the symbolic union of heaven and earth, the great 'world-parents' of many mythologies.

From this more refined perspective, we can make a more detailed model of our template designs and the philosophical ideas upon which they are formulated:

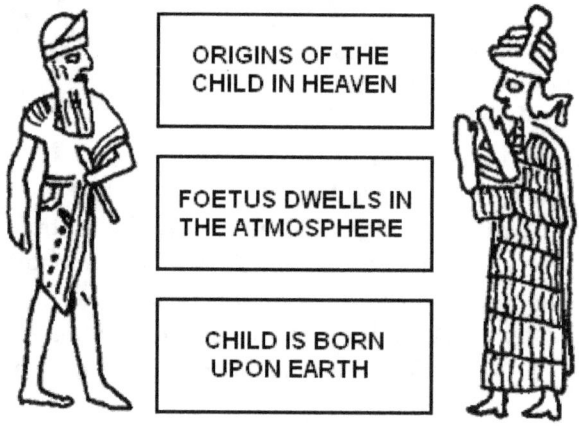

A revised model of our template designs

Animal Metaphors

Alongside the major metaphors of the descending bull-calf and the celestial waters, there are a number of less common metaphors that picture the child in the guise of yet more animal symbols. Although these metaphors play a lesser role in the overall system, they are still very relevant as they present us with a number of variations all based upon the same basic themes.

The Bird & Chick

Just as heaven can be symbolised by a cow and the child as its calf, so too can the celestial realms be represented by a bird that gives birth to the child in the form of a chick. I haven't managed to find a single template design that combines the mother-bird with her chick but there are a number of such designs that treat them separately:

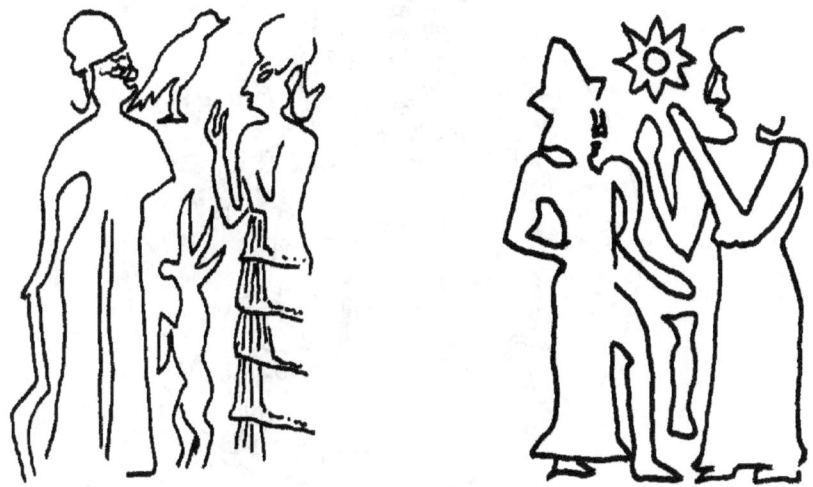

12 & 13 Heaven is symbolised as a bird and the child as a chick [1]

In the first illustration (*fig 12*), the Lama goddess directs her prayers to the celestial powers in the form of a bird set in the upper 'heavenly' register of the design. As we will see in the next chapter, the Lama goddess is praying that the Lord is blessed with the virility of the wild goat rather than a child. The second image completes the picture by portraying the child as a tiny chick placed in the lower register of the design. As we have already seen, the mother-bird is usually depicted as a flying bird with outstretched wings but another distinctive feature of her form, seen in fig 12, is that she has very long legs with which to carry her charge.

---

[1] Left, Stein 1993, detail of fig 684. Right, Stein 1993, detail of fig 21. Both sealings from Nuzi, circa 14th Century BCE.

Animal Metaphors

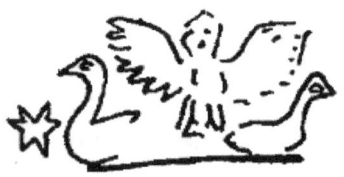

14 Anzu with her chicks [2]

Although the mother bird with her chicks doesn't seem to appear in our template designs, it is a common enough icon in the wider artistic tradition, where we sometimes see the image of a lion-headed eagle with her chicks (*left*).

Western scholars often call this type of design by the rather misleading title 'master of the animals'. On the contrary, I would designate it as one of many icons of the heavenly mother bringing new life to the animal and human worlds. Sometimes the bird descends from the skies to 'touch' the earthly mothers with her divine feet; in other images the bird carries her children in the form of calves or chicks.

The argument between 'master' and 'mother' can be settled by the remarkable image seen below. The Near Eastern icon of the lion-headed bird reappeared thousands of years later in the Archaic art of Greece as the gorgon-faced bird-goddess.

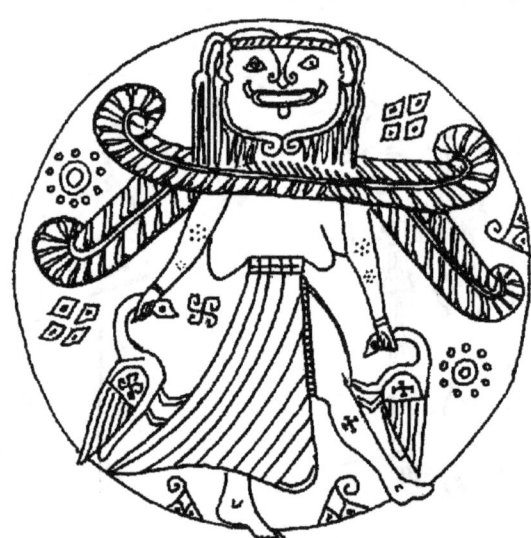

15 Greek Gorgon with her chicks [3]

The Sumerians embedded these symbolic ideas in the writing system that they invented in the latter part of the 4th millennium BCE. As we have already seen, the sign for 'calf' (**Amar**) has an extended set of meanings beyond the simple calf's head that it explicitly depicts. We have already seen that this sign can refer to human children and to the 'youngsters' of any animal – another of the **Amar**-sign's well attested meanings is to represent the 'chick' of any bird.[4] This is highly significant, as the correspondence

---

[2] Amiet 1961, plate 82, detail from fig 1093.

[3] Harrison 1962, fig 33 on page 193.

[4] PSD: AMAR [young] The range of meanings applied to the Amar-sign is ' calf; young, youngster, chick; son & descendant'.

between our icons of the child and the Sumerian lexicon gives us some confidence that there is an articulate and purposeful system underpinning all this varied material.

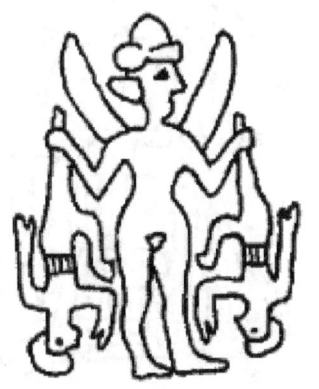

16 A winged goddess with her children [5]

The 'reality' behind all these symbolic designs is seen in figure 16 (*left*), which shows a winged goddess flying down from the heavens carrying two young boys in her hands. This single image can be regarded as a 'master key', which reveals the underlying meaning of so many icons found in ancient art.

Ultimately, this image proves that the relationship between heaven and the child can be defined as one of a mother and her children. We will return to this icon, and the seal it is drawn from, later on, in the next part of the book.

The Frog

Our next set of designs continues the aquatic themes of the celestial waters as it is centred upon a creature that is either a frog or a turtle. It is difficult to be precise about the nature of the creature, however, the way its back legs are fashioned does suggest a frog.

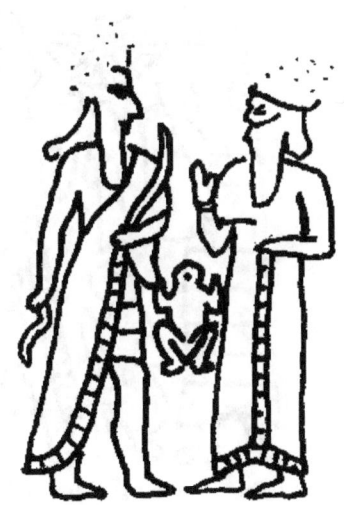

17 The frog as symbol of the child [6]

Here the 'frog' is simply placed before the Lord in our so-called 'place of the child'. A male figure, probably a lesser nobleman due to his less ornate dress, is praying that the Lord is blessed with a child.

Although it is an entirely negative argument, I would say that unless the frog is a symbol for the child, it is well nigh impossible to make any other meaningful interpretation of this otherwise very bizarre image.

---

[5] Detail from an Assyrian Seal, 1600-1400 BCE. Louvre collection AO7296. Winter 1987, Abb 379.
[6] A Kassite seal. Collon 1987, fig 652 on page 150.

Animal Metaphors

Fortunately, a positive argument can also be made. Another design (*right*) shows the true nature of the celestial waters. A goddess, enthroned upon a goatfish, dispenses her waters and the life-within-the-waters, besides being directly represented as the descending child, is also figured as our frog.

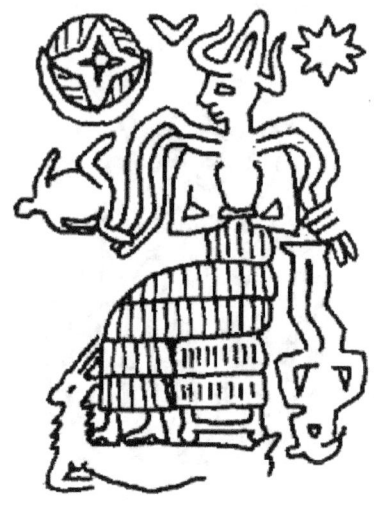

18 The celestial waters [7]

The icon of the 'descending child' is another touchstone that proves that these designs are all about the creation of the human child as it is a direct depiction of the human foetus while still in the womb.

The rationale behind the descending child and the symbolism of the descending calf is perfectly clear to any mother. Before emerging into the world, the unborn baby turns around within the womb, and manoeuvres its head downwards, for its headfirst descent into the world. This is referred to as 'head engagement' in medical literature but in more everyday terms it is called 'baby drop' as the expectant mother often feels that there is nothing holding her baby back from falling straight out of her womb.

The Monkey

Our first design (*right*), while still retaining the fish symbol of the celestial waters, adds a crouching monkey into the mix. The monkey is a common symbol in ancient art, appearing in many diverse contexts, but here in our template designs it is evidently a symbol for the foetal child.

In this image, the heavens are symbolised by a winged disk rather than the sun and moon so typical of previous examples. This symbol is a very apt symbol for the heavens as its central circle represents the solar disk,[9] and its outstretched wings embody the aerial powers of the winds and the rains.

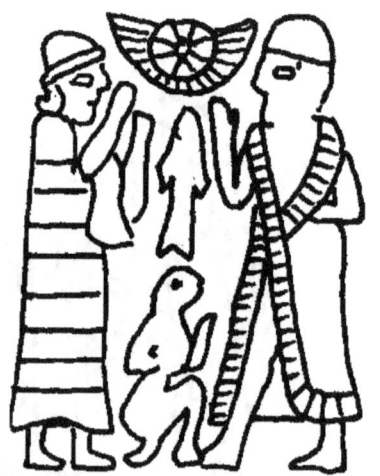

19 The monkey & fish as foetal child [8]

---

[7] Detail of an early 2nd millennium seal. Collon 1987, fig 4 on page 6.

[8] Syrian seal (2000-1500 BCE). Collon 1987, fig 189 on page 49. Fig 11, sealing from Nuzi circa 14th century BCE. Stein 1993, detail of fig 22.

[9] Dalley 1986, pages 88-89.

Animal Metaphors

In our next design (*right*) the format changes again as the heavens are here represented by the radiant sun and the Lord petitions a figure called the Naked Goddess. Like the Syrian goddess we met with earlier, the Naked Goddess is functioning as a representative of the heavens who has the power to grant the Lord a child. We will meet her again in Part Two of the book.

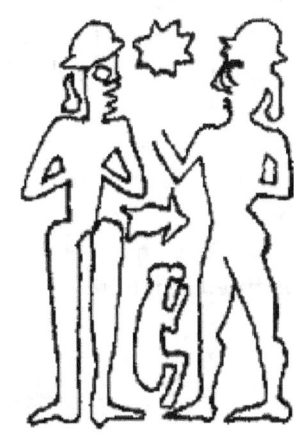

20 The Lord prays to a naked goddess [10]

Compared to the fish, which arguably alludes to the earliest stages of the embryo, the monkey is used to represent the later stages of development when the foetus has grown head and limbs and has assumed a basic hominoid form. This is confirmed by the way that the monkey is typically depicted in a crouching posture, which purposefully echoes the crouching pose so characteristic of the human foetus.

The idea of identifying the child with monkeys and fish is not as strange as it may at first appear. Afterall, a comparable conception is current in the familiar idiom of modern English where young children can be likened to 'little monkeys' and even 'small fry'. Common phases such as these reflect the thought patterns of the ordinary people – they are very often the key to understanding the meaning of ancient art and design.

The monkey is a very common symbol, appearing in many of our birth-related images; a typical example being the following Assyrian design, which places it beside a winged genie carrying a pair of descending calves:

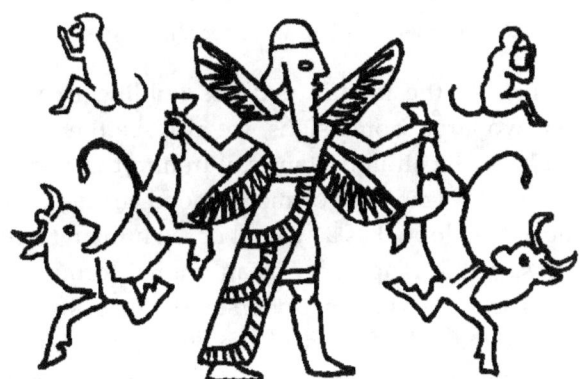

21 A winged genie with descending bull-calves and monkeys [11]

---

[10] Sealing from Nuzi circa 14th century BCE. Stein 1993, detail of fig 22.

[11] A Neo-Babylonian seal. Collon 1987, fig 374 on page 81.

Animal Metaphors

Here the heavens are represented by a winged genie whose four wings arguably represent the four winds of the cardinal directions. So it is apparent that this genie is not just another generic symbol of the heavens but is intentionally fashioned to represent the aerial realms. He is performing the function previously assigned to the flying bird and winged goddess, and can therefore be understood in terms of the idea that the child is conceived in the ethereal realms of the heavens and is then gently brought down to earth towards its birth.

The theory that monkeys represent unborn children is supported by artistic evidence of a different nature:

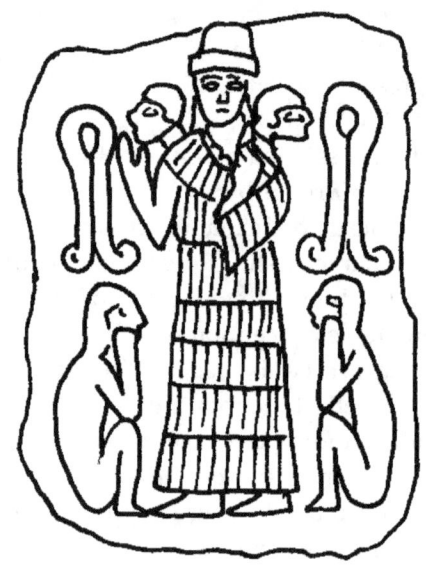

22 A mother-goddess with her children [12]

This clay plaque portrays the mother goddess holding two young children. But sitting at her feet, under two large womb-signs, we also see the crouching forms of two foetal children. Here we have the all-important children in their born and unborn states under the care of the goddess. This icon of motherhood makes it easy to see how the crouching monkey came to be adopted as a symbol of the human foetus.

Now that we have seen the range of protean animal forms used to represent the unborn child, it becomes much easier to understand the basis upon which they all operate. The symbols employed – the fish, frog, the bull calf and monkey – all represent the successive stages of human foetal development. They broadly agree with the modern understanding that the human foetus does indeed evolve from a fish-like embryo with

---

[12] Black & Green 1992, fig 109, page 132.

gills, through stages equivalent to amphibians, reptiles and mammals, until it finally assumes its apelike and humanoid form.

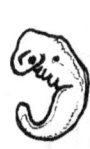 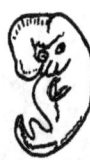 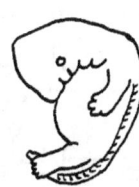 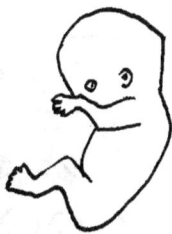

The stages of human foetal development (not to scale)

We know from ancient omen collections like *Šumma Izbu*,[13] which lists an endless variety of deformed births or miscarriages alongside their ominous meanings, that the peoples of Mesopotamia were avid observers of the birth-processes of the human and animal worlds. In their own way, these ancient peoples appreciated the unity of life on earth and like us, they marvelled at the mysterious process of foetal evolution in the hidden interior of the mother's body.

This concludes our survey of the animalian forms applied to the human child. However, one more symbol for the child still remains.

The Ankh

The Egyptian symbol known as the Ankh became popular in Assyrian art in the 2nd millennium BCE. In Egypt, the Ankh has two principal meanings according to modern lexicons and dictionaries. In a religious context it roughly means 'eternal life', but in a more ordinary sense, it simply refers to the 'physical life' of an individual.[15]

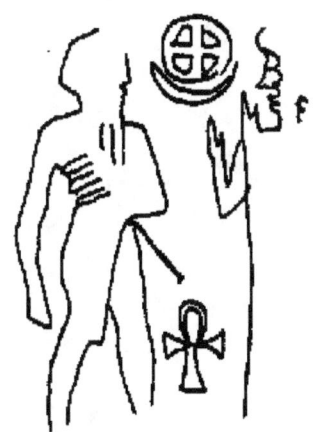

23 The Ankh representing the child [14]

The somewhat timeworn impression seen in fig 23 (*left*), depicts the familiar scene of the Lord and the Lama-goddess praying on his behalf, but the place of the child is now occupied by the figure of an Ankh. In this design there is therefore every reason to think that the Ankh is being used as a symbol to represent the 'physical life' of the child; all the more so as the doctrine of eternal life didn't hold sway in historical Mesopotamia.

[13] *Šumma Izbu* is available in a modern English translation, see the bibliography under Leichty, 1970.
[14] A seal from Alalakh, Turkey (2000-1500 BCE). Collon 1975, fig 122
[15] Bunson 1995, page 23, under Ankh.

Animal Metaphors

Another example (*below*) incorporating the Syrian goddess with her sacred bird, appears to use the Egyptian symbol in much the same manner:

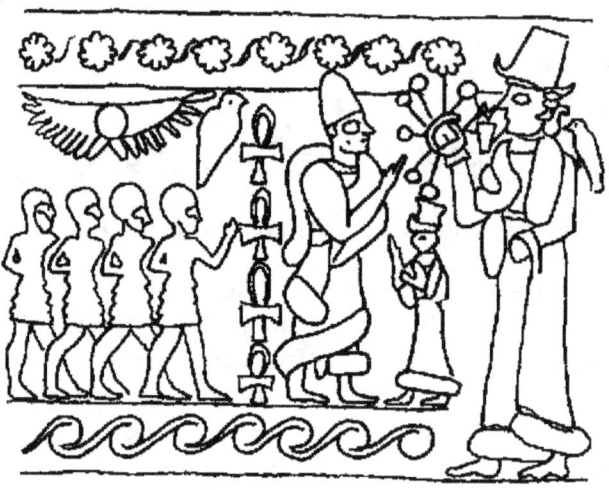

24 Four Ankhs representing four children [16]

In this image you'd have to argue that the four Ankhs piled up in a stack must refer to the four children standing in a row behind them. It is also interesting to note the dual appearance of the bird – one, the mother bird, perching on the shoulder of the Syrian goddess and the other, presumably representing her chicks, set above the children.

In the next chapter we will explore the final set of reproductive metaphors – the fertile trees and flowers.

---

[16] A seal from Alalakh (Southern Turkey) Collon 1975, fig 12.

The Seed of Mankind

The symbolic imagery applied to the child is not limited to the world of animals. Trees, plants and flowers abound in the traditional arts, and ancient artists used their imagery to express ideas on the origins of the child and the mysteries of human generation. As we will see in the course of this chapter, the manifold seeds produced by the trees and flowers are understood as 'the seed of mankind', the germinal state of human children.

Before exploring the primary metaphors of the seed-laden trees and flowers, we will be well served by looking at the more basic powers contained within the plant kingdoms.

The Plant of Fertility

Beyond their obvious use as foodstuffs and building materials, plants and trees have many properties useful to man, perhaps the most important being their medicinal uses. The very fact that plant-based concoctions can effect the health or wholeness of man led early cultures to ascribe a certain living power and vitality to plants. Their potency was not to be underestimated, afterall plants can kill as well as cure.

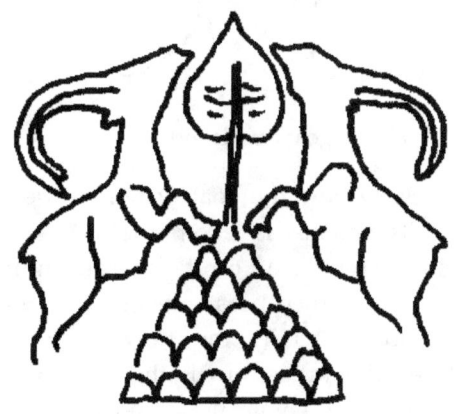

25 The mountain top tree [1]

According to the ancients, certain plants also had the power to increase or restore the sexual potency of men. Mythic texts sometimes speak of the 'plant of birth', which had the power to grant a son to a man.[2] Echoing the same fertility symbolism in the animal sphere, the annals of ancient art are replete with images of horned beasts browsing upon all sorts of plants and trees. The basic motif is depicted simply and elegantly in our first design seen on the right.

Two mountain goats, set in symmetric poses, are stretching up on their hind legs to browse from a stylised tree. The tree stands on top of an equally stylised image of the mountains. This icon, in one form or another, is one of the commonest among the entire corpus of ancient art. The basic motif of the horned beast eating from a sacred plant is found in the earliest art of Mesopotamia and has remained a mainstay of traditional art and design ever since.

[1] Amiet 1961, plate 35, fig 542.
[2] Dalley 1989, page 196. Myth of Etana, end of tablet 2.

The Seed of Mankind

The imagery of the fertile tree is developed in the next design (*right*). Now the same trees are adorned with graceful 'S'-shaped fronds, which appear to be new shoots and saplings born from the parent tree. Even the mountains are strewn with new plants. The vibrancy and vitality of all this new growth is beautifully expressed through their graceful curving forms.

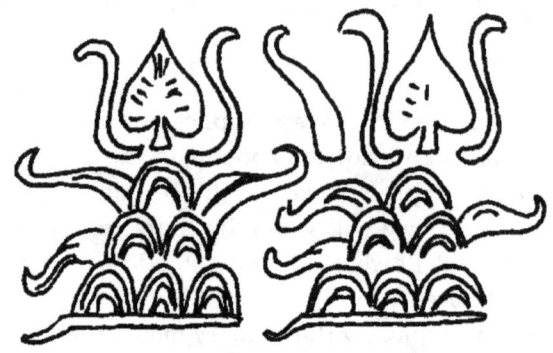

26 The verdant mountains [3]

This same curvaceous energy is what is absorbed by the wild goats and other creatures that browse upon the tree. The effects of this plant vitality upon the wild beasts is particularly apparent in the Billy-goats seen in fig 27 (*left*).

They have eaten from the 'plant of fertility' and its energy is now made manifest in their magnificent twisting horns and their cascading beards. These features can only point to the animals gaining their own 'seed' or sexual maturity.

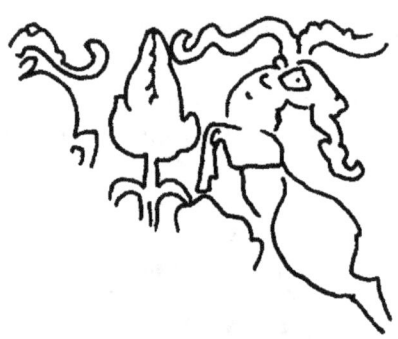

27 The goats made fertile [4]

Precisely how the goat or horned beast acquires its potency is a common subject in traditional artwork. As can be seen in figure 28 (*right*), the horned beasts devour the fresh foliage and especially the flowers of the sacred tree. Regardless of whether these wild goats are male or female, what they are doing is assimilating the seed-like powers of the tree, which will ultimately bring them their own fertility and a healthy progeny of youngsters.

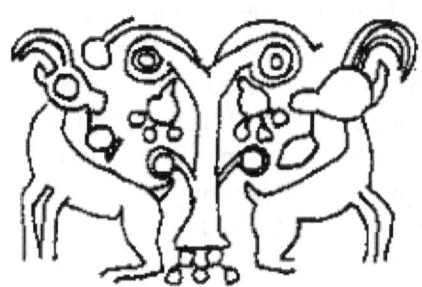

28 The tree of fertility [5]

---

[3] Amiet 1961, plate 31, fig 497.
[4] Amiet 1961, plate 38 bis, fig I.
[5] Collon 1975, detail from fig 224.

The Seed of Mankind

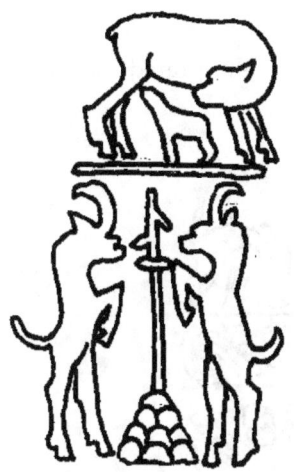

29 The tree of birth [6]

The male and female sides of the goat's sexuality are clarified in the next design (*left*). In the lower register, two male goats stretching up on their back legs have eaten the tree back to its branches, thereby gaining all its potency for themselves. And above them, we see the sought-after effects of that fertility – the female goat tenderly suckling her newborn kid.

The same principles also apply to mankind as is shown by the kneeling figure of a man seen in fig 30 (*below*) The same energy that resides in the horns and beard of the wild beasts has also made the man's hair and beard curl up. He is the man of virility, a figure representing the potency of the fathers. And to demonstrate his attainment of sexual maturity, he grasps the tail of the bull – a polite metaphor for an erection and the act of procreation. [8]

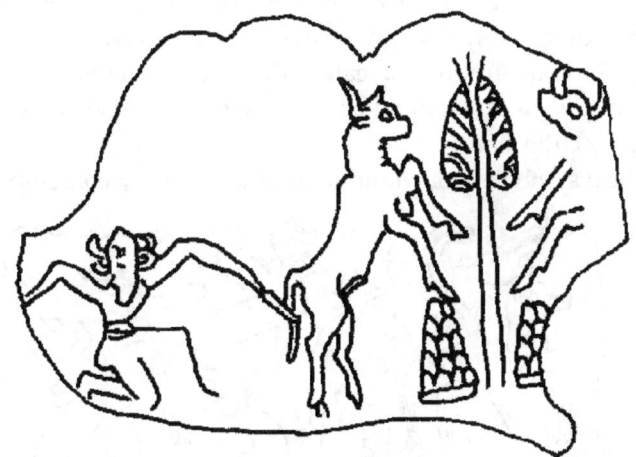

30 The curly-haired man gains his fertility [7]

Because the wild goats gain their vitality and sexual 'seed' from eating the plants and assimilating their powers, it should come as no surprise that both the tree and the standing goat should also be used as independent metaphors for the creation of human children.

---

[6] Frankfort 1939, plate XXVI, detail of fig l.

[7] Akkadian sealing. Boehmer 1965, Tafel XXIII, fig 262b.

[8] Veldhuis 1991, page 9.

The Seed of Mankind

The Standing Goat

The fertile figure of the standing goat appears to have migrated into the formulary of our birth related designs:

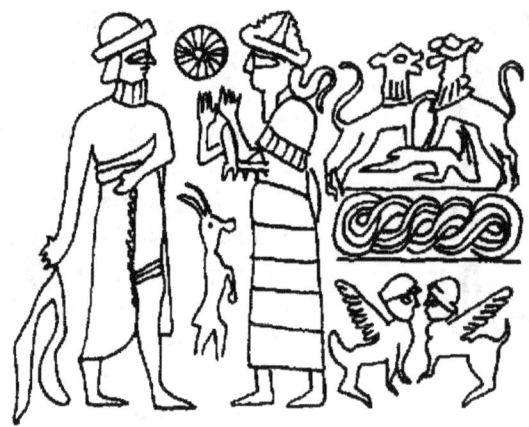

31 The metaphor of the standing goat [9]

In light of what we have just learnt about the standing goat and the tree, this design is probably using the goat as a symbol of male potency. The erect posture of the goat and its horns, which are timeless symbols of sexual virility, show the standing goat to be a symbol of the masculine power to procreate rather than the child itself. Accordingly, the Lama-goddess may now be understood as praying that the gods bless the Lord with the power to father many children.

Almost identical symbolism is found in another roughly contemporary seal design:

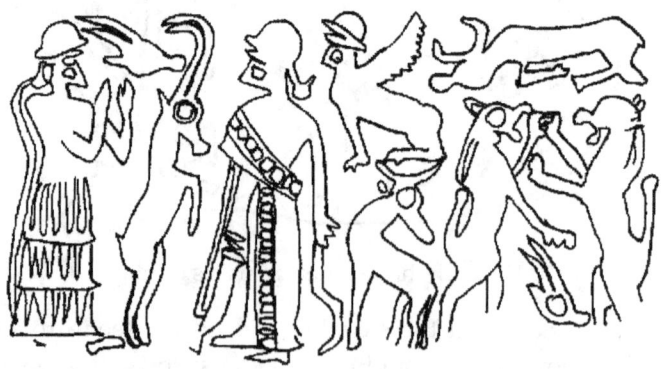

32 The standing goat from another seal design [10]

The fertility of this goat is shown by the way in which a kid's head springs into life from its horn.

---

[9] Mid 2nd Millennium BCE, Alalakh (southern Turkey). Collon 1975, fig 189.
[10] Mid 2nd Millennium BCE sealing, Nuzi (Iraq). Stein 1993, fig 2.

The Seed of Mankind

Even though the last two designs were discovered hundreds of miles apart, the similarities between them are remarkable, even down to the background images of human-headed sphinxes and pairs of lions apparently contesting over the body of a goat. The correspondence of such details, hailing from such far-flung locations, is a convincing argument that the basic symbol system underpinning these designs was part of a broad tradition present throughout the whole of the Ancient Near East.

The Tree of Life

Folklore, mythology and ancient art all abound in extraordinary trees. From cosmological trees that span heaven and earth, to trees of knowledge, and the fabled tree of life with its sacred fruit, the symbol of the tree spans both the cosmic and intimately human levels. Rather than survey, or even summarise, the vast and varied literature on the subject, we shall get back to basics and that means going back to the imagery of trees in our birth-related designs.

The type of tree that typically occurs in our specific field of interest is a tree laden with seeds. I shall refer to this particular tree as the 'Tree of Life'. Our first design (*below*) is a very good example as it places the tree alongside a whole host of familiar symbols.

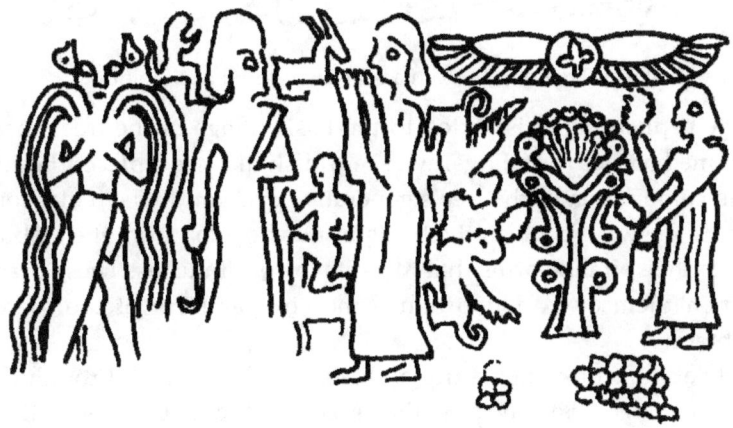

33 The Tree of Life alongside symbols of human fertility [11]

At first sight this design presents a confusing mass of symbolic images. But starting in the centre, we can immediately see the figures of Lama and the Lord, and surrounding the Lord we can recognise the child-symbols of the monkey, goat-kid and the kneeling child. This shows that we are on the familiar territory of human fertility. Behind the Lord, the celestial waters are represented by a phallic male figure with twin out-pourings of water flowing from another invisible vase. All in all, this half of the design is a neat summary of the birth metaphors we have already explored.

---

[11] A seal from Assur, latter half of 2nd millennium BCE. Frankfort 1939, text fig 54 on page 184.

The Seed of Mankind

In the other half of the design, we see the sacred tree set upon a rocky mass that represents the earth and the mountains. The tree itself is adorned with a mass of curving fronds and shoots, all embellished with their circular seeds. Above it, the winged disk intimates that the crown of the tree stretches upward into the realms of heaven.

As this image proves, the lions and sphinxes that have appeared in some of our earlier designs are equally at home with the Tree of Life. Both creatures also appear in our next image of the tree:

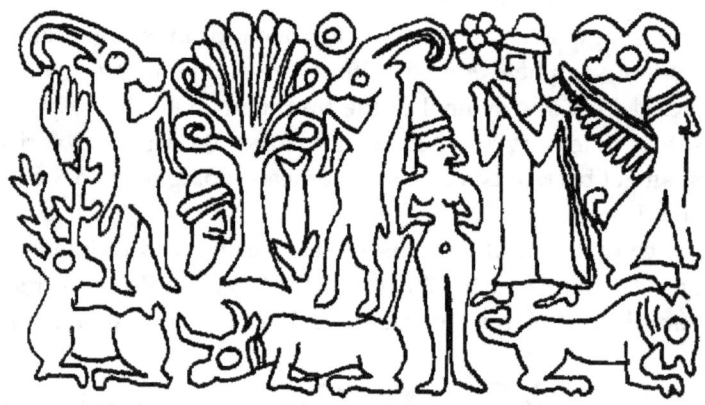

34 The Tree of Life from a seal discovered at Megiddo [12]

Here more explicit detail is added to the basic image of the tree. Focussing on the tree and its immediate surroundings, we see a disk-like seed placed besides its crown. The seed is the culmination of the tree's generative cycle and its circular form is perhaps foreshadowed by the way in which the tree's fronds develop from the globular buds seen in its crown into the spiraline arms that form its lower branches. These branches seem to curve back upon themselves and produce the circular form of the seed within their protective embrace.

Either side of the trunk, the nature of this seed is described through the agency of a human head and a fish. Simply put, the 'seed' of the tree is the self-same 'seed of humanity', which contains the germ of the fish-like embryo and the potential of the human child.

In the ancient world, the germinal state of the child was often referred to as 'the seed of humanity. The sign used to write 'seed' (**Numun**) [13] (*right*) was most commonly used in reference to cereal seeds but like so many Sumerian signs it also has its human side, being used to refer to human 'semen', 'offspring and descendants'.[14]

The **Numun**-sign

[12] Ornan 2005, fig 43.

[13] PSD: NUMUN [seed]

[14] In its Akkadian equivalent, *zēru* see CDA.

The Seed of Mankind

The seed is the essential symbol in these designs but its tiny size creates something of a problem for visual artists. This difficulty was overcome by developing the visual icon of the seed into a dotted circle. Even so, it is still easy to overlook such a small symbol. Perhaps this is why the inner, symbolic, nature of the 'seed' is sometimes made very explicit in ancient artwork, as is the case with the beautifully simple design seen below:

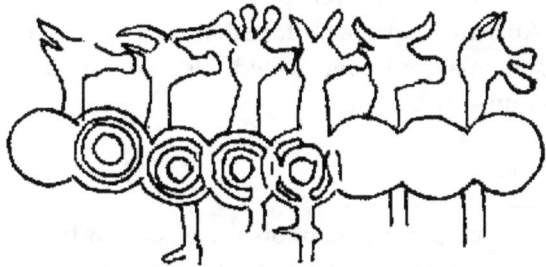

35 The life within the sacred seeds [15]

These seeds evidently carry the germinal forms of the kids and calves. They are the seeds of life, the seeds of humanity, that are formed in the upper reaches of the tree. Stretching as it does between heaven and earth, the Tree of Life once again intimates that the conception and formation of the child is considered a truly cosmological event.

The next design is a remarkable summary of the birth metaphors we have been exploring. Dating to the Early Dynastic period (3100-2390 BCE) this image is testament to how old these basic fertility metaphors are and how long they have been closely associated with each other.

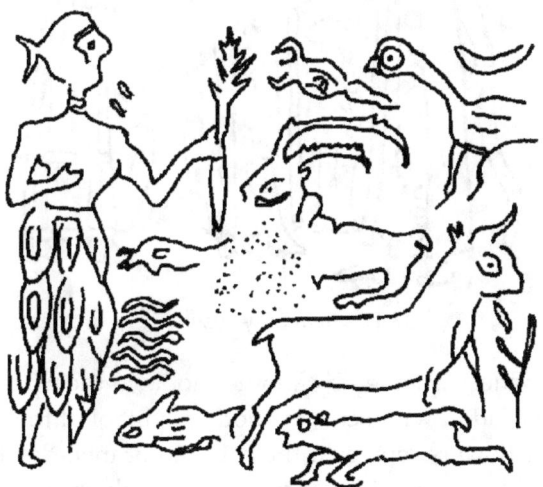

36 An early summary of the birth metaphors [16]

---

[15] Stein 1993, fig 273.
[16] Early Dynastic seal-design. Amiet 1961, plate 87, fig 1141.

The Seed of Mankind

With the plant of fertility in his hand, this man is surrounded by three of the primary metaphors of human procreation. Before him, the celestial waters are seen with their twin fish; in the skies a heavenly bird carries its goat-kid; and in the foreground a cow has given birth to its calf after eating from the sacred seed-bearing plant.

Over succeeding millennia these metaphors of fertility, their themes and variations, have been endlessly reworked and recombined to form the enduring basis of the traditional arts in the Ancient Near East. More than any other set of symbols, these birth motifs are a form of perennial and deep-seated wisdom, based as they are on the most fundamental drives of humanity.

The Flower & its Seed

The last of the principal plant metaphors centres upon the rosette or flower, which appears to be used as an alternative way of representing the fertile heavens in many of our designs. One of the clearest examples (*below*) portrays two children, a boy and a girl, each under their own radiant flower.

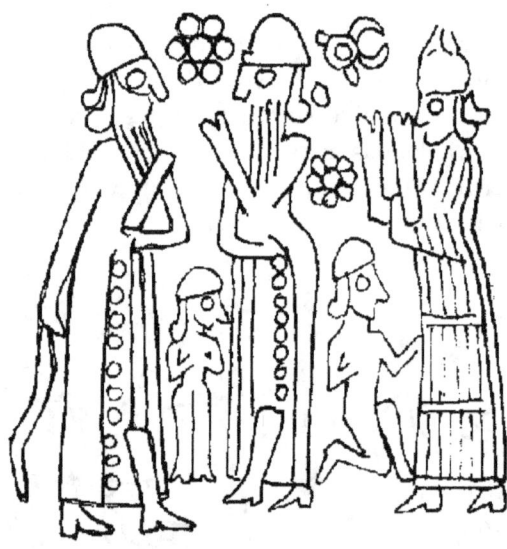

37 The heavenly rosettes [17]

Here the Lama-goddess is joined by another noble in their prayers for his Lordship. The flower, like the tree laden with seed, is another symbol of the heavenly mother. The seeds that fall from her flowers represent the children of men descending from the skies to be born upon earth. This arcane idea is rendered visible in the next design, where the three diskettes set above the child represent the heavenly seeds falling from the skies:

---

[17] Assyrian seal, 1500-1000 BCE. Collon 1987, detail of fig 855 on page 180

The Seed of Mankind

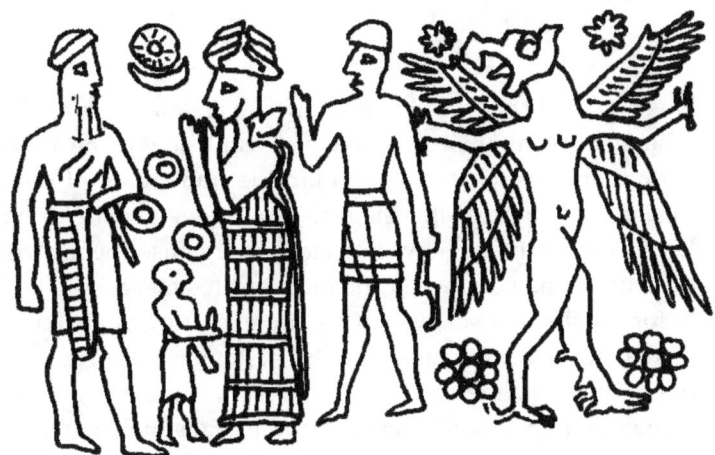

38 The 'Seed of Mankind' metaphor [18]

The most fascinating part of this design has got to be the monstrous demon seen on the right-hand side. Its inclusion in this design, between the rosettes and stars, marks it out as a highly significant figure. Its grotesque form points to a much more archaic and primitive strata lying behind the rather standardised formats of our template designs.[19]

Naturally the same ideas also hold true in the animal world. In our final image the heavenly flower has cast down one of its seeds which simultaneously manifests itself as the newly-born kids that seemingly fall from the skies.

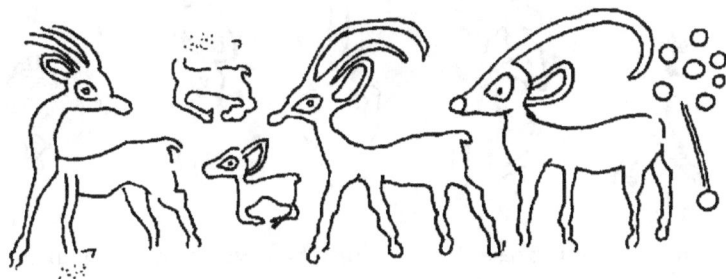

39 The seed falling from the flower [20]

Behind all the varied symbols, a simpler set of models is starting to take shape. Now we know that the fundamental mother-and-child pairing can be depicted in so many ways – the cow and its calf, the bird and its chick, the flower and its seed – the rationale behind the whole system starts to become obvious.

In the next chapter I shall summarise the major points of our exploration so far.

---

[18] A 2nd millennium seal discovered in a shipwreck off the coast of Turkey Collon 1987, fig 570 on page 136.

[19] I will briefly return to this figure in Part Three, at the end of the chapter 'The Fall of the Goddess'.

[20] Pre-dynastic seal. Amiet 1961, plate 22, fig 375.

The Symbol System

So far we have looked at nearly 40 images, which are all informed by one or more of our child metaphors. Even at this early stage, I think it will be useful to present a summary of our findings and to set them within the framework of the broader symbol system. All we really need to do at this stage is group together the principal symbols of the child and the heavens and see how they start to organise themselves. Only then do the underlying structures and common principles start to emerge into the light of day.

Fortunately for us, the symbol system we are exploring is actually quite simple in nature. I believe that this is intentional, as the system was purposefully designed to convey, rather than conceal, its message.

The varied imagery of our seal designs naturally falls into two distinct categories – on the one hand we have naturalistic figures like the Lord, Lama goddess and the child, and on the other hand we have fully symbolic images like the bull-calf and monkey. Using these two categories to organise our material helps us to distinguish between the symbols and the realities they represent.

We will start by summarising the varied forms used to represent the child.

Human Forms of the Child

The human forms of the child come in a variety of shapes and sizes:

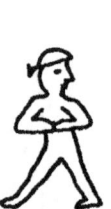 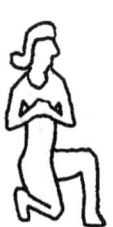 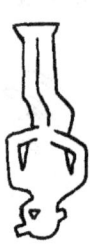 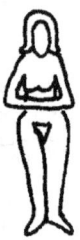 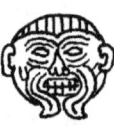

Most often the child is represented as a tiny boy who is either walking or kneeling in a crouching position. However, some designs do feature a young girl, who is generally seen in full frontal posture. An occasional variant of the boy-child sets his figure in an upside-down position – a motif that I have already suggested relates to the head-first emergence of the child at birth.

In addition to these completely formed figures, the child is also represented by its head alone. The icon commonly known as Humbaba's head (*far right*) fulfils this role in several designs – I believe that his ugly wrinkled face is ultimately derived from the wrinkled up face of the newborn baby.

The Symbol System

Symbolic Forms of the Child

Beyond the wholly human figures of the infant seen above, the child can also be represented by a variety of animal symbols.

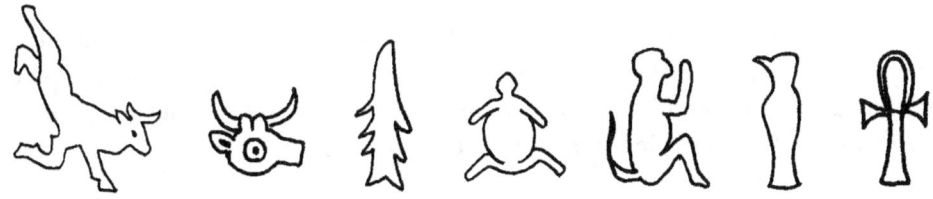

One of the commonest animal symbols for the child is what I call the descending calf or kid; I believe it is the animalian equivalent to the upside-down child. And parallel to the baby's crumpled up face we also find a calf's head. Other animal symbols for the nascent child are seen in the form of the fish and the frog, which naturally allude to the celestial waters that contain the seed of the embryonic child. Then we have the monkey whose crouching posture consciously echoes the form of the foetus within the womb. And finally, the chick of the heavenly bird and the Ankh complete the principal symbols used to represent the child.

It is only natural to start forming sets of mother and child pairings from these independent icons. Behind the idea of the calf-child is the mythical notion that the heavens are symbolised as a fertile cow. In the same way, the child is born to the heavenly bird in the form of her chick. Underpinning these very simple icons is the far-reaching philosophical idea that the child is a microcosmic copy of its heavenly mother.

Glyphs of the Heavens

The divine realms of heaven are most commonly represented by a combination of the sun-disk and the lunar crescent.

  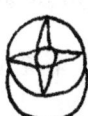 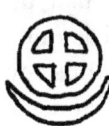 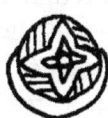 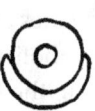

In all of these examples, the sun is depicted as a circular disk set in conjunction with the crescent moon. The sun-disk is typically portrayed as a radiant star, which is most often based on a four-fold geometry. Other variations include the solar wheel and the simple dotted circle, which is reminiscent of the symbolic form of the seed.

The Symbol System

Another group of heaven symbols omit the moon and just use the solar disk.

 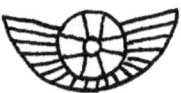

These three examples indicate that the radiant sun is the essential defining feature of the heavens and not the moon. The sun-disk is also incorporated into the icon known as the winged disk. The formulation of this particular symbol shows that the concept of 'heaven' also extends to the realm of the winds and rains.

Animalian Symbols of the Heavens

Beyond the rather graphic symbols of the sun and moon we also encounter a well-defined set of animalian figures that express the nature of the archaic heavens.

 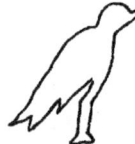 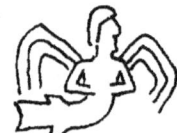 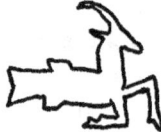

Like the winged disk, the flying bird with its outstretched wings invokes the notion of the winds that forever circulate around the skies. As we saw in an earlier chapter, the flying bird often carries the calf down from the skies or touches the mother directly; this is why the mother bird is typically rendered with extended, even oversize, legs (*see figs 7 & 8*). Another less common variant of the heavenly bird found in some more localised traditions shows it alighted with folded wings; but it can still be distinguished from the chick by its characteristic long legs.

While the bird alludes to the winds of heaven, it is something of a surprise to see that the heavens can also be symbolised by the watery symbols of the fish-man and goatfish. Both icons, through their fish tails, allude to the celestial waters that flow through the skies and eventually fall as rain.

The symbolism of the heavens thus revolves around three different sets of ideas. In the first place, the heavens are characterised by the celestial light that emanates from the sun and moon; in the second place, the aerial realms of the winds are referenced by the various birds and the winged disk; and the final aspect of celestial symbolism revolves around the watery figures of the fish-man and goatfish. These seemingly disparate notions are all aspects of the same fundamental conception which I refer to as the 'fertile heavens'. In the next part of this book we will start to see how these diverse symbolic strands are woven together in the traditional artwork of the Ancient Near East.

The Symbol System

Dual Icons – The Heavenly Carrier & the Child

The symbols we have been exploring are often used as individual icons in their own right. Nevertheless, it is also a common practice to combine them with other symbols thus making what I call 'dual icons'. The two images seen below are excellent examples of this practice.

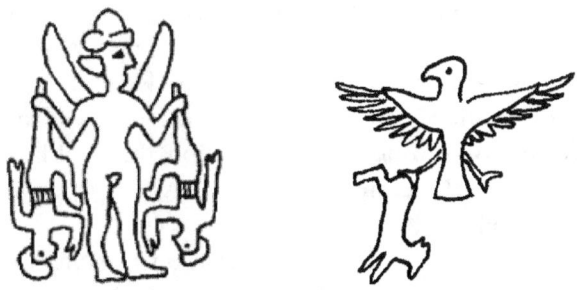

These two icons represent the very essence of our symbol system – not only how it operates as a visual communication system but also the core meanings embedded in the symbolic forms employed.

The first icon is what I would call a 'master image' as it depicts the fundamental equation of our study in as naturalistic a way as is possible – the winged goddess descends from the skies carrying her human charges. The second icon is simply a symbolic version of the same idea in which the bird and calf are counter-changed for the goddess and her children. In Part Two we will explore these icons further and present more material that confirms the inherent identity between them.

I believe that the original idea behind these dual icons was that the celestial realms were regarded as the mother of the child and that they, in esoteric terms, depict the descent of the immaterial soul into the realms of physical reality which culminates in the birth of a child upon earth.

In later times, the same fundamental conception of the heavenly progenitor was often expressed in a variant form in which the heavenly carrier is depicted as a distinctly masculine entity. Two of our seal designs follow this model:

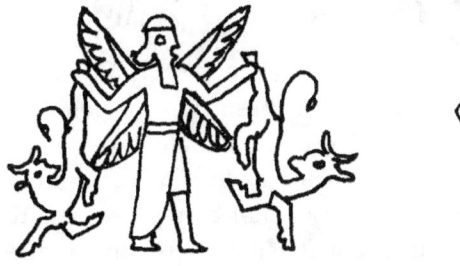 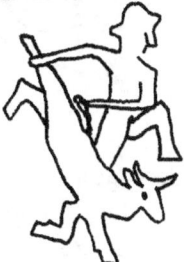

The Symbol System

As both figures are self-evidently carriers of the calf, they have to be regarded as heavenly beings. The first icon featuring a winged genie fulfils this condition as his four wings arguably relate him to the four directional winds. The second design, seemingly depicting a kneeling child with a bull-calf, appears to contradict the relationship of parent and child that I have posited for these dual icons. I believe that this icon is part of a later development that recast the waters of heaven as a masculine potency. This kneeling figure is very closely related to the virile man with curly hair we met earlier (*fig 30*). He represents the fertile Fathers that reside in the heavens. We will try and unravel something of his nature in Part Three of the book, when we will meet him again.

These male-orientated images are not my central concern as far as this book goes. I regard them as derivative of a much older tradition that holds to the idea that the heavenly progenitor is decidedly feminine in nature. And it is my principal aim to map out these older feminine models.

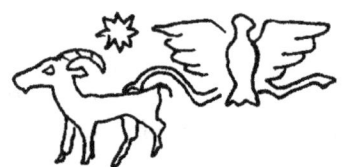

A variant on the bird theme (*left*) shows the bird of heaven touching the mother beast to impregnate her with her child. Here the child is invisible but is alluded to by the radiant star which indicates that the child has descended from heaven to take its place in its mother's womb

While most of the dual icons we have summarised so far have used the metaphors of cattle and goats, the other major metaphor for the birth of the human child – the celestial waters – uses the figures of watery creatures like the fish and frog to represent the nascent child:

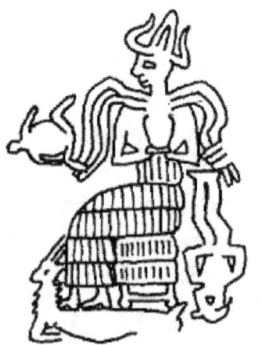
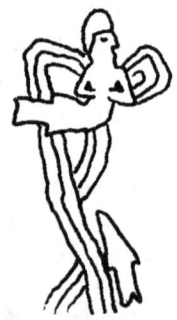

I think there is every reason to regard these two images as dual icons of the heavenly progenitor and their children. The first example is particularly convincing as both a frog and a descending child are depicted as the emergent life-in-the-waters. The second example takes the aquatic symbolism further by representing the heavens by the image of a fish-being. There isn't sufficient detail to tell if this figure is a merman or mermaid, but the essentially feminine nature of the waters would suggest that the original idea would be the mermaid. Regardless of the creature's gender, its intrinsic nature defines it as a denizen of the waters of heaven not the salt-water seas that encircled the earth.

Behind the manifold imagery employed in these dual icons we can see a common pattern of ideas – the child, or rather its soul, starts its life in the eternal realms of the heavens and through the agency of a 'carrier' it descends to earth to be born among men. This idea can rightly be defined as 'archetypal' in nature as it is manifest in the most diverse icons. Furthermore, this archetype of the celestial mother and her child can be found throughout the entire history of art in the Near East.

The same fundamental pairing of heavenly mother and child is also at the heart of our final set of metaphors – the trees and flowers.

The Dual Icons of Trees & Flowers & their Seed

Far from being decorative motifs, the trees and flowers that abound in ancient art are an intrinsic element in the overarching symbol system. They can also be treated as dual icons of the heavenly mother with her children, who are represented by the plant's innumerable seeds.

Even though the visual forms of the trees and flowers are entirely different from the animalian symbols already seen, they still follow the same archetypal pattern previously mapped out. The crown of the tree, or the flower atop its stalk, represents the heavenly realms where the all-important seed is formed. The similarities continue as the generative process is brought to its culmination when the seed finally falls to earth. Thus the visual icon of the seed falling to earth is a direct parallel to the calf or child descending through the skies.

Cuneiform Signs

Alongside all this purely artistic symbolism we have also encountered various signs drawn from the cuneiform writing system. Even though the signs we have met with so far are entirely non-human in their visual formats, some of them do have a distinctly human side to them in terms of their meanings. This is a significant finding as it shows that at least some of the signs of the writing system can also operate like symbols.

The Symbol System

The three most important signs, and their principal meanings, are rendered in the table below:

COSMOS	SIGN	MANKIND
Calf, chick or youngster.	**AMAR**	The child, son or descendant of man.
Water in all its forms.	**A**	The semen & amniotic fluids of male & female, descendants.
The seeds of cereals and wild plants.	**NUMUN**	The seed of man is semen and progeny.

These three examples show how some cuneiform signs can act as symbols. They are the connecting link between man and the universe. And by inter-connecting with more mythical paradigms like the heavenly cow, the flying bird, the tree of life and the celestial waters, these signs weave a web of meanings that goes way beyond the level of simple metaphor. This inter-connected web of meanings, where metaphors collide and combine, can only be grasped by the intuition. This is how a symbol system works.

We have now finished our brief survey of the symbol system. To take our study further we need to leave the realms of folk symbolism seen in our birth designs and delve into the arena of mythical and religious art. The purpose of this is to prove our central proposition: that the heavens were originally understood as female and decidedly fertile in nature as they contain the massed 'seeds' of humanity. Along the way, we will also try and shed some light on the process of how the heavens later came to be dominated by the masculine powers.

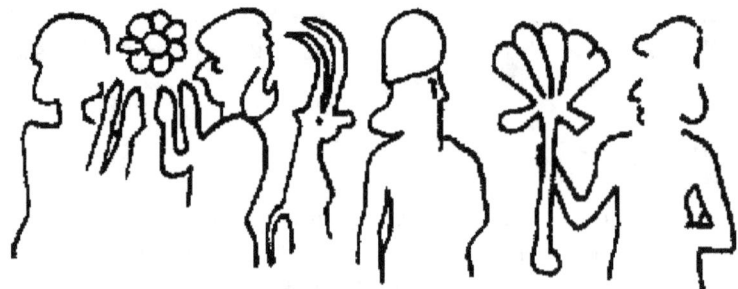

40 Symbols of animal and plant fertility [1]

---

[1] Seal design from Alalakh (1500-1000 BCE). Collon 1975, fig 198.

PART TWO:
The Goddess of the Skies

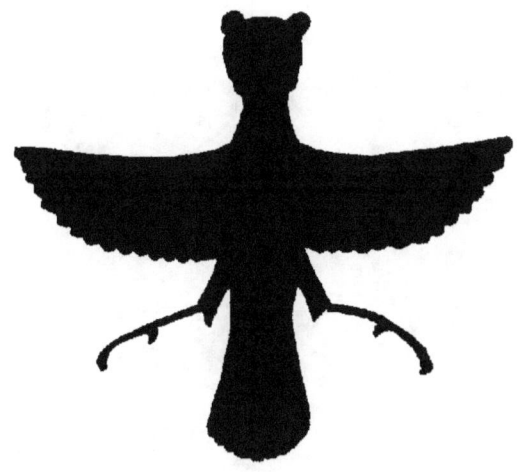

The Goddess of Life

The various symbols of the child that we have explored in Part One of the book can be treated as a starting point from which to expand our studies. The assorted child motifs can be used as a diagnostic tool to survey a much wider range of ancient designs. If a particular design is dominated by our key motifs – if, for instance, it incorporates images of monkeys, bull-calves and fish – then we can make a provisional assumption that the whole design relates, in one way or another, to archaic ideas concerning human conception and the creation of the child.

Applying this very basic method to survey a more diverse range of designs, we can see that beyond the appearance of the Syrian goddess and a naked goddess (*see figs 6 & 20*), various other goddesses are regularly associated with our child motifs. The first such goddess, who I call the 'Goddess of Life', most often appears enthroned as is the case in our first design:

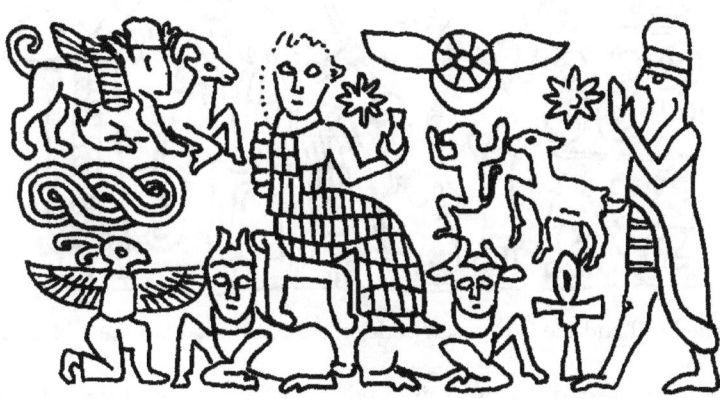

41 The Goddess of Life [1]

This design shows the Lord praying directly to the enthroned goddess without the intervention of the Lama-goddess who is entirely absent from the scene. The combined motifs of goat-kid, monkey and Ankh all show that the Lord is praying to the goddess to grant him the boon of children. The inclusion of the winged disk and the shining stars is another familiar pattern.

Taken together, all this contextual imagery leads to the inevitable conclusion that the goddess at the centre of this design holds the power to confer children upon the Lord, and presumably the rest of mankind. This may explain the small vase she holds aloft. With a radiant star placed next to it, this vase is probably another way of representing the celestial waters. (*See also the next illustration, bottom left*)

---

[1] Old Assyrian seal. Metropolitan Museum, Gallery 403, ascension # 1991:368.5

The Goddess of Life

Here we also have a new set of mythical creatures that all combine human and animal components. The enigmatic figures of the bird-man, the human-headed sphinx and the bison-men, are all part of the mythical entourage of the birth goddesses.[2]

The bison-men, upon which the goddess has set her throne, arguably represent the generative powers of the fathers. They first appear in ancient artwork at the dawn of the 3rd millennium BCE. We will meet them again, in a more procreative role, a little later in this chapter.

Enthroned upon the fertile fathers and holding the life-giving powers of the celestial waters, our goddess is presented as a high-ranking divinity ruling over human conception and procreation. She is set centre stage in the next illustration, which also features another one of our birth goddesses, who I call the 'Courtesan.

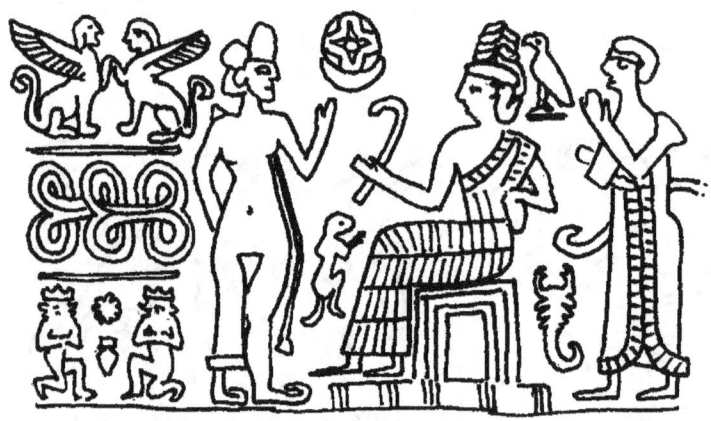

42 The Lord and the Courtesan petition the enthroned Goddess of Life [3]

Here the enthroned goddess is petitioned from both sides – by the figure of the Lord behind her and by the semi-naked Courtesan who stands before her. It appears that the Courtesan has taken on the intermediary role previously assigned to the Lama-goddess and is petitioning a greater power on behalf of the Lord.

In this design we also see three of the goddess' sacred symbols strewn around her. We have already met with the foetal monkey and the heavenly bird that delivers the child, but here we also find a scorpion. In Babylonian astrology, the constellation of the Scorpion was generally considered as a symbol of war, destruction and death – largely due to all its weaponry and its armoured body segments. But contrary to these warlike aspects, the constellation was held sacred to a great goddess called Išhara. She was worshipped throughout the Near East as a goddess of love and the marriage bed,[4] and this naturally points to a rather different, fertility orientated, meaning to the scorpion.

---

[2] I intend to explore their symbolism, along with the other animal symbols of the goddess in another book.
[3] Collon 1987, fig 778 on page 168.
[4] Leick 1991, page 94.

The Goddess of Life

The annals of ancient art provide several very relevant images that illustrate this unexpected aspect to the scorpion; one of the most striking and instructive is the Assyrian design seen below:

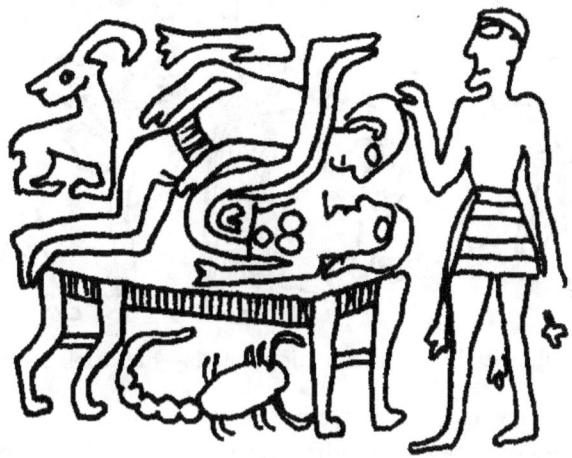

43 The goddess' scorpion under the marriage bed [5]

As this design shows, in the realm of the fertility goddesses, the symbolism of the scorpion is all about human conception and impregnation. From the presence of the crouching goat-kid and the fish we can conclude that this ceremonial rite of the marriage bed is intended to secure a fertile union between the newly wed parents.

The Goddess of Life seen in figs 41 & 42 can be identified as the Babylonian goddess known as Gula by symbolic crook that she wields. Gula, the 'Great One', is regarded as another great goddesses, the 'mistress of life',[6] and her crook identifies her as the ward and shepherdess of her flocks, who represent mankind. In Babylonian astrology, Gula was known as the Nanny-Goat, and her constellation figure was cryptically known as the 'cattle-pen of Gula'.[7] These attributes mark her out as another aspect of the Great Mother as the 'cattle-pen' was the sacred enclosure where calves were born.

In the pantheons of the 2nd millennium BCE, Gula had the ultimate say on granting offspring to humanity, and this function, extrapolated from the concerns of the individual to the universal scale, is formulated in one of Gula's primary mythical attributes: 'you are the one who created mankind'.[8] The fertility aspects of Gula are apparent in depictions of the goddess, where she is typically accompanied by rampant goats and the tree of life.

---

[5] Winter 1987, Abb 366, dated to the 15th century BCE.

[6] BPO2, text II, line 7 ff.

[7] CAD: *tarbaşu*

[8] Reiner 1995, page 129.

The Goddess of Life

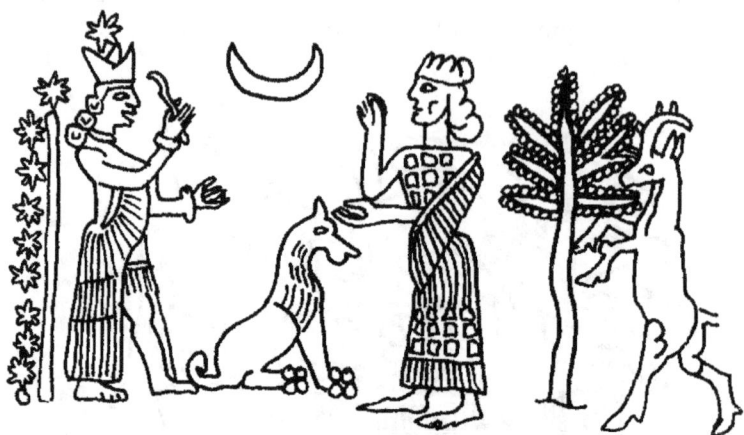

44 The goddess Gula with her characteristic symbols – the crook, sitting dog & goat [9]

In later times, Gula was the chief deity of medicine and the healing arts, but in origin she was patroness of pregnant mothers and midwives.[10] The more practical side of her medical arts would have been directed towards problematic deliveries and the birth-related injuries that commonly befell the mother. Gula not only ruled over the health of mother and child through the whole pregnancy but she also set the destiny of the child at its birth. At the end of a magical incantation designed to aid the birth of a child, Gula is petitioned to 'determine the destiny' of the child 'once she has cut the umbilical cord'.[11]

The next design reveals further aspects of the fertility symbolism associated with the Goddess of Life.

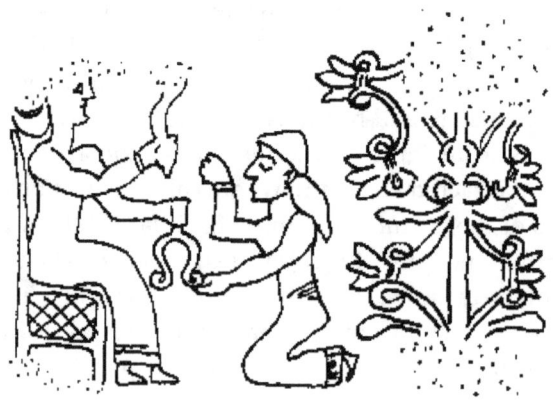

45 A supplicant petitions the Goddess of Life [12]

---

[9] Neo-Assyrian cylinder seal. Collon 1987, fig 793.

[10] ETCSL A sir-gida to Ninisina (Ninisina A) lines 1-14 & 74-82.

[11] Cunningham 1997, page 72, quoted text lines 49-50.

[12] Ornan 2005, fig 24.

The Goddess of Life

The kneeling supplicant raises one imploring hand to the goddess and with her other hand she touches the foot of the goddess' omega-symbol (*see below*). Behind, in the background, is an ornate tree replete with its flowers and circular seeds. The narrative behind this design is probably that the supplicant is asking the goddess to implant her own womb with the 'seed' from the tree and thus make it fertile and bear children.

The images so far encountered have concentrated on the 'Goddess of Life', whom we have identified as the Babylonian goddess Gula. As a Babylonian goddess, Gula, arguably came to prominence in the course of the 2nd millennium BCE. Before this time, the figure that I call the 'Courtesan' could occupy her exalted position as the creatrix of mankind.

The following design, dating to the earlier half of the 2nd millennium BCE, sets the Courtesan as the central character among a group of familiar child symbols. Not only that, she is evidently very closely associated to the bison-men we saw earlier, who are now revealed in their fertile phallic forms.

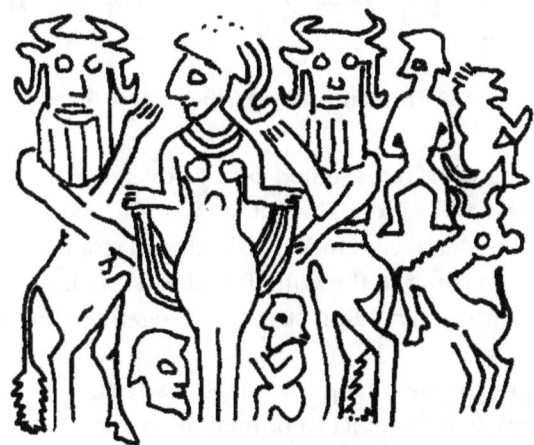

46 The Courtesan as mother of humanity [13]

Although one of our previous images (*fig 42*) set the Courtesan in an apparently lesser role as a 'petitioner' before the enthroned Goddess of Life, this design tells another tale. This image proves that the Courtesan performed exactly the same roles and functions as the Goddess of Life. The array of child symbols around her – the crouching child, the human head, and in the background the bow-legged baby, monkey and bull-calf – attest to the fact that she rules over all aspects of human conception, pregnancy and birth. Indeed, to judge by this image, the Courtesan can be thought of as the mother of all humanity just as much as the Goddess of Life.

---

[13] Early 2nd millennium BCE seal, Cappadocian. Frankfort 1939, detail of text fig 75.

The Goddess of Life

Our final image (*below*) doesn't actually portray the goddess herself – only her oversize arm. Nevertheless, it provides an excellent illustration of the goddess' essential functions in the realm of human birth and procreation:

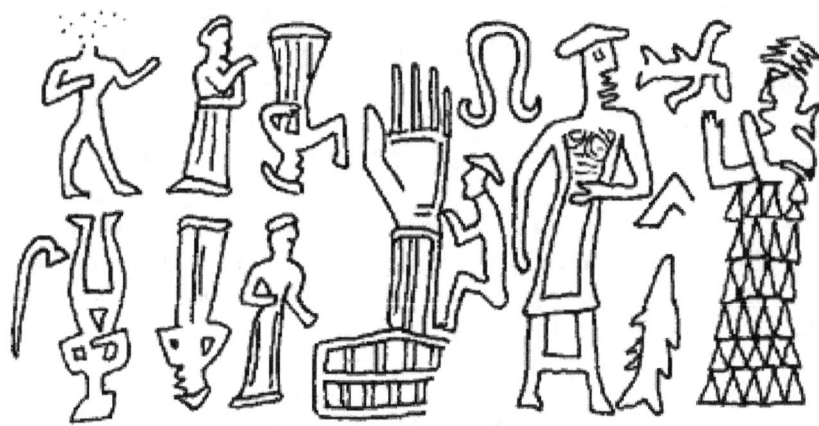

47 The hand of the birth goddess [14]

The birth goddess is only represented by her oversize arm, which dominates the central portion of the design. In the realms of symbolism, the human hand by itself has connotations of a person's capacity to act, direct and control; the hand shapes and manipulates the world according to the will of the individual. Here the goddess' hand is combined with the firm arm of enabling strength – together they describe the operative power of the deity.

The cuneiform writing system helps us out again in the form of the A₂-sign (*right*), which depicts a human hand and forearm. As well as directly referring to a human 'arm' and a bird's 'wing', the sign has the more derived meanings of 'strength, ability, power and labour'. [15]

The A₂-sign

What work the goddess' hand actually performs has to be worked out from the rest of the design. Over on the left-hand side of the image we see a group of boys and girls, half of which are portrayed upside down. Their upside-down format identifies them with the motif of the descending calf, and that, according to the theories mapped out in this book, makes them unborn children still within the womb. In terms of the imagery employed in this design, they are waiting for the hand of the goddess to bring them to birth. While the group of children patiently await their turn, the hand of the goddess safely delivers the tiny figure of a crouching

---

[14] Frankfort 1939, text fig 42. I have relocated the crook to the opposite side of the design in accordance with Frankfort's drawing.

[15] PSD: A [arm] and CDA: *idu*.

The Goddess of Life

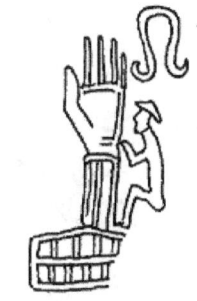

child (*right*) from the omega-like womb above. Thus the actions performed by the divine hand of the goddess define her as the great midwife of humanity.

Sad to say, the protective influence of the goddess didn't always succeed in keeping mother and child safe from harm. Alongside the many miscarriages, abortions and infant deaths, serious injuries to the mother could easily lead to her death. Such is the theme of a heartfelt poem that describes how a pregnant mother was snatched away by cruel fate on the day of her giving birth:

'The day I bore the fruit, how happy I was
Happy was I, happy my husband.
The day of my going into labour, my face became darkened
The day of my giving birth, my eyes became clouded.
With open hands I prayed to the Lady-of-the-Gods,
"You are the mother of those who have borne a child. Save my life"
Hearing this, the Lady-of-the-Gods veiled her face saying:
"Why do you keep praying to me? ……..
Death came creeping into my bedroom,
It drove me from my home,
It tore me from my husband'.[16]

---

[16] Nemet-Nejat 1999, page 93.

The Bird Goddess

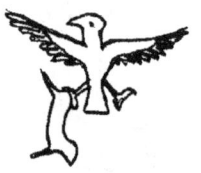 In Part One of the book we encountered the symbolic calf or kid being carried by flying birds (*left*) or other aerial beings like a genie with four wings (*fig 21*). The air-borne nature of these icons relates back to the idea that the calf, the foetal child, originated in the heavens and, from there, descended through the skies to be born upon earth.

These images are but parts of a bigger picture that places the calf-child in the hands of a heavenly carrier. In our terms of reference, we could define the flying bird as another symbol of the fertile heavens; ultimately it is a symbol of the celestial goddess who brings all life to birth. The clearest expression of this idea is the figure that I call the 'Bird Goddess'; she is the central character in our first design:

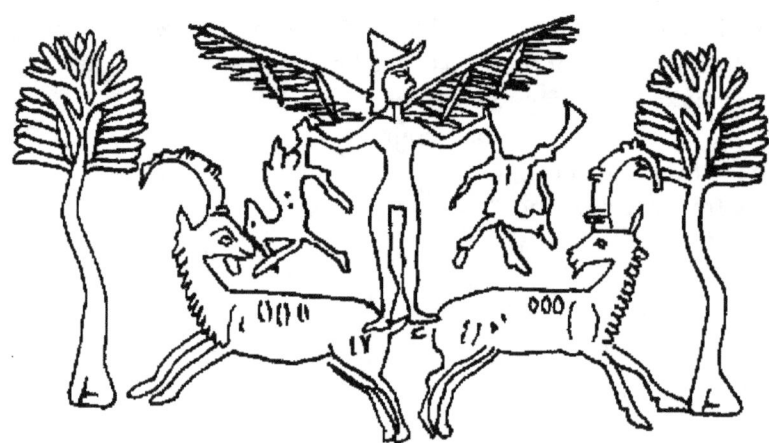

48 The winged goddess brings newborn kids to their parents [1]

The goddess is completely naked but for her horned headdress, however, the most striking thing about her is the massive set of wings that sprout from her shoulders. She has evidently descended from the high heavens and alighting upon the rumps of the mothers-to-be she delivers her heaven-born kids.

In fact, you could describe the winged goddess as a human variant of the flying bird that so often delivers the calf-child to its mother on earth. We can actually take the comparison between the winged goddess and the bird much further. Because the flying bird and goddess have exactly the same function, and share the all-important attribute of wings, we can go so far as to say that one can be identified with the other. The identification is based on the combination of shared features and identical functions –

---

[1] Ornan 2005, fig .33

The Bird Goddess

these are the basic rules of identification within the realms of symbolic art. Just as the child has his animal forms, so too, does the goddess.

Ancient artists developed various master icons that depict the whole process of the heavenly mother bringing her calves and kids to their earthly mothers. By setting two such images next to each other, the underlying pattern is much easier to grasp:

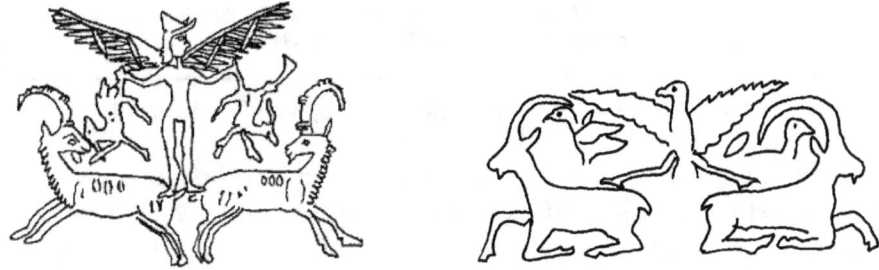

Master icons of the heavenly bird delivering youngsters to their earthly mothers [2]

In both these images the mother bird is seen alighting upon the rumps of the mother beasts – this sacred 'touch' of the goddess is what imparts the child to their wombs. At first sight the next pair of images (*below*) look pretty much the same but I would argue that they show the two different aspects of our master images seen above.

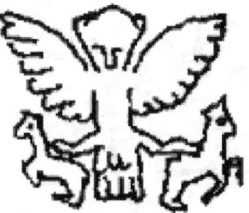 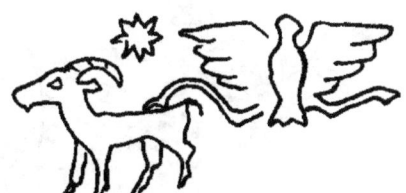

49 & 50 Icons of the bird delivering calves and touching the mother [3]

The first design (*left*) shows a lion-headed eagle carrying its calves and the second image shows the mother bird landing on the mother beast, and thus blessing her with child. Now I hope that the reader can appreciate that all these images are intimately inter-related aspects of the same narrative; they only start to make sense when seen as parts of a variegated series rather than as isolated icons.

As these images show, there are actually three bird-like figures that descend from the heavens to impart calves and kids to their mothers. Alongside the winged goddess and the eagle-like bird, we also see a truly mythical creature in the form of the lion-headed eagle known in mythology as Anzu or Imdugud, the 'great storm bird'.[4]

---

[2] Detail of fig 48 and repeat of fig 7
[3] Left, Amiet 1961, plate 80, detail of fig 1062. Right, Amiet 1961, plate 58, detail of fig 792.
[4] Anzu being the Akkadian name, and Imdugud 'the powerful storm bird' the Sumerian name. See Jacobsen 1976, pages 128-129.

The Bird Goddess

To summarise this set of identifications, it is perhaps useful to present them in a more schematic fashion:

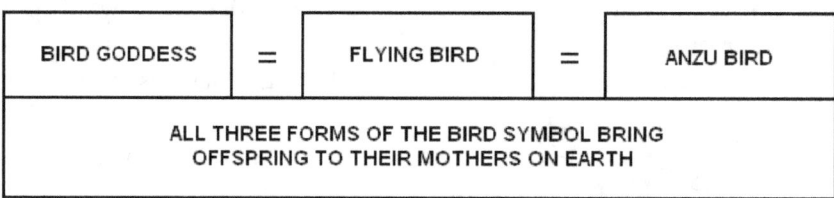

Identifications of the bird goddess through her fertile functions

This way of presenting related sets of symbols is eminently simple and practical, but above all else, it stresses the structured way in which symbolism works behind the facade of its variegated imagery. There are many ways of expressing the same message in archaic art and this schematic way of representing motifs makes it easier to focus on the essential features.

The identification of the bird with the heavenly mother is the fundamental paradigm of our study. This explains why the following image of Anzu landing on a pair of antlered deer was an icon of the great goddess known as Ninhursag.

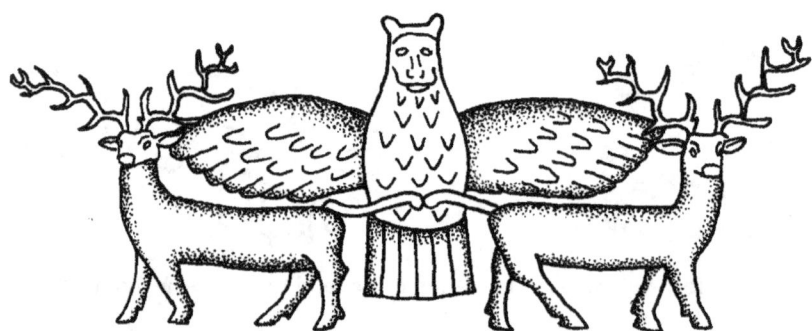

51 Anzu and two deer, from a bronze panel set above the entrance to the temple of Ninhursag [5]

Ninhursag, one of the most important goddesses in Mesopotamia, was 'the Lady of the Steppes'. In the pantheon of the 3rd millennium BCE, she governed the fertility of the wild plants and animals found in the foothills of the mountains. As Ninhursag was also known as 'the Mother of all children' we can understand that her sacred herd animals must symbolise the mass of humanity. The grasslands that her herds have roamed since time immemorial were known as the 'high plains' [6] – a term which can also be understood as the 'plains of heaven'.

---

[5] Mid 3rd Millennium, Roaf 1966, page 86.
[6] PSD: ANEDIN [steppe]

The Bird Goddess

To be more precise, Ninhursag governed the fertility of the four-legged creatures [7] such as the gazelle, deer and onagers rather than the carnivores. This is because the goddess herself is the lioness. We get a hint of this in a hymn to the goddess which describes her awesome nature: 'You, O Queen, become equal to Heaven (**An**), wearing a terrifying splendour'.[8] The nature of the goddess' terrifying visage is made plain in a hymn to another aspect of the mother goddess who goes under the name of Nintur – the Queen of Birth: 'Nintur, supreme mother of all the lands, has appeared with the hair-raising fearsomeness of a lion'.[9]

Even though Anzu is sometimes associated with Enlil, the king of the gods – Enlil sets Anzu's destiny and is even figured as the bird's father [10] – the great bird of heaven is more properly treated as a symbol of the heavenly mother goddess.

The very human and feminine nature of the bird goddess is fully manifest in our next design, part of which we met earlier (*fig 16*):

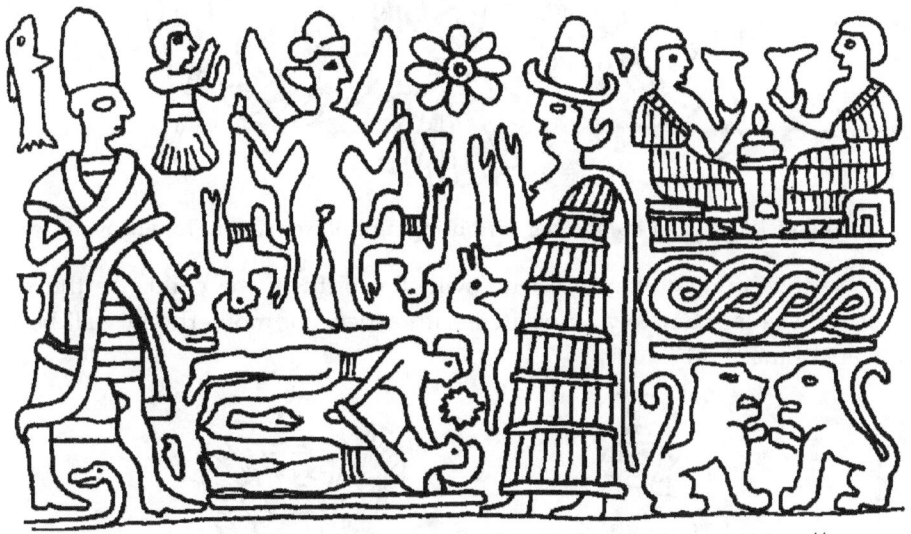

52 The winged goddess descends to earth with her sky-born children [11]

This design places the winged goddess within a wholly human context, and a very specific human context at that. The earthly parents, to whom the goddess delivers her children, are in the act of making love. Previously I had talked about the bird-goddess as delivering the child to their mothers at birth, afterall, the newborn child is described as a calf fallen upon the ground. However, this depiction of the goddess shows her connection to the human birth process is much broader, and this forces us to re-evaluate

---

[7] PSD: NIĜURLIMMU [creature]. The Sumerian term is literally 'things with four legs'.

[8] ETCSL: Ninurta's Exploits, lines 390-410.

[9] ETCSL: Nintur A, lines 20-35.

[10] ETCSL: Lugalbanda & the Anzu-bird, lines 90-110.

[11] Detail from an Assyrian Seal, 1600-1400 BCE. Louvre collection AO7296. Winter 1987, Abb 379.

The Bird Goddess

our ideas about the goddess. This design is not actually about birth but about the moment of conception, the very beginnings of the pregnancy. And it is the winged goddess that evidently effects the inception of the whole process of human conception.

The Greek conception of the bird-goddess followed the same Near Eastern model and repeats the same statement that the bird-goddess, with her fearsome Gorgon-like face, is the heavenly mother of human children:

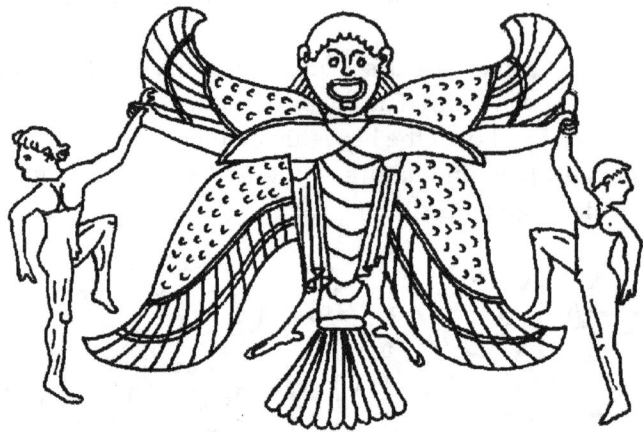

53 A Greek design of the mother-bird bringing children down from heaven [12]

Nor do the goddess' concerns end with the birth of the child. As the following images show, she is intimately associated with aspects of motherhood well beyond the safe delivery of the child:

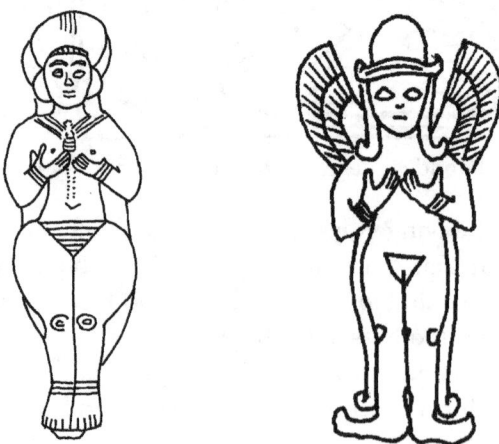

54 & 55 Two goddesses of motherhood [13]

---

[12] Harrison 1962, fig 19 on page 177.

[13] Left, mould-made figurine, Susa, Iran 12th century BCE. Right, detail from a Hittite rock mural at Carchemish. Ornan 2005, detail of fig 88.

The Bird Goddess

These goddesses' massive thighs and the emphasis on their vulvas certainly identify them as goddesses of childbirth but the way both figures cups their breasts also points to the production of milk and the ongoing care of the infant child.

The bird goddess evidently governs all aspects of motherhood. The winged goddess thus has two major aspects – through her affinity with the birds she is the embodiment of the skies and of heaven itself, and she is the celestial mother of the human child. She governs the whole reproductive process from the time of the child's inception to its successful birth and beyond. In essence, she is the creatrix of the child, the personification of the innate powers of the woman's body to create and nurture a new living being within her – if you like, she is the 'natural intelligence' of the womb that forms the child.

Surveying the varied forms of the bird goddess impresses upon the modern mind the many diverse ways in which the birth metaphors were represented. In many respects these designs constitute a sort of folk magic – they are fertility charms in their own right – and their endless renditions and variations spread over the millennia, are testament to the pervasive presence and power of the heavenly goddess.

The common factor in all these icons of the bird goddess is their outstretched wings. As a symbol, wings naturally pertain to the aerial realms; their presence on a mythical being implies that they are flying through the skies. There are actually slightly different types of 'Winged Goddess' – some with even more unusual features – which are evidently part of the same jigsaw puzzle:

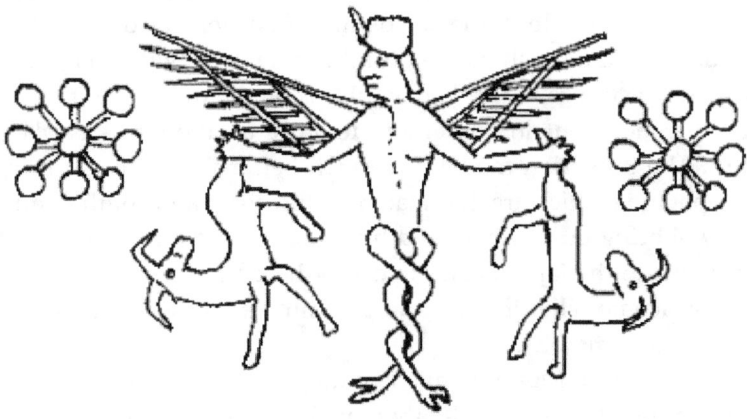

56 A winged goddess with twisting legs [14]

Fortunately modern scholars have investigated this strange goddess with twisting legs. They have managed to identify her as an image of the South Wind. In the traditions of the 2nd millennium, the South Wind was female by nature; she was the primary wind

[14] Detail from an Assyrian seal design, 1500-1300 BCE. The Walters Art Museum (online) Fig 29, Accession number 42.671

The Bird Goddess

of Mesopotamia, always listed first and was regarded as the sister of the other three directional winds.[15] Her form varies according to time, place and artistic imagination but one of her common characteristics is her twisting or even coiling legs:

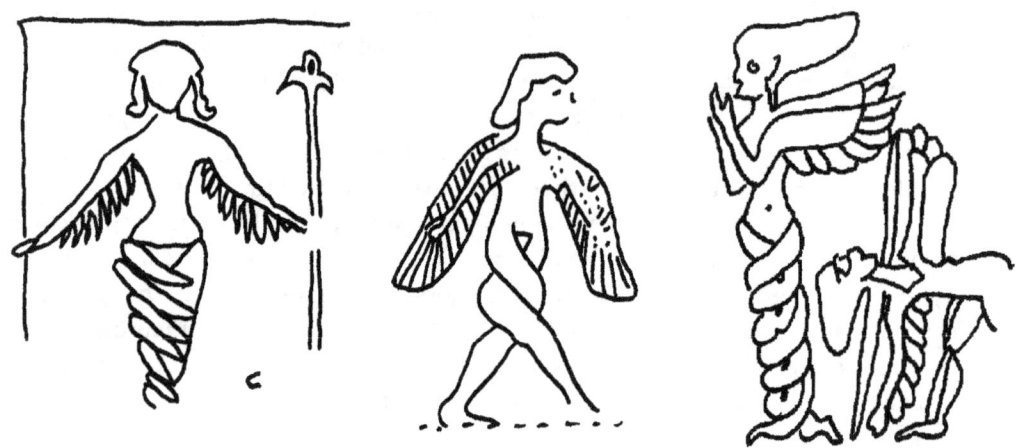

57-59 Three renditions of the South Wind; one example (*right*) alongside the West Wind [16]

The strange form of this goddess' legs may be a visual analogue to the Akkadian word for the 'south wind' – *šūtu* – which is derived from a root meaning 'to circle around' like a flying bird.[17] Similarly, the West Wind's unusual posture may be related to descriptions of the west wind as being 'not straight'. Aside from these visual puns, seemingly based on literate ideas, the winds are often portrayed with their hair swept back by the winds – this is a much more natural way of conveying their essential nature.

In later Akkadian culture we find an emphasis on the traditional four winds defined by the cardinal directions but in Sumerian literature all the stress is placed upon just north and south. The Sumerian model is a much better match to the primary weather patterns of Mesopotamia which are dominated by the north and south winds. In summer, the south wind will bring intense heat and humidity – called the 'fever', but in winter it brings welcome rains to the farmers and livestock-herders. The north wind is cooling by nature, bringing welcome relief in the stifling summers but striking with frost and chill winds during the winter months.

The weather pattern of Mesopotamia is thus polarised between the seasons and the winds. This same principle is self-evidently manifest in the astrological lore attributed to the Anzu-bird, whose constellation figure was associated with the extreme temperatures of summer and winter: '*If the front star of the Anzu-bird is very red: if it is winter there will be frost, if it is summer there will be heat*'.[18]

---

[15] Wiggermann 2007, pages 125-165. Horowitz 1988, pages 196-198.
[16] Wiggermann 2007, right, fig 16c; middle, fig 31c; left, fig 9.
[17] Wiggermann 2007, page 127
[18] BPO2 Text XVI, line 10.

The Bird Goddess

We naturally think of the winds as being a very limited part of the overall conception of the heavens. We think of it in terms of the atmosphere, a thin layer of gases, surrounding the earth that only extends a few miles above its surface. But in ancient cosmology, the winds stretch all the way to the realm of the sun and the stars. This is implied by the figure of the winged disk, which simply attaches the outstretched wings of a bird onto the solar disk. This formulation implies that the winds extend into what we would call the celestial and stellar realms.

Such a grand conception of the winds, stretching all the way to the heavenly vault, is beautifully expressed in our next design:

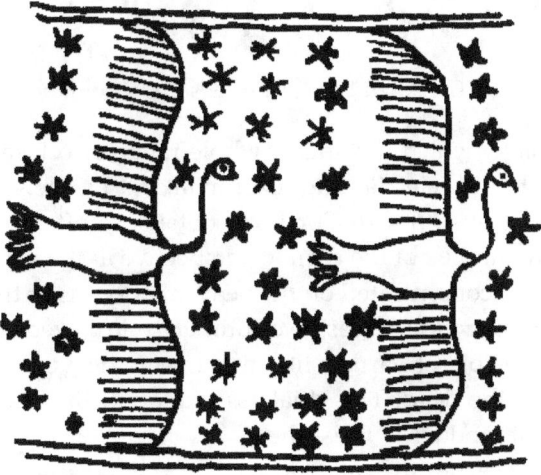

60 The mother birds fly among the stars [19]

Given the celestial origins of the human soul, this image of the mother bird flying through a field of stars must surely allude to the very first stages of the soul's cosmic descent. It is easy to imagine these birds 'plucking stars' from the firmament and bearing them down to earth. The basic idea that the soul is a star fallen from heaven can also be found in the *Epic of Gilgamesh*, where the birth of Enkidu is so described in one of Gilgamesh's ominous dreams.

Gilgamesh dreamt that 'the stars of heaven appeared above me, and like a rock from the sky one fell down before me'.[20] His mother correctly interpreted that the falling star was Enkidu, Gilgamesh's future friend and companion. As many scholars have pointed out, Enkidu is really a representative of 'primal man'. He was of superhuman strength and was born in highlands, where he was fostered by the wild herd animals.

The idea that a child's soul falls to earth as a shooting star is a truly poetic metaphor for the creation of a new life. And we should not forget that the falling star bears with it the imprint of the whole of heaven within which it dwelt for timeless ages.

[19] Halaf period bowl, 5th millennium BCE. Goff 1963, detail from fig 80.
[20] George 1999, page 10 (Tablet I, lines 247-8)

The Bird Goddess

This is why a whole array of celestial orbs are sometimes set around the icon of the mother bird:

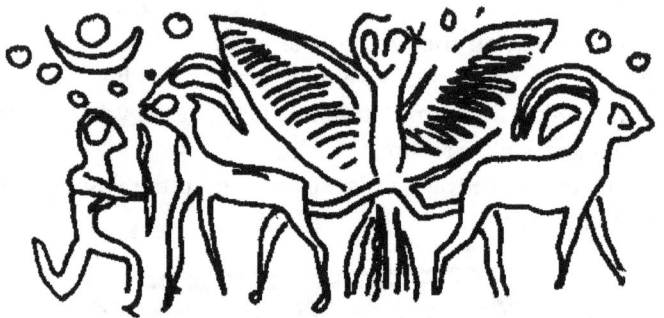

61 The Anzu-bird carries descends from the heavens [21]

Unlike this image, which includes a whole range of celestial bodies, ancient artists often referred back to the celestial origins of mankind by the simple device of placing a single star in their designs (*fig 50*). Such tiny details, so often overlooked, are extremely significant as they remind us of the cosmic perspective at the very heart of our study.

Thus far we have concentrated on the heavenly origins of the child, but the converse is also true as the bird goddess was also intimately involved in the death of mankind. Beyond being the crucible of earthly life, the archaic heavens were also the realm that received the souls of the dead. This dual association of life and death makes the bird a symbol of the great goddess. It is the bringer of life when it carries the calf from the skies, but it is also the bird of death carrying the discarnate soul back into the starry realms of the night.

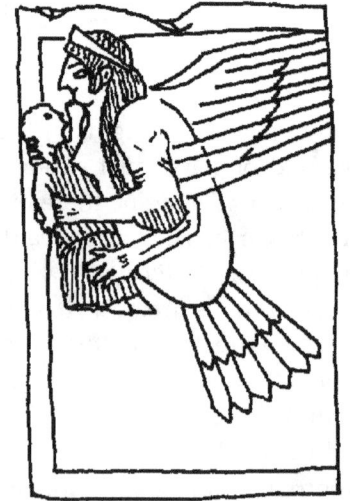

62 A Greek Harpy with a baby [22]

The Greeks assimilated much of the bird-goddess' symbolism into their conception of the Harpies, who were a group of bird-women that, like the Anzu-bird, brought on violent squalls, winds and storms.

In Greek mythic tradition the Harpies or 'Snatchers', as their name implies, were thought to carry off the souls of the dead, but as figure 62 (*right*) shows they also carried the souls of children to and from the heavenly realms.

---

[21] Amiet 1961, plate 94, fig 1239.
[22] Harrison 1962, fig 20 on page 177.

68

The Bird Goddess

Significantly, this image was carved on a gravestone, which again points to the liminal role of the bird-goddess in the creation and dissolution of human life. The tenderness and intimacy with which this Harpy carries her charge certainly suggests that she is the celestial mother of the tiny infant dressed in its swaddling clothes.

This image of the Greek bird-goddess shows that she facilitates both the coming to birth of mankind and his cessation. The Harpies carry souls back and forth between heaven and earth.

In Mesopotamia too, Anzu played out the same dual role of creatrix and transporter of the dead. The deathly side of Anzu is seen in the next image (*below*), where it is pictured carrying off a group of men with their arms tied behind their backs.

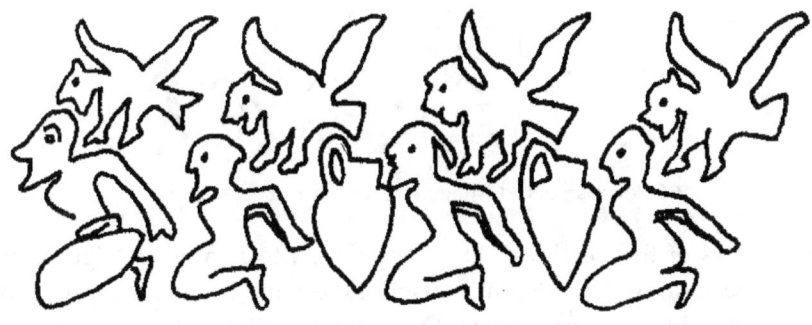

63 Anzu-birds carry off bound men [23]

That these men are dead or as good as dead is shown by another literary parallel drawn from the *Epic of Gilgamesh*. When Enkidu dreamed of his impending death, he dreamt that he was struck down by a demon with the face of an Anzu-bird. The demon overpowered him, then bound his arms behind his back and forcibly rendered him to the 'house of dust' – a name for the underworld, set way below the earth where the buried corpses of mankind moulder away to dust.[24]

All this imagery shows that Anzu, like the Harpies, carried off the souls of the dead as well as acting as the bringer of new life. But unlike the underworld destination of Enkidu's dream, the bird-goddess carried the dead back to the heavenly realms from which they originated.[25]

The origins of such ideas can be traced back into the Neolithic period. The famous village of Catal Huyuk, now in modern-day Turkey, contained three separate houses that contained wall paintings of enormous vultures set among headless human corpses. There are also images of excarnation towers (*overleaf*) where the birds picked the flesh from the bones of the dead.

---

[23] 4th millennium BCE seal. Collon 1987, fig 887.

[24] George 1999, pages 60-61 (Tablet VII, lines 165-184)

[25] We will return to the idea of heaven and the underworld being very different realms of the dead in Part Three of the book.

The Bird Goddess

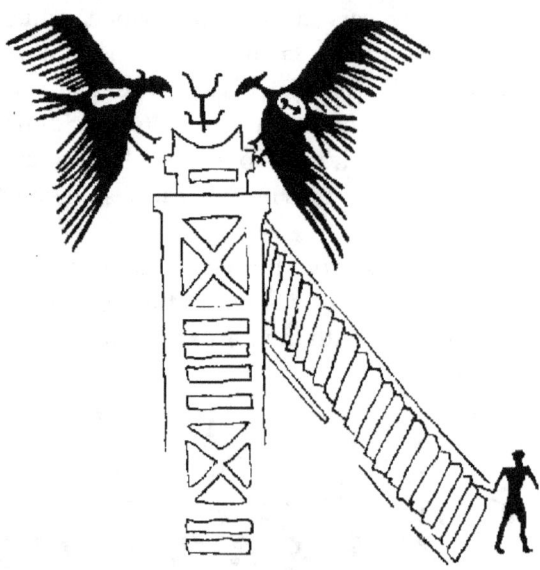

64 Reconstructed image of an excarnation tower [26]

These vultures of the dead are set in opposition to another intriguing icon of the goddess that appears in seven different houses of the same village. One such goddess, set above three clay bull heads, even appears to be giving birth to a tiny calf (*below*).[27]

The bizarre imagery of the goddess overshadows a more sombre purpose as the bones of men, women and children were also discovered in these shrines. This assemblage of artefacts therefore places a naked goddess in the dual context of life and death, and more significantly, they appear to describe mankind in terms of cattle.

It is impossible to tell if this birth goddess is a sky deity of any sort but she is typically placed high up in the shrines while the bull's heads are down at floor level, and the bone burials below. It may not be too much of a stretch for the imagination to understand her outstretched limbs as harkening back to the outstretched wings and legs of our bird goddess.

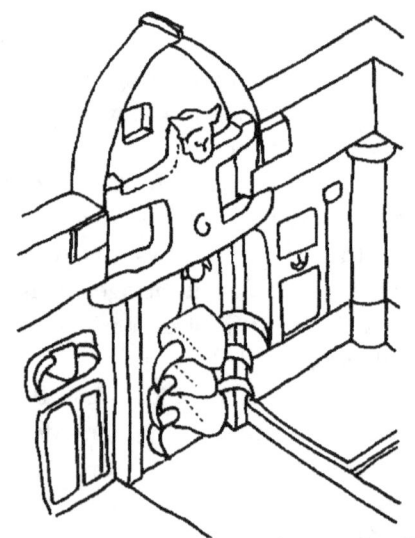

65 A burial shrine from Catal Huyuk [28]

---

[26] From an internet search for 'Catal Huyuk'– a disputed image based on Mellaart's drawings.

[27] Mallowan 1965, caption 58 b, page 109. The excavator described it as giving birth to a male lamb.

[28] Mallowan 1965, fig 58b, page 109.

The Bird Goddess

Man's concept of himself inevitably plays the fundamental defining role in the myths he creates about his own origins and ends. Archaic artwork paints a picture in which the child's soul descended from the heavenly realms to be born on earth, and returned to the heavens after its worldly end. This cycle of birth and return can be mapped out as follows:

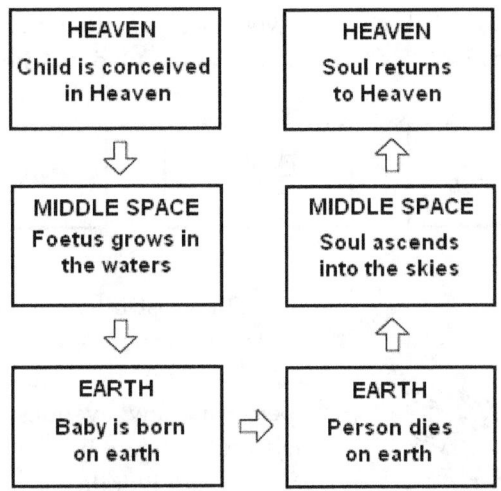

Diagram of the archaic model of man's creation and end

This highly symmetrical model of man and the universe is also the basis of Vedic philosophy. The Vedic heavens were the cradle of human life. Yama, the first man, was the first-born child of the sun god and he described his own origins as being with 'the divine youth in the waters and the woman of the waters'.[29] Translating this into our own terminology, the first man was born from the sun and the celestial waters. After his death, he became lord of the dead. However, the Vedic realm of the dead was not below the earth but located in heaven above. The 'path' that Yama established was subsequently followed by the massed ranks of the dead. Those that travelled its way attained the highest heavens where the dead were reunited with the ancestral fathers. In the words of another Vedic poet: the discarnate soul 'returns home, leaving all imperfection behind, he merges with a glorious body'.[30]

I hope this Vedic interlude illustrates how the whole system worked and, more importantly, that it is a viable model, which has definite precedents in other advanced cultures of the archaic world with a penchant for developing complex symbolic schemes.

We will continue with the aerial theme in the next chapter, which explores the symbolism of the storm goddess.

---

[29] O'Flaherty 1981, page 248, verse 4. (Book 10, hymn 10) The divine youth may well be related to our lineage figure.

[30] O'Flaherty 1981, page 44, verses 7 & 8 (Book 10, hymn 14)

The Storm Goddess

In the last chapter, I made a general identification between the winged goddess and the various forms of the flying bird. This identification was founded on the combination of their shared features, such as wings and bird-feet (*fig 56*), and on their identical functions of transporting the calf-child between heaven and earth.

As before, the basic identifications can be represented in schematic format:

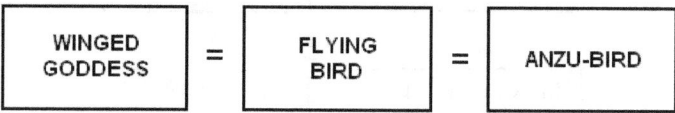

The most intriguing part of the equation is the incorporation of the lion-headed bird known as Anzu (*left*). Its inclusion in our birth motifs opens up new avenues of exploration as this mythical creature has a very well-defined nature in surviving literate sources.

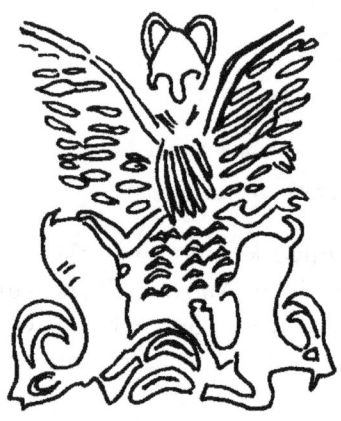

66 Anzu with its calves [1]

In the earliest written traditions, the lion-headed eagle was described in cosmological terms – its foot was set upon the earth while its hand reached up to heaven; its enormous wings spanned the very skies. The high god, Enlil, assigned the bird the power to decree 'the destiny of the rolling rivers',[2] for the Anzu-bird was the 'powerful storm-bird',[3] and the roar of its lion-head was thunder. Anzu was the bringer of rains and floods, fogs and mists,[4] and the winds were born of its flapping wings.

All this diverse material shows that Anzu is a 'unitary symbol' of the skies, by which I mean it incorporates manifold aspects of the weather and the skies into its nature. Anzu's leonine head is arguably a symbol of the sun in the midst of heaven, and as an embodiment of the storm, lightning is said to flash from its eyes.[5]

What this all boils down to is that the flying bird is a symbol of the skies and all the weather it holds. The nature of the storm bird as bringer of the rains is only rarely met

---

[1] Amiet 1961, plate 87, detail of fig 1147.
[2] ETCSL: Lugalbanda & the Mountain Cave, lines 111-131 and 90-110.
[3] 'Powerful storm-bird' is the meaning of its Sumerian name Imdugud. Jacobsen 1976, pages 128-129.
[4] Black & Green 1992, page 107. See the PSD: MURU [rainstorm] which also means 'mist & drizzle'.
[5] ETCSL: Lament for Unug, lines 11-20.

with in ancient art, I believe the association is so strong that ancient artists purposefully avoided combining the two motifs. What they did instead was combine the image of the descending waters with other icons of the skies such as the winged disk. The illustration seen below is a typical example of this practice, as it clearly shows the heavenly torrents falling from the body of the winged disk.

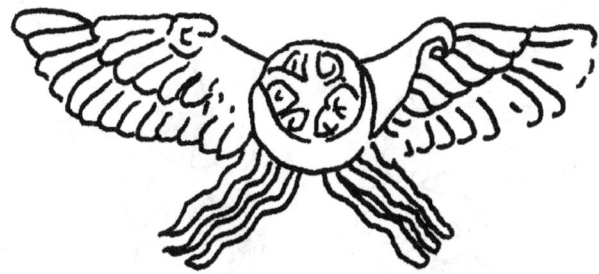

67 The winged disk emanates the celestial waters [6]

Some of the most striking artwork of the 4th millennium BCE hails from what is now modern-day Iran. One of the favourite themes of these early artists was the symbolism of the celestial waters. They sometimes incorporated the storm bird into their designs (*below*), where it flies across the skies, bringing forth the waters of heaven.

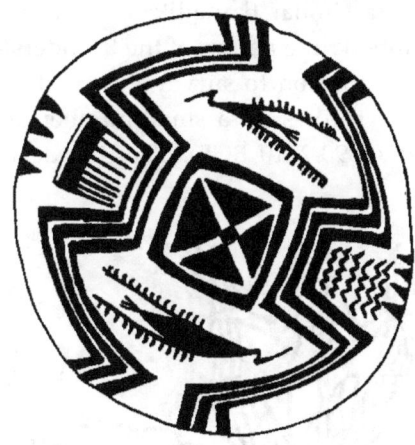

68 Storm-birds fly through the skies [7]

If the bird is such a fundamental symbol of the rains and storms, then by the terms of our identifications, the winged goddess, who evidently partakes of the nature of the winds, must also be a goddess of the weather-bearing skies and the storms.

---

[6] Wiggermann 2007, detail of fig 20.
[7] Book of Iran. Ayatollahi, 2002, fig 15.

The Storm Goddess

Before looking at any icons of the major goddesses, it is an instructive exercise to go back to the more primitive imagery of the personified winds. If it can be shown that the winds are also embodiments of the storm, then the argument is already halfway to being proven. A 2nd millennium BCE carved stele (*below*) provides us with the answers we are seeking. This monument incorporates very clear figures of all four traditional winds, even if modern scholars have had some difficulty working out which is which:

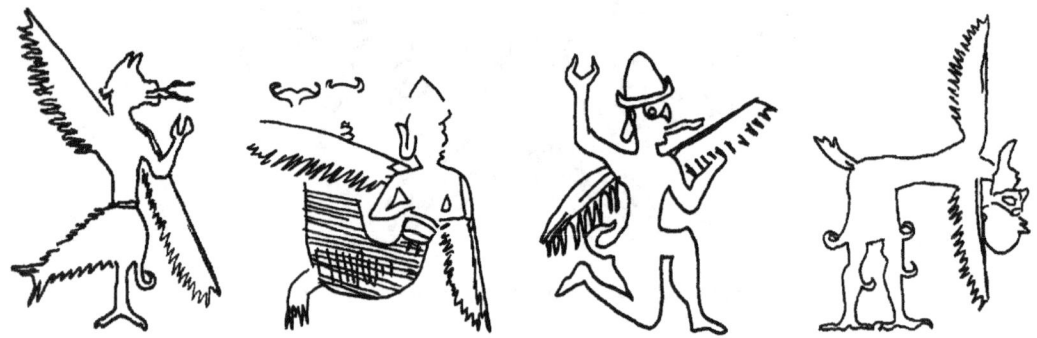

69 Figures of the four winds from an Assyrian stele [8]

The first and third examples, probably portraying the South and East winds, are the pertinent figures. The first appears to have a lightning bolt emerging from its mouth, while the third example has a similar flame-like or watery emanation – both of which indicate that these beings embody the nature of the thunderstorm.

Now we are in a better position to survey the artistic record for goddesses of the rains and storms. The survey throws up a small number of very promising images, all dating to the Akkadian age (2390-2210 BCE). The first design features the storm god's chariot:

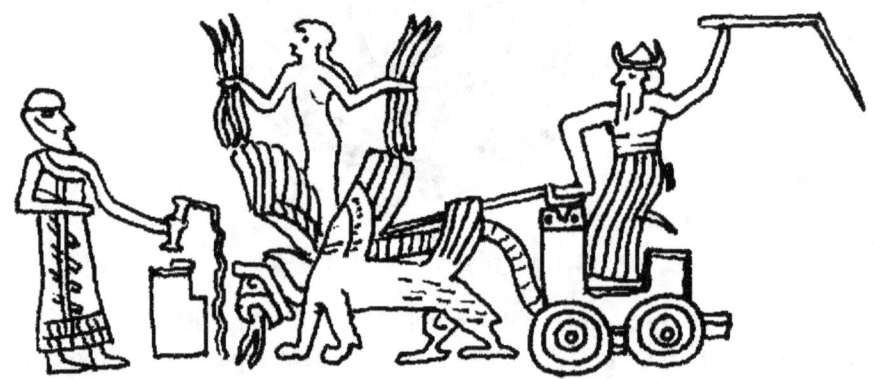

70 The storm deities of the Akkadian age [9]

---

[8] Stein 1993, fig 659, details. I would identify the winds, from left to right, as South, North, East and West. Wiggermann 2007, page 147 (note for fig 17) reverses the attributions of North and South.

[9] Boehmer 1965, fig 373.

The Storm Goddess

But it isn't the storm god who draws our attention – it is the seemingly naked goddess who stands upon the storm-griffin. It is she, rather than the storm god, that holds the essence of the storm in the form of her lightning bolts. Indeed, she can be regarded as the embodiment of the storm striking with her lightning bolts just as her sacred griffin disgorges the floodwaters of heaven.

This goddess has all the credentials of an independent deity of the storm. In fact, the storm god and his rumbling chariot look like they have been added on to the icon of the goddess and her griffin. The next image helps to confirm our suspicions as it omits the storm god's chariot altogether and instead depicts both deities riding on their own storm-beasts.

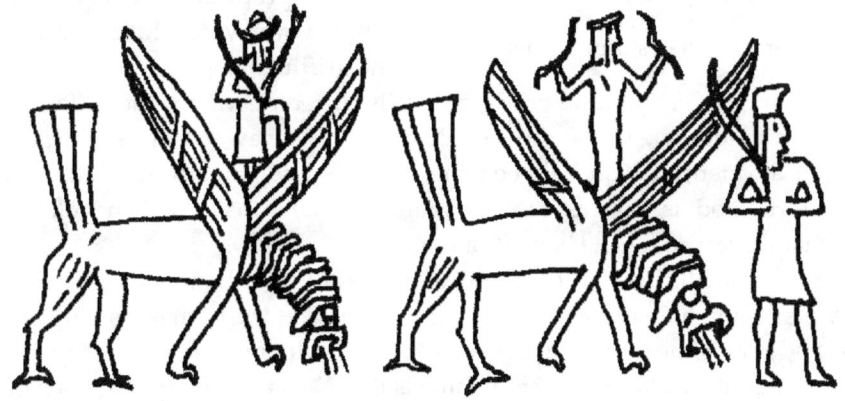

71 Riders of the Storm; male & female storm deities on their griffins [10]

The creature we have called a 'storm-griffin' is obviously very close, both in form and function, to the Anzu-bird. As symbols of the storm, their lion heads roar with thunder, their wings whip up the tempests and they both bring on the rains. The only appreciable difference between the two beasts is the relative preponderance of eagle and lion in their composition – the griffin having the larger share of a lion. Thus the storm-griffin and the storm-bird can also be identified with each other.[11] As the sky-bird and storm-griffin merge into one entity, so does the figure of the winged goddess harmonise with our storm goddess. By riding the storm-griffin, the storm goddess is already flying through the skies; it is just the case that her wings are attached to her symbolic storm-beast rather than herself.

Going back to the image of the storm god's chariot, it is a worthwhile diversion to look at the way in which the two deities relate to the griffin. The goddess with her lightning bolts is as much an embodiment of the storm as the griffin. They are kindred spirits, wild and wilful.

---

[10] Boehmer 1965, fig 367.

[11] The same conclusion is drawn from art and text in Watanabe 2002, page 128 & her fig 48.

The Storm Goddess

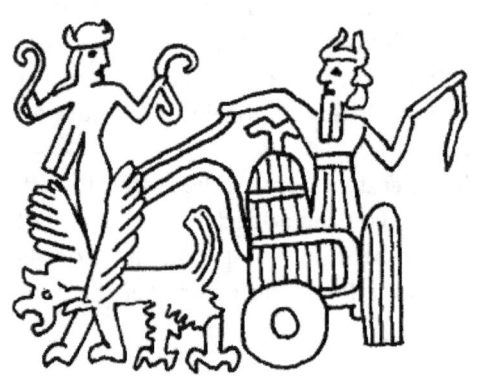

72 Another Akkadian storm chariot [12]

On the other hand, the storm god comes across in a completely different manner. He has used all the latest technology to harness the griffin's tempestuous nature. The god controls the beast through his reins and cracking whip. The god has bound the elemental powers of the storm to his chariot. The seal depicts him as the 'driver of the storm' and his characteristic weapon is very appropriately deemed to be the whip, with which he relentlessly drives the griffin on.

The two deities relate to the griffin in totally different ways – the difference reflects two entirely different views of the world. The worldview of the goddess posits an affinity, even an identification between the goddess and the storm-beast, on the other hand, the storm god is cast as the conqueror of the beast – a benevolent god that harnesses chaotic nature for the benefit of man.

Seeing as how all these Akkadian designs date to the literate era, there must be a good chance of being able to name the storm goddess. In truth, there is only one realistic candidate, and that is the Sumerian goddess known as Inanna.

The popular understanding of her name is that she is the 'Lady or Queen of Heaven' (**Nin-anna**). Various Sumerian hymns dedicated to the goddess describe the manifold aspects of her character. In several hymns she is directly envisioned as the storm, coming forth from heaven, riding upon the storm clouds that are called her 'seven great beasts'.[13] The nature of her beasts is revealed in another hymn that describes the goddess riding through the heavens with the stormy south wind before her, and a swirling dust storm following on behind.[14]

These references certainly provide a good match our seal designs. They picture Inanna riding through the skies among the winds and storm clouds. Her true nature, as the storm itself, is finally made explicit in a passage that describes her alongside the storm god: 'You (Inanna) charge forward like a charging storm. You roar with the roaring storm, you continually thunder with Iškur' (the Sumerian storm god).[15] More succinctly, another hymn to the goddess backs up the idea where it proclaims: 'Inanna, in heaven, you are lightning'.[16]

---

[12] Collon 1987, detail from fig 726 on page 160; also Boehmer 1965, Tafel XXXI, fig 372.

[13] ETCSL: Inana (D), lines 99-108.

[14] ETCSL: Inana & Šukaletuda, lines 185-193. See Horowitz 1998, page 198. The south wind is considered to be the most violent wind, often bringing thunderous tempests and at times severe rainfall.

[15] ETCSL: Exaltation of Inana, lines 20-33.

[16] ETCSL: Inana D, lines 44-56.

The Storm Goddess

Inanna's rulership of the storms was even sanctioned by the high god Enlil. In one of her hymns of self-praise, Inanna recounts that 'He (Enlil) gave me the storm wind and he gave me the dust cloud'.[17] The seal designs we have seen in this section, by setting Inanna alongside the storm god, may well reflect this 'official version' of the pantheon as endorsed by Enlil.

The two storm deities commonly appear with each other in Akkadian artwork, as is the case in our next design that depicts a bull sacrifice:

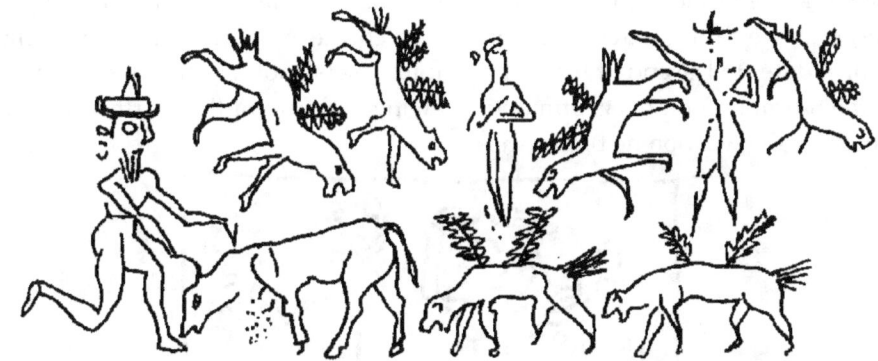

73 A god performs the bull sacrifice as the storm griffins mass [18]

To judge from the context of the whole design, the bull sacrifice, carried out by the kneeling god on the left-hand side, must bring on the winter rains as the gathering storm clouds are represented by the massed griffins that descend from the skies. They are opening their mouths to unleash their thunderous roar and let loose the floodwaters.

Continuing with the same theme, another Akkadian design very neatly depicts the culmination of the bull sacrifice and the sought-after rains.

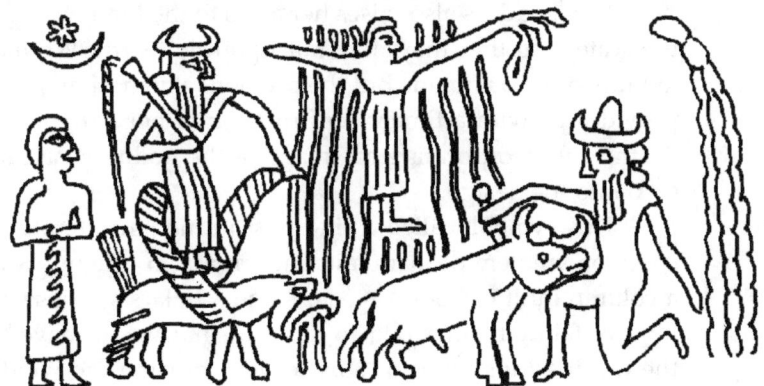

74 The bull sacrifice brings on the rains [19]

---

[17] ETCSL: Inana (F), lines 4-13.
[18] Boehmer 1965, Tafel XXX, fig 364.
[19] Collon 1987, fig 780 on page 168; and Boehmer 1965, Tafel XXXI, fig 369.

The Storm Goddess

The goddess stands in the middle of the sky with arms held aloft; she is unleashing the rains that have been brought on by the sacrifice. Like our previous images of the storm goddess, which all held thunderbolts, this goddess is also a very direct embodiment of the storm as she stands right in the midst of the maelstrom while the storm god stands idly by.

Inanna also appears as a goddess of the rains in literate sources. One hymn to the goddess describes the arrival of her foreboding clouds: 'When with the storm you reduce everything to a mere shadow, Inanna when you cause the rain to fall all day long ...' [20]

Images of the rain goddess are not limited to the Akkadian era. The design seen below, which dates to the end of the 3rd millennium, sets another form of the rain goddess between the Storm god on his griffin and the winged figure of the North wind, who can be identified by the weapon he brandishes.[22]

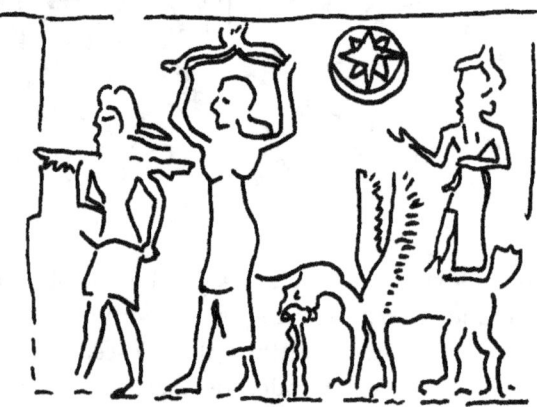

75 The powers of the sky – the north wind, the rain goddess and the storm god [21]

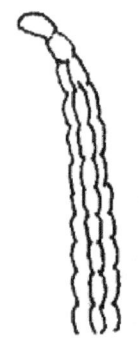

Detail of fig 74

This goddess also raises her arms to the high heavens and frees the waters so that they may fall upon the earth. We have already identified her as Inanna but the previous illustration (*fig 74*) actually provides us with a timely confirmation of her name. It manages to do this by incorporating an image of the goddess' sacred standard (*left*) into the design.

This symbol, called a ring-post in modern literature, is a very common emblem of Inanna in ancient art; in origin it was probably a column built of bound reeds. Some scholars suppose it had some kind of fabric banner tied to its head that would have fluttered in the winds – thus acting as a basic weather vane and wind gauge.[23]

---

[20] ETCSL: A hymn to Inana as Ninegala, Inana (D) lines 58-65.
[21] Wiggermann 2007, fig 6.
[22] Wiggermann 2007, page 129.
[23] Cohen 2005, page 131.

The Storm Goddess

The symbol of the ring-post 'migrated' from the arena of the visual arts into the realm of writing, where it was adopted as the **Muš₃**-sign (*right*). This sign, prefixed by the star-sign for divinity, is invariably used to write the name of Inanna in all manner of texts.[24]

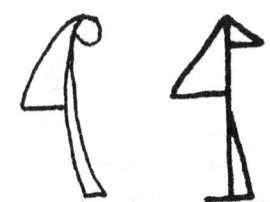

Two examples of the **Muš₃**-sign

In light of the Anzu-bird causing summertime heat and wintertime chills, it surely can't be a coincidence that the **Muš₃**-sign and its variant forms have a wide range of weather related meanings attributed to them including 'frost and ice', 'winter' and 'cold weather'.[25]

I hope that the foregoing discussion has proved the reality of an early goddess of the skies and storms in Mesopotamia. As an added bonus, we have also been able to discover that her name was Inanna. Her imagery and the testimonial of her hymns prove that she is a true counterpart to the animalian creatures of the sky, like the Anzu-bird and griffin, who embody the powers of the storm.

Behind the diverse imagery of the storm goddess and the metaphors of the child there is actually a surprising decree of consistency. The common pattern shows that the heavenly powers, symbolised by birds, not only bring the rains and winds from the skies, but they also foster and ultimately deliver the children of mankind to their mothers on earth.

It is best to contemplate the dual powers of the heavens in their iconic forms:

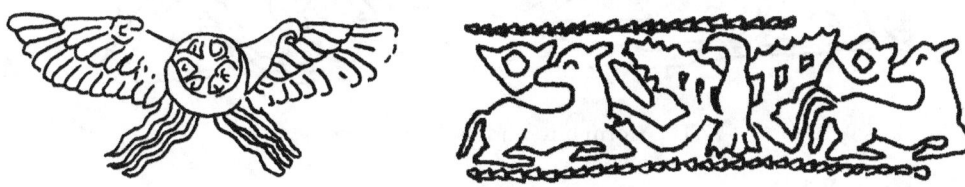

76 Dual conception of the fertile heavens:
The water-bearing winged disk and the flying bird bringing new life down from the skies [26]

The two powers accorded to the heavens – the formation of the child and the creation of rain – appear so utterly unrelated to the modern mind. To the archaic mind, however, the rains were emblematic of the celestial waters, and these waters contained the 'seed of mankind'. The diverse powers attributed to the heavens can only be

---

[24] Labat 1988, # 103, on pages 84-85, and page 293 under Ištar.

[25] PSD: AMAGI 'frost, ice'. HALBA 'frost, ice, cold weather, to be cold. MABI 'frost'. SED 'to be cold, to cool, winter'.

[26] Amiet 1961, plate 56, detail of fig 767.

The Storm Goddess

reconciled when the waters of heaven are understood as the living waters that bear the nascent child. When this truth is understood, the connection between the sky goddess and the earthly mother becomes self-evident: The storm goddess' thunderous roar and the deluge that follows are parallel to the mother's screams in childbirth and the breaking of her own waters. The dome of heaven is thereby likened to the swollen belly of the mother, and the waters within both hold the essence of the protean child.

As I mentioned before, images of the storm bird dispensing its waters are relatively rare as the association is just too obvious. Nevertheless, a single Assyrian design very helpfully combines the dual symbolism of the storm bird into one succinct image:

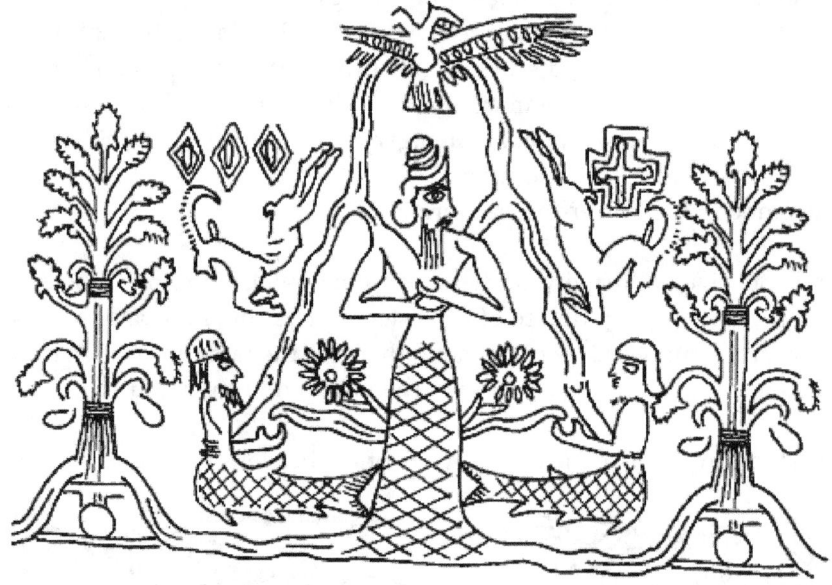

77 The storm bird and its fertile waters [27]

Twin streams of water pour from the storm bird and the living essence they contain is symbolised by the graceful mountain goats that descend with the waters to the earth. This design introduces the masculine element of the man-mountain; his potent waters mingle with the deluge in mid-heaven and thereby fertilise them. Via the celestial mermen, the waters eventually fall upon the mountain slopes and bring the flowers to life. Then, as we have seen (figs 25-30), the goats climb the mountains to eat these same flowers to gain their own fertile seed. Thus do the skies bring life to the earth and all its inhabitants.

The incorporation of the male element, as we will see in Part Three of the book, is the invention of a later age, what is important to recognise here is that the celestial waters are essentially female in nature and bear the descending spirit of the child.

---

[27] Kassite seal design. Ornan 2005, fig 17; and Annus 2002, fig 8, on page 125.

The Storm Goddess

The fundamental idea that the skies are feminine in nature and laden with a seed-like essence is perfectly illustrated by another Assyrian design:

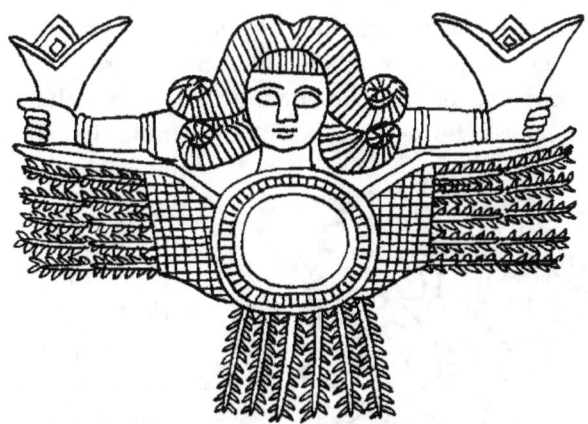

78 An Assyrian image of the female winged disk [28]

Although the winged disk is most often inhabited by male divinities, there are a number of lesser-known examples that unequivocally show its female side. This goddess is the living embodiment of the winged disk. She is a goddess of the fertile heavens, whose wings span the skies and bring the fertile rains. The plants she holds in her outstretched hands allude to the familiar idea that the rains carry the seed of life.

Contemplation of these images lead us to the inevitable conclusion that the great mother of humanity is not a goddess of the earth, no, on the contrary, she is a goddess of the fertile skies.

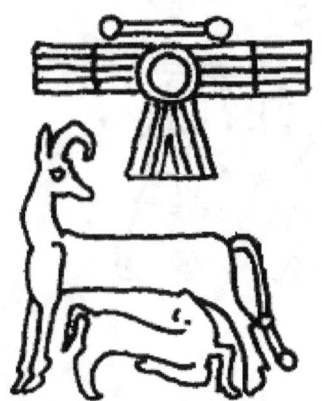

79 Detail of an Assyrian seal [29]

The same idea of the life-nurturing heavens was often expressed by setting the beautiful icon of the mother and child under a symbol of the fecund skies. The example seen in figure 79 (*left*) uses the winged disk and deer but many other combinations were used to express the self-same idea.

What all these designs are really saying is that the child has two mothers. Besides the earthly mother that physically bears the child to the world, every child also has a celestial mother who shapes its foetal form within its mother's womb and brings it to birth. In the bigger picture this celestial goddess is, of necessity, the goddess that forms the foetal children of all mankind.

[28] IDD website under Dictionary Entries – Female Solar Deities, fig 1, page 1.
[29] Frankfort 1939, plate XXXIV, fig i.

The Storm Goddess

The proposition that the heavens are fertile and female in nature has become the first and most fundamental principle in our study. It is at odds with general opinion on ancient religion, at least that conveyed to us by literate sources. This is one of several points in our journey where ancient art tells a different story from the written traditions. And we shall follow the narrative of symbols rather than words.

A very useful property of 'fundamental principles' is that they are constantly repeated in different pictorial terms. The essential formula that the sky goddess is also the mother of all humanity can be proven in a most convincing manner by simply placing two images of the Courtesan side-by-side.

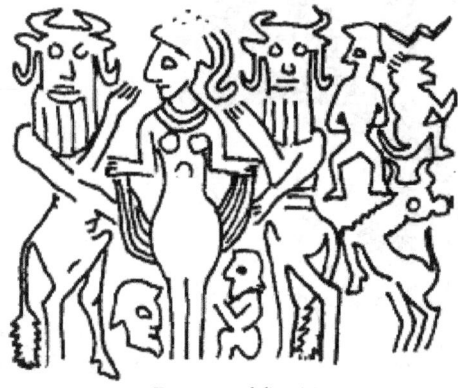

Repeat of fig 46

First of all, we have to go back to an earlier design (*left*). This semi-naked goddess, standing between the phallic bison-men and surrounded by images of the child, can certainly be identified as the mother of all children and therefore of all mankind.

The very same goddess, and there is no mistaking her, appears in her astral aspect below, where she is set between more ordinary renditions of the fathers:

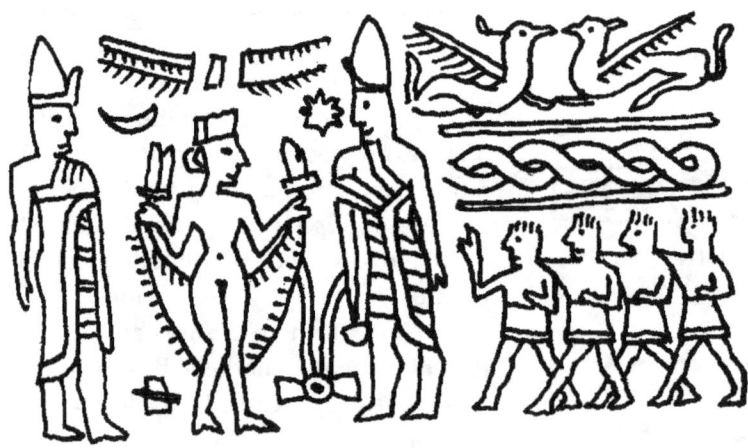

80 The storm goddess as celestial mother [30]

Here we see the Courtesan in all her celestial glory. She wields the lightning bolts of the sky goddess and is crowned with the heavenly symbols of the sun, moon and winged disk. She embodies all of heaven from the storms to the realm of the stars.

---

[30] Winter 1987, Abb 269.

The Storm Goddess

Being presented with the astral side of the Courtesan, we can be in little doubt that she is an icon of Inanna, the great goddess of heaven and the wellspring of all earthly fertility. And it is as a goddess of heaven that the Courtesan's ever-present shawl starts to make sense. I believe it is referring to night and day. When the bright goddess unveils her body she illuminates the skies creating day, but when she veils her body she manifests as night, resplendent with her shining stars.

Taken together, this pair of images proves beyond any doubt that the sky goddess also functioned as the mother of humanity.

The inherently fertile nature of the sky goddess is encoded into her name. Even though Inanna's name was always written with her ring-post sign, this way of writing it obscures its real meaning and derivation. Ultimately she is ^(deity) NIN-ANNA, the 'Lady or Queen of Heaven' (*right*).

The **Nin**-sign has the meaning of 'lady or queen'. This sign is itself a composite sign, made up from the feminine vulva on top (*see below*) and the sign for 'noble' below, which may depict a seat of some sort. Together they connote a 'noble woman'.

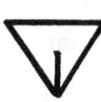

The womb-sign (*left*), has two principal readings – read as **Munus** it refers to a 'woman' and the 'female' gender in general; and read as **Gala** it specifically means 'womb or vulva'.[31]

The following **An**-sign is used to connote the 'heavens' which Inanna rules, and the final sign (**Na**) is used as a grammatical element that conveys the possessive case. Thus the whole name can be understood as 'the Queen of Heaven', but a more nuanced rendering could equally be 'the noble womb of heaven'.

Before ending this chapter it may prove useful to summarise our findings and set them within the broader framework of the emergent symbol system.

We started this chapter with a basic proposition that the winged goddess could be identified with the different forms of the flying bird. We have further seen how this bird, representing the fertile heavens, brought all life to earth in the form of the waters it disburses and the symbol of the child it so often carries. Now we can add the winged disk to our list of symbols that represent the fertile skies as it too pours forth the heavenly waters and carries the child to its mother (*fig 79*). Thus our set of identifications for the heavenly powers grows. What is more, our investigation has started to reveal an additional layer of symmetry to the structure, as the different symbolic forms of the bird goddess can now be set out in a very orderly relationship to the two primary metaphors of the child.

---

[31] PSD: MUNUS [woman] & GALA [vulva]

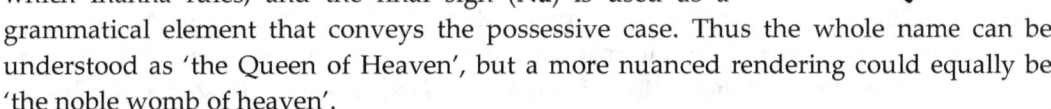

The Storm Goddess

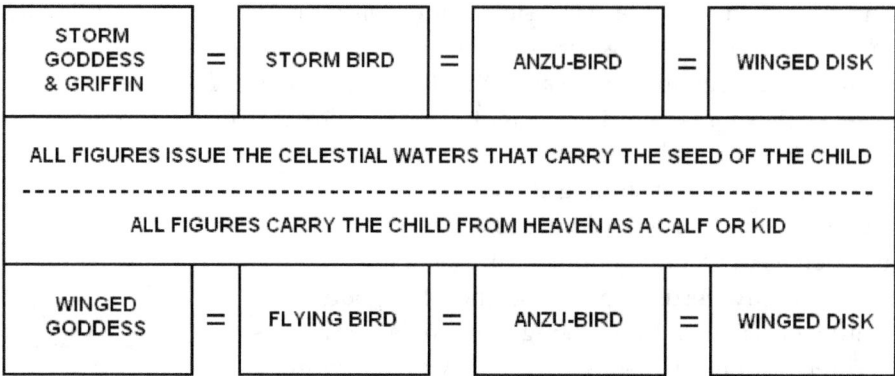

Diagram mapping out the relationship between heavenly symbols and the child

This diagram maps out the essential core of our emerging symbol system. The binary nature of the system is self-evident and acts as a countercheck for completeness. We can also speculate on the basis of this diagram that the sphinxes and griffins we have started to see in some of our designs are part of this same structure – but we will have to wait until another time before we are in a position to prove this proposition.

The fact that very specific symbols, like the lion-headed eagle and winged disk, can be 'exchanged' from one set of paradigms to another demonstrates that there is an implicit order underpinning the artistic traditions. In truth, the degree of symmetry exhibited by the model, forces you to call it a 'symbol system'.

Composed of *metaphors* like the celestial waters and the descending calf, and sets of *identifications* like the various avatars of the bird-goddess, the structural layout of a symbol system is comparable to a fabric woven from a horizontal woof and a vertical warp. And like the finest Persian carpets, there is a beauteous symmetry in its formulation. That is part of the intrinsic appeal of a symbol system and the basis upon which we can start to decipher it. Individual symbols express small links in much bigger chains. The bigger picture only starts to emerge when you start to pull the several threads together and look at the resulting patterns. Behind its diverse imagery is a unitary scheme, which largely bypasses the analytical and logical faculties of the mind. It is only realised when the separate pieces of the puzzle fall into place and reveal the underlying patterns of thought.

The ancients seem to have had more dexterity than us moderns when it comes to the symbolic realms. Nevertheless, I believe that the principles and the practice can be relearned. Personally, I have found that drawing or copying the images is the best starting point as this brings the imagery to life within one's own imagination.

Although we have made considerable progress in our study of the goddess, we have by no means circumscribed her nature. Beyond the realms of the weather-bearing skies, the goddess also manifests herself in the higher, more refined, worlds of the celestial orbs. This is the subject of the next chapter.

The Celestial Goddess

As goddess of the storm Inanna certainly ruled the weather-bearing realms of the skies. Needless to say, this domain was only the lowest part of the skies. High above the vagaries of the storm-winds, in the upper reaches of the archaic cosmos, the great luminaries circled around the earth.

In the earliest literary texts, the goddess manifested herself among the celestial bodies as the planet Venus; even today the planet of love and all things female. This Venusian goddess should properly be called Inanna-Ištar as she is actually a fusion of two different goddesses – our Sumerian goddess Inanna and an Akkadian deity known as Ištar. The two goddesses were fused together, that is syncretised, in the Akkadian period (2390-2210 BCE). Their union is part of a broader cultural phenomenon that saw the older Sumerian pantheon being merged together with a whole host of new Akkadian gods.

It is generally assumed that the principal deities being merged together shared significant attributes in common – thus Utu, the sun god of the Sumerians was merged with the Akkadian sun god Šamaš, and the two water gods came together as Enki-Ea. Naturally these gods of the sun and the waters were akin to a greater or lesser degree as they shared the same 'physical manifestations', but there would have been differences, perhaps significant differences, between the god-forms of two so different cultures.

The process of merging the Sumerian and Akkadian pantheons could, in theological terms at least, be a very cutthroat affair. In contemporary artwork, scenes of god slaying god attest that there were irreconcilable differences between the two cultures and their views on the divine.

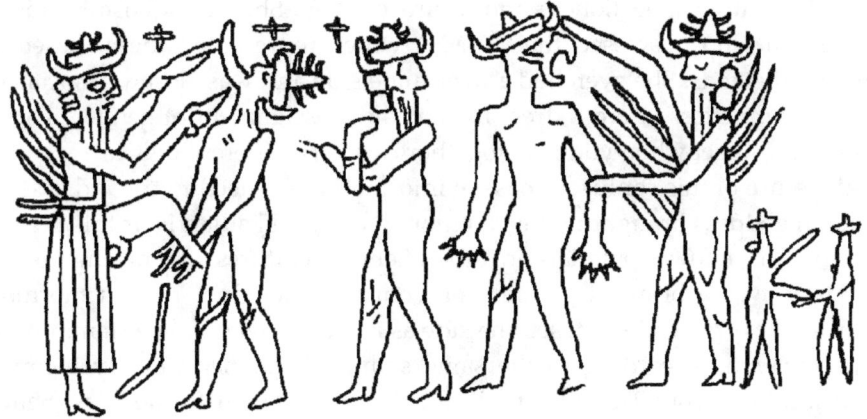

81 The capture and slaughter of the archaic gods from an Akkadian seal [1]

---

[1] Boehmer 1965, Tafel XXVI, fig 307; & Goff 1963, fig 717.

The Celestial Goddess

While some of the archaic powers were brutally dispatched, and their worship presumably suppressed, other Sumerian figures were transformed by being merged with Akkadian gods and goddesses. The merging of the pantheons, and the overall rise of Akkadian culture, shifted the whole worldview of Mesopotamia and had a profound effect on how the ancient goddess was perceived.

As I mentioned before, Inanna, the Sumerian goddess we have started to explore, was fused together with an Akkadian goddess called Ištar. The resultant figure is the syncretic goddess Inanna-Ištar that we know about through literate sources like myths and hymns. Both goddesses appear to be associated with love and procreation but beyond that, the more you learn about them, the more diverse they appear. In fact, the reason why the two goddesses were fused together was not actually based on their similarities but upon a political expediency – Ištar was the tutelary goddess of the new Akkadian rulers and Inanna was the chief goddess of the Sumerian populations.[2] By combining the two goddesses, the Akkadian kings sought to legitimise their reign over the land of Sumeria. It is therefore not surprising that modern commentators describe this dual goddess as a complex and even contradictory character.

The classical Inanna-Ištar is represented as a fiercely independent goddess whose wrath was feared by all. Her love of battle was legendary yet she was also a goddess of love and courtship. In the animal realm she was a goddess of fertility; she also brought abundance to the orchards and fields. But in the realm of human sexuality she was more ambivalent – an erotic figure, a temptress and a lover who ultimately destroyed those who loved her. Symbolised as the Hierodule she represented the erotic function on a cosmic scale; any motherly role seems to be entirely lacking.

Even this welter of ideas doesn't exhaust the multitude of attributes assigned to the goddess. She was the goddess of the storm and the planet Venus, she was the holy cow of heaven as well as an exalted lioness and a bird of prey. She had a cosmic side as the Queen of Heaven who possessed the '50 **Me**', which represented the amassed sacred powers held by the gods. She even had a masculine side and was closely associated with transvestites, the practices of cross-dressing and the reassignment of gender. This is just the kind of mess you get when you fuse together two very different deities!

To make sense of this confused mass of information we need to try and assess what each individual goddess brought to the equation. For the Akkadian Ištar this is relatively simple, as she has known parallels in other Semitic cultures. According to modern authorities, Ištar was a bisexual goddess of Venus. In her dual role as morning and evening star 'she' expressed her masculine side as patron of war and her feminine side in love and procreation. According to the same sources, Ištar had already incorporated another god into her orbit. This was the Venusian god known to the West Semites as Aštar,[3] he presumably brought the patronage of war into Ištar's symbolism. So Ištar was

---

[2] Leick 1991, page 87 & 96.

[3] Leick 1991, page 96 & 15 (see also section on his mother, Aštart, for a potential solar-motherly goddess)

The Celestial Goddess

actually a dual deity in her own right, before her fate was ever inter-twinned with that of Inanna.

What Inanna was like before the fusion is much more difficult to say because no pre-fusion texts about her have come to light and, to make matters worse, she has no known relatives outside Mesopotamia. To make any progress we will have to adopt an alternative strategy. Basically, we need to remove the known attributes of Ištar from the mix of elements found in the syncretic goddess. This method of mental subtraction has obvious limitations and dangers; for one thing it won't furnish us with a ready-made description of Inanna but it should give us a simple list of decent possibilities. If we can then correlate these possibilities with artistic and textual material we should be in a position to start reconstructing the nature of the Sumerian goddess with a degree of confidence.

So far we have proved, in art and literature, that Inanna was a goddess of the rains and storms. The varied description of Inanna-Ištar further suggests that Inanna may be the sacred bird and the divine cow goddess who ruled the entirety of heaven rather than a particular planetary power like Venus. More than anything else, I believe that Inanna was characterised as the great goddess of fertility, the heavenly mother of mankind, which is in stark contrast to the warlike and childless Ištar.

Although this separation of the goddesses is an entirely theoretical model, I would argue that both goddesses are now, not just simpler but also, much more coherent

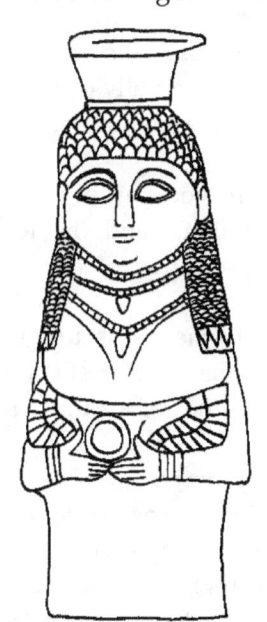

82 The Goddess of heaven [4]

figures. The basic attributes that I have posited for Inanna fit quite well with the ideas of the goddess and child we have been exploring.

For instance, the idea that Inanna embraced all of heaven resonates with the beautiful Assyrian water vase (*left*) carved into the form of the sky goddess. Given that the wings of the winged disk represent the winds and storms, and its central disk is another glyph for the sun, this goddess is conceived on a truly cosmic scale.

This cosmic vision of the goddess is articulated in the aptly named *Exaltation of Inanna*, where the poet declares: 'Be it known that you are lofty as the heavens. Be it known that you are as broad as the earth'.[5] A more astronomic take on the same idea, that Inanna was the goddess of all heaven, is found earlier in the same hymn: 'You are the great lady of the horizon and zenith of the heavens'.[6] In other words, Inanna embraces all the heavenly stations and spheres.

---

[4] IDD website, Female Solar Deities, fig 50a, on page 2.
[5] ETCSL: Inana B, lines 122-138.
[6] ETCSL: Inana B lines 109-121.

The Celestial Goddess

Even this quick sketch of Inanna has helped us make some significant progress with our understanding of the goddess. What is more, Inanna's well-attested attribute 'cow of heaven' is very likely related to all the calf symbolism we have seen applied to the child. This idea may well be expressed in the next design, which returns to the imagery of the Courtesan:

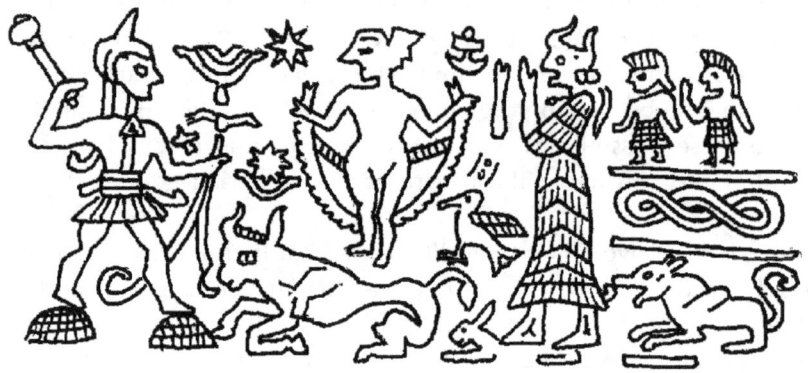

83 The Courtesan and storm god [7]

The goddess is surrounded by symbols, known and unknown. Her association to the cow is made plain even if we can't be sure if this is an adult cow or an over size calf (which could be argued from the flying bird at its tail). The other symbols around her are more elusive – the two star symbols before her speak of her celestial aspect but tell us little more. Similarly, the tiny icons arrayed around the goddess are equally obscure, but there is a possibility that they may represent some of the **Me** – the sacred powers of the gods.

The seemingly diverse elements of this design – the storm god striding over the mountains, the starry realms of the skies, sacred cows and lions, and the fertility symbolism of children – are all mirrored in our proposed description of the ancient Inanna.

The mysterious figure that I call the Courtesan is evidently the connecting thread between all Inanna's symbolism. We have previously met her as the 'mother of mankind' and as the goddess of the skies and storms, now we see the outlines of a truly celestial goddess emerging from the visual sources.

The Courtesan is a curious-looking figure. She is usually posed opening up her shawl to reveal her nakedness, but at other times she appears in a strange state of semi-dress. With her ornate hairdo, and the occasional detail like her curving slippers (*fig 42*), she presents a rather exotic figure combining the airs of high-class and cultural refinement with a mix of eroticism and cultic spectacle. The figure that I have called the Courtesan can be none other than the Hierodule, the great mistress of the gods – who was supposed to be a goddess of sensuality and eroticism rather than motherhood.

---

[7] Assyrian sealing. Reference lost. See Walter's Art Museum, fig 30 Ascension # 42.450 for a similar design.

The Celestial Goddess

The contexts in which the Courtesan appears in ancient art show her to be very compatible with the nature of the Sumerian goddess, Inanna. The varied symbolism surrounding the Courtesan – the storm gods and bison-men, the stars and the **Me**, the celestial cattle and children – all point towards the original identity of Inanna as the heavenly mother of mankind.

Two of our pivotal Courtesan designs (*figs 80 & 83*) are embellished with astral symbols – radiant stars, a moon and winged disk – and it is to the high heavens that we turn to next. In the next design we see the mythical mountains of the east where the sun god rises. Among a group of well-known mythical characters, a wonderfully enigmatic goddess stares us in the face.

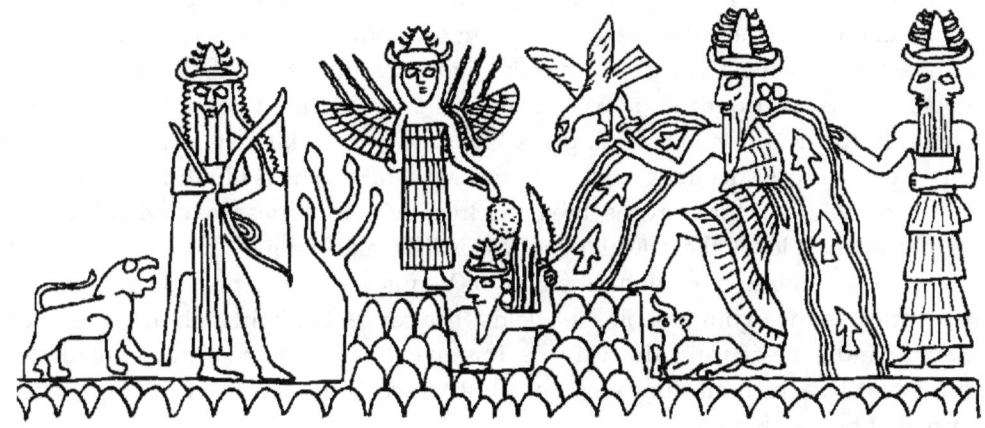

84 The 'Mountain of Sunrise' [8]

The scene is set at dawn just as the sun god rises and starts his ascent into the skies. The goddess has risen ahead of him and this, even by itself, suggests she is either a goddess of the dawn or, much more likely given the Akkadian context of the design, she is meant to be Venus manifesting as the morning star.

Although she is now fully dressed, the goddess still retains more primitive features like her outstretched wings, in marked contrast to the fully human gods around her. The rays of light that emanate from her shoulders point to the great luminaries of the upper heavens. At a very basic level, her symbolism shows her to be a goddess of heavenly light. This depiction of the goddess extends the scope of her influence from the weather-bearing clouds and winds into the more refined realms of the celestial orbs. The attribution of light is a highly significant addition to the goddess' symbolism; we can learn a lot more from literate sources.

The rays of light given to this goddess are doubtless paralleled in divine hymns by the symbolic torch that is the commonest symbol attributed to celestial Inanna. As I cannot ever recall seeing any images of a goddesses from the Ancient Near East holding

---

[8] Boehmer 1965, Tafel XXXII, fig 377; & Goff 1963, fig 720.

The Celestial Goddess

flaming torches, the convention of placing flames directly upon the goddess' shoulders must make the goddess herself the flaming torch. This is all the more likely as one particular hymn to Inanna does indeed directly address the goddess as 'the holy torch' who illuminates the heavens.

Other hymns treat the torch as a straightforward attribute of celestial Inanna: 'A shining torch is assigned to you, the light of the land'.[9] And the light of this torch is further said to 'light up the corners of heaven, turning darkness to light'.[10] Another hymn specifically addressed to the Venusian goddess even states that 'heaven and earth are filled with her huge brilliance'.[11] These are rather over-stated qualities for a planet like Venus. Venus may well be the brightest planet, and brighter than any star, but she hardly turns 'darkness to light', nor displays a 'huge brilliance' that fills the worlds.

A selection of further passages drawn from the goddess' hymns show that Inanna's torch, in fact, represents all forms of celestial light including the light from the sun and the moon. This is spelt out in one particular hymn: 'At night ...(Inanna) ... appears like moonlight. In the heat of noon she appears like sunlight'.[12] The texts could not be more explicit – Inanna is celestial light in all its forms. Most often, she is identified as sunlight – 'the holy torch who fills the heavens, the light, Inanna, who shines like daylight'.[13]

At the deepest level, the celestial goddess is light and the light-filled expanse of the heavens. She is sunlight, moonlight, the light of Venus and the stars; and that same light is also manifest in the lightning bolt she wields. The concept of light embraces the essence of the storm and the essence of the heavens. It is an entirely appropriate symbol for deity, as light is that by which all things are seen but which is unseen itself; it is an invisible brilliance that pervades all heaven.

As a symbol of heavenly light, the flaming torch is widely attributed to the many solar deities of the Ancient Near East. I stress the term 'solar deities', rather than 'gods', as there are several significant solar goddesses in the region. Among the Hurrians, Canaanites and the pre-Islamic Arabs, the sun was female.[14] The sun goddesses appear to be earlier than the sun gods as even the Akkadian sun god Šamaš is meant to have mysterious feminine origins. The earliest hard evidence for Šamaš in Mesopotamia comes from the Early Dynastic period where his name occurs in personal names – and some such names like 'Ummi-Šamaš' literally meaning 'My mother is Šamaš', obviously imply a feminine solar deity.[15]

One of the best known sun goddesses was Šapaš, whose name is closely related to Šamaš (both derive from the Semitic root – šmš – meaning 'sun'). She was the sun goddess of Ugarit, an ancient city-state on the Mediterranean coast. Her principal title

---

[9] ETCSL: Inana (D), lines 1-8.

[10] ETCSL: Inana (D), lines 209-218.

[11] ETCSL: Iddin-Dagan (A), lines 1-16.

[12] ETCSL: Iddin-Dagan A, lines 112-121.

[13] ETCSL: Iddin-Dagan (A), lines 1-16.

[14] Leick 1991, page 147.

[15] Leick 1991, page 147 under Šamaš

The Celestial Goddess

was the 'torch of the gods', and with her all-seeing eyes she could see everything that happened upon earth [16] – these attributes are basic solar traits that are faithfully reproduced in the imagery of all the solar deities, be they male or female.

In the Mesopotamian traditions, the sun gods adopt exactly the same symbolism: '…youthful Utu, who like a torch illuminates the land from the holy heavens'.[17] Likewise, the Akkadian sun god, Šamaš, is repeatedly said to 'bring light in the darkness'.[18]

The torch may be an all-embracive symbol of celestial light, but more specifically it is a symbol of the sun and its radiant light. Put bluntly, that means that one of celestial Inanna's primary aspects was as a goddess of solar light. If Inanna does indeed have a strong solar aspect it would naturally be preserved in the artistic record, even if literate sources are largely silent on the matter.[19] In fact, the very centrality of the sun in the archaic worldview should make it a common occurrence in the symbolism of the sky goddess, even in later times.

One of the commonest icons of the goddess does indeed fulfil these requirements. The icon in question can be called 'celestial Inanna' as it features a figure of the goddess set among the radiant forms of the heavenly bodies. It represents the Queen of Heaven in her sacred sanctuary, **E-Anna**, the 'House of Heaven'.

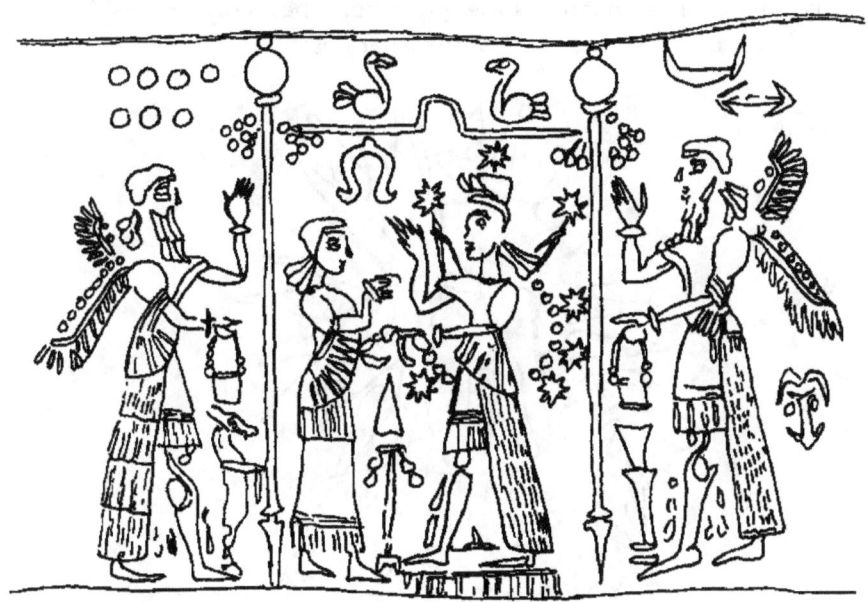

85 Inanna within her heavenly shrine [20]

[16] Leick 1991, page 149, under Šapaš

[17] ETCSL: Šulgi (Q), lines 1-11.

[18] Finkel 'Necromancy in Mesopotamia' (Archiv fur Orientforschung XXIX) page 9, line 6 of translated text.

[19] See the IDD website under 'Female Solar Deities' for a similar situation in Neo-Assyrian times where sky and solar goddesses are well-known in art but not in literature.

[20] Black & Green 1992, fig 49.

The Celestial Goddess

The heavenly stage is set by the appearance of the crescent moon and the seven stars of the Pleiades shining from above. But where is the sun? It can only be the large disk set behind the goddess. The goddess herself is the sunlight, the fruitful radiance of the sun. Surrounded by the sun, moon and stars, this image gives us a complete rendition of the light-generating powers of the heavens.

This interpretation that Inanna's great disk is solar in nature is, I believe, entirely new as in modern literature this symbol is widely referred to as a 'nimbus of stars' even if some examples (*below & fig 140*) don't actually have any stars adorning them!

The way that Inanna's shrine is portrayed defines the nature of the heavenly goddess. The two small birds perching upon its roof are the emissaries of the goddess that transport the soul between the upper and lower worlds. Likewise, the womb symbol that adorns the heavenly vault unambiguously points to the heavens being the womb that brings the child to birth.

The radiant light of Inanna is a very direct, non-symbolic, way of talking about the nature of the fertile heavens. For the archaic mind, visual metaphors, especially animal symbols, were the natural way to express these same spiritual realities. And the light of the sun, as we have intimated before, can be symbolised as the great lion of the skies. This is why the hymns speak of Inanna as the 'great light, heavenly lioness'.[22] Now we can understand the next design of the goddess for what it is:

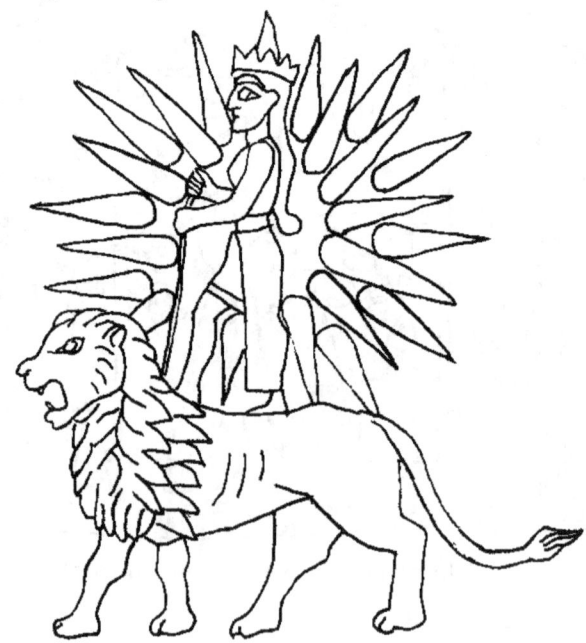

86 Celestial Inanna with her radiant sun-disk and solar lion [21]

---

[21] Parpola 1997, plate XXX, fig c; after Stephanie Beaulieu on the Matrifocus website. There are several more images of the goddess in her halo of stars on the IDD website under the title 'Figure in Nimbus'.

The Celestial Goddess

Here we see the celestial goddess in all her dazzling glory. This is Inanna, the heavenly light. Now there can be no mistaking the radiant sun-disk behind her; nor the purport of the solar lion she bestrides. Our celestial Inanna represents the heavens filled with the effulgent light of the sun.

It is possible to make comparisons between Inanna with her celestial lion and other goddesses who are all associated with the great carnivore, such as Cybele in her lion-drawn chariot or the host of Greek goddesses who were also depicted alongside a lion, even if ancient and modern commentators remain in the dark about its ultimate significance. But it is far more novel to look to the not so distant past of Northern Europe, to the mythic tradition of the Norsemen, which as a young man, first ignited my imagination and my interest in archaic symbolism.

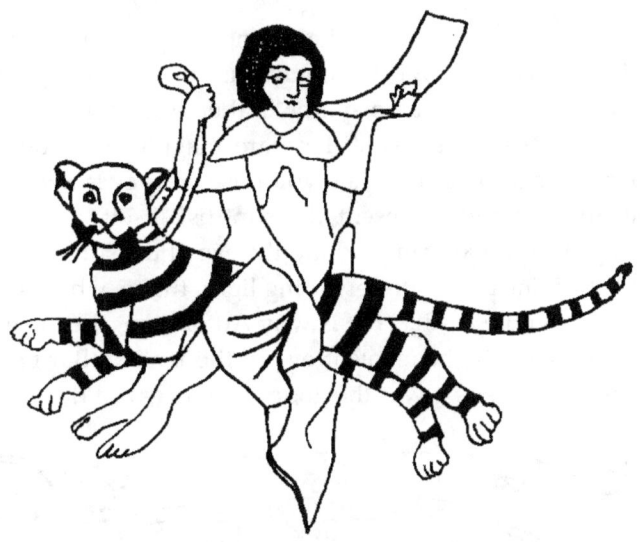

87 The Norse goddess, Freya, from a medieval mural [23]

Riding upon a vibrant tiger of all things, this Scandinavian goddess rightly holds the horn of fertility; she is evidently the North European counterpart to the life-generating goddesses of the Near East.

Returning to Mesopotamian sources. Apart from comparing Inanna to sunlight on a number of occasions,[24] literate sources say next to nothing of the solar goddess. However, one remembrance of the goddess' sun-disk does surface in the literature of the late 3rd millennium. A single quote from the Gudea inscriptions, stands out as it is so explicit. King Gudea was building a great temple and he demanded tribute of all kinds from the

[22] ETCSL: Inana D, lines 1-8.

[23] Jones 1991, page 12. From Schleswig cathedral.

[24] For instance, ETCSL: Iddin Dagan A lines 195-202. In the Sacred Marriage section, 'she shines like daylight' and makes the king position himself next (?) to her like the sun'.

The Celestial Goddess

outlying cities to help furnish the temple. Among the demands he made was for a 'sun-disk (**aš-me**) emblem of Inanna'.[25] This term **Ašme** refers to an ornate sun-disk typically made of precious metal that was used in cult, however the term's principal Sumerian meaning is 'radiance' which again indicates that the all-pervasive light of the sun is the central concern rather than the physical disk of the sun itself.[26]

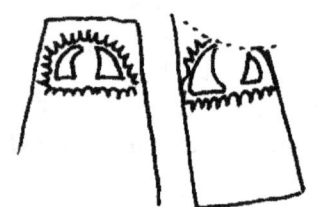

88 The eyes of the sky goddess [27]

Apart from being represented by radiant stars, and flaming torches, the light of the sun could also be symbolised by the eye and its potent gaze.

As eyes, seeing and light are so inextricably bound up with each other, the sun and the light it radiates are very appropriately symbolised by the all-seeing eye of the sky.

The rising of the sun god was poetically described as him 'lifting his gaze over the mountains', or as him emerging from the great below and gazing upward.[28] The same symbolic theme is found in the lore of Inanna, where one of her hymns declares: 'You alone are magnificent, you are the great cow among the gods of heaven and earth. When you raise your eyes they pay heed to you'.[29] More to the point, the eye can represent the sun-disk itself, as in a description of a foreboding solar eclipse: 'as the day grew dark, the eye of the sun was eclipsing'.[30]

The 'sight' of the divine eye is all-pervading light, that is why the sun, as eye of sky, sees all that happens upon the earth. That is why An or Anu, the male personification of heaven, was also known as 'the benevolent eye of the land'.[32] But before Anu assumed nominal rulership of the heavens it was the goddess who gazed down from on high:

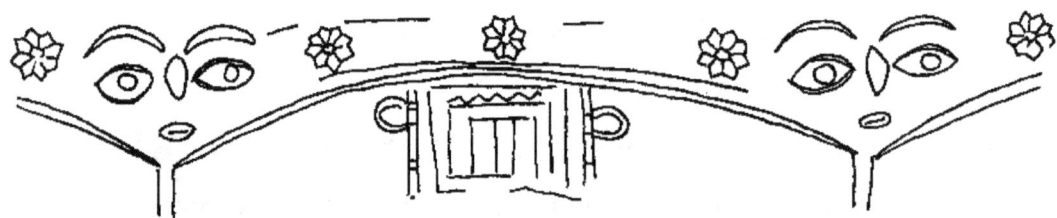

89 The face of the heavenly goddess [31]

---

[25] ETCSL: The Building of Ningirsu's Temple – Gudea A & B line 385, where **Ašme** is inexplicably translated as 'rosette' (**Gurun**). No modern Sumerian or Akkadian dictionaries (PSD, CDA, CAD) give 'rosette' as a meaning of Ašme. However, both signs are cross-like in their general appearance (see page 120) See also, Price 1927, Gudea A, section 14, line 27 where the line is translated as here.

[26] PSD: AŠME [radiance] & CDA: *šamšatu*.

[27] Jemdet Nasr period. Goff 1963, fig 346.

[28] ETCSL: Hymn to Utu (Utu B) lines 32 and 1.

[29] ETCSL: Inana C, lines 182-196.

[30] ETCSL: Lament for Sumer & Urim, lines 303-317.

[31] Amiet 1961, plate 48, fig 681; see also Goff 1963, fig 370 (photo).

[32] ETCSL: Išbi-Erra C, lines 18-22.

The Celestial Goddess

It is the goddess' all-seeing eyes that adorn the face of heaven: 'from the midst of heaven my Lady (Inanna) looks down with joy'.[33] These images reveal the true beauty of the great goddess whose radiant face and benevolent glance grace the heavens. They are remembered in a Sumerian phrase that occasionally appears in royal inscriptions: 'with joyful eyes and a radiant brow' the goddess is said to look upon the king with favour.[34] If the light of the goddess' eyes is sunlight then her radiant brow or shining forehead would represent the dome of heaven filled with her sacred light.

The goddess' all-seeing eyes find their most startling expression in the innumerable 'eye-idols' found in sites all over the Ancient Near East. Tens of thousands of such idols, carved from stone or shaped from clay, were discovered in the north Syrian temple at Tell Brak, which dates to the late 4th millennium BCE. That they are idols of a goddess is shown by the occasional necklace etched upon them.

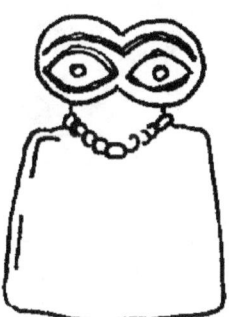 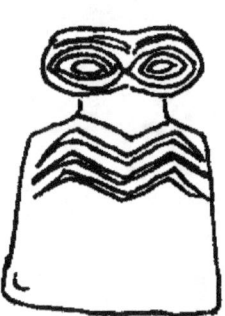 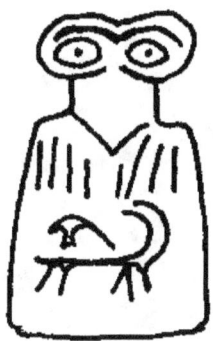

90-92 Eye-idols, one adorned with a necklace, and one with the symbols of the bird & calf [35]

The conception of the fertile heavens even holds true for these eye-idols as one of them (*far right*) is decorated with the icon of the calf and bird – this goddess of the sunlit skies is evidently pregnant with her sacred child.

This fertile aspect of sunlight immediately reminds us of the nature of the sun god's gaze. The most significant aspect of the sun's gaze was that it induced fertility in the herds: 'when you gaze upon the bulls in the cattle-pen, bulls fill the cattle-pen. When you gaze upon the sheep in the fold, sheep fill the fold'.[36] The same text goes on to talk about its effects on man 'When you have gazed upon the man ...' but sadly the final line or two have been lost. Even so the implication should, by now, be obvious.

This little quote rather subtly compares the fertile light of the sun to the 'glint' in a person's eye. The lusty connotations of the glint-in-the-eye work as well in Sumerian as they do in English. In a passage from another Sumerian poem a wise mother gives her

---

[33] ETCSL: Iddin-Dagan A, lines 223-225.
[34] ETCSL: Šulgi R, lines 82-90. the translation reads 'with joyful eyes and shining forehead, Ninlil ... looks upon king Šulgi'. See also PSD: IGI SAĜKI ZALAG BAR [look favourably]
[35] Left, Goff 1963, fig 653. Middle, Goff 1963, fig 652. Left, Goff 1963, fig 654. (Not to scale)
[36] ETCSL: Utu E, lines 60-66.

The Celestial Goddess

daughter some timeless advice as to the lustful ways of men: 'his eye is bright, he will look at you. Straightaway he will want to have intercourse, he will want to kiss! He will be happy to pour lusty semen into the womb, and then he will leave you to it'.[37]

But the men don't always get their way. In one charming song the Sumerian sun god, Utu, who was sometimes known as 'the youth with shining eyes',[38] tried to seduce his sister Inanna by getting her drunk. But the goddess rejects his incestuous desires and coyly feigned complete innocence of kissing and as having no knowledge of any such thing as making love![39]

These entertaining excerpts of lust belie the underlying truth that they convey – that the sun, or rather its all-pervading light, contains the living seed of all creation. It ultimately identifies the sunlit heavens as the matrix that brings the human child to birth.

---

[37] ETCSL: Enlil and Ninlil, lines 13-21.

[38] ETCSL: Lipit-Eštar B, lines 1-14.

[39] ETCSL: Utu F, lines 35-38. See also Black & Green 1992, page 184.

The Fertile Skies

The archaic heavens are the wellspring of all life on earth. They are full of the life-giving waters and they are full of light. The ancients used visual symbols to express these numinous ideas. By doing so, they rendered the potentialities of the invisible worlds into a tangible form. This, at heart, is what archaic symbols are all about; they can be defined as images of the formative, of potential becoming manifest.

Our previous studies have shown that the sacred icons of the bird-goddess carrying her calves is one way of expressing this potentiality of the fertile skies:

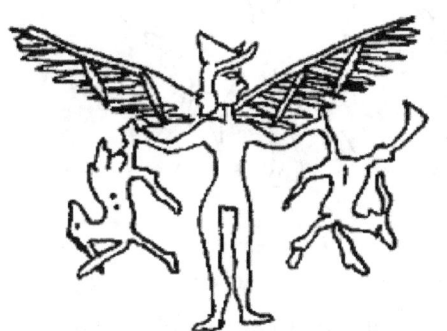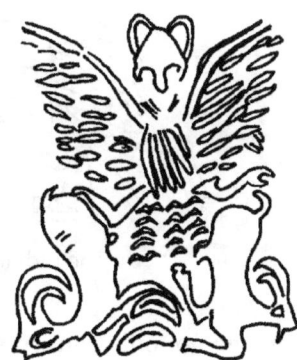

Two icons of the life-engendering heavens [1]

It is the main purpose of the present chapter to show that the calf-child can also be understood as being carried down to earth on the rays of the sun. This is because sunlight, like the celestial waters, was also conceived of as the matrix within which all life took shape. In mythic texts, the fertile nature of sunlight was symbolised as the gaze of the sun, which brings cattle to the fold. This beautiful idea is realised in one of the commonest icons found in ancient art – the mother beast and her calf set under a radiant sun (*right*).

Given that literate sources specifically describe the sun god's gaze in terms of the cattle metaphor we can infer that this design is all about the light of the sun carrying the calf to its mother on earth.

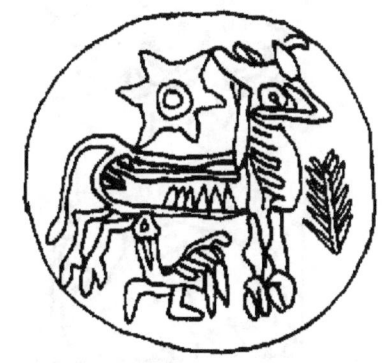

93 The radiant sun as bearer of the calf [2]

---

[1] Left, detail of fig 48. Right, Amiet 1961, plate 87, detail of fig 1147.
[2] Ornan 2005, fig 214.

The Fertile Skies

The truth of this proposition can be demonstrated by showing that other major glyphs of the fertile heavens, like the **An**-sign, the winged disk and solar cross, also play out the same role of carrying the calf down from the skies. A brief survey of illustration sources quickly produces all the designs we need, starting with the sign for 'heaven' itself:

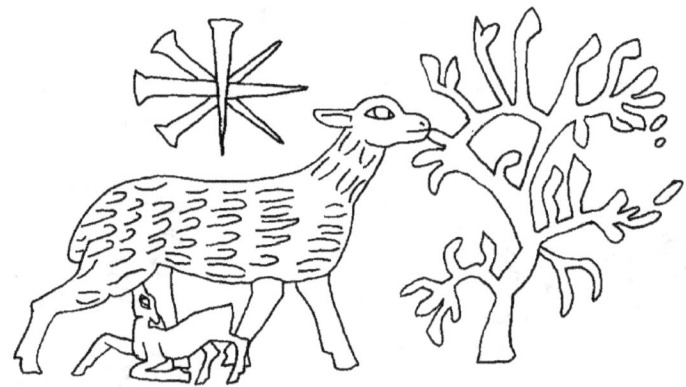

94 The radiant heavens as bearer of the lamb [3]

This image not only confirms our basic hypothesis that the radiant heavens are the crucible of all life on earth but it also shows us that the **An**-sign, which is used to write 'heaven' is another glyph of the central sun with its fertile rays radiating across the skies.

Our next design (*below*), which is in a slightly different format, introduces the winged disk as the heavenly symbol that inculcates new life (*see also fig 79*).

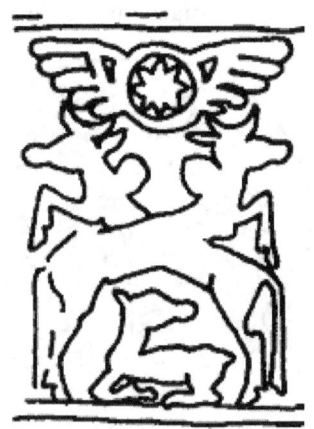

95 A Winged Disk carries a calf [4]

This design rightly sets a fiery sun within the winged disk. Its light has delivered the newborn calf to its parents.

This image also conveys the idea that the child actually has three parents – their physical mother and father on earth and the goddess in heaven. This, in turn, may throw some light on why Gilgamesh described himself as being two-thirds god and one-third man; unlike mere mortals, Gilgamesh's human mother was counted as the goddess of Uruk, Ninsun – the Lady Wild Cow.[5]

---

[3] Parpola 1997, plate XXXVIII, fig 17. After Stephanie Beaulieu on the Matrifocus website.
[4] Frankfort 1939, text fig 53.
[5] George 1999, page 2 (Tablet 1, lines 47-48)

The Fertile Skies

Alongside the winged disk, the equal-armed cross also transmits the calf from its heavenly abode down to its parents on earth:

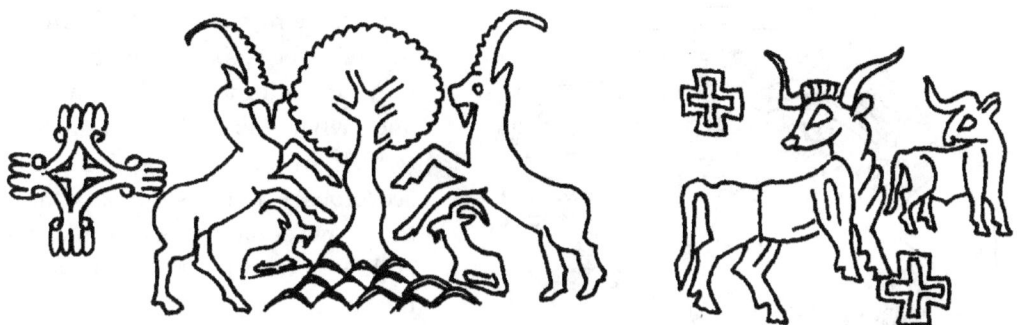

96 & 97 The solar cross causes the herds to breed [6]

From its continual appearance in scenes of animal fertility you could infer that the equal-armed cross is an independent symbol of one generation creating another. However, the use of the cross as a symbol of the fertile skies shows that its inherent power is solar in nature. Its involvement in animal reproduction is therefore likely to be based on the idea that the annual breeding-cycle of the herds is ultimately and very intimately driven by the seasonal cycle of the sun.

The solar nature of the equal-armed cross is made explicit in the Sumerian sign used to write 'sun-disk' (**Ašme**). The lexicon gives this sign two meanings, one referring to actual cult objects made of bronze, silver and gold, while its other principal meaning is given as 'radiance', which once again indicates that the radiating light of the sun, rather than the sun-disk itself, is the central concern of our heavenly symbols. [7]

However, it is the written form of **Ašme** that really makes sense as a solar symbol:

✝ AŠ-ME	The Sumerian sign **Ašme** is made up from two independent signs. The single vertical stroke at the top is the **Aš**-sign, which is commonly used to write 'one or single' or 'first one'. This is then joined to the **Me**-sign, shaped like a letter 'T' thus forming a cross. The **Me** were conceived of as archetypal powers, symbols and rituals. The lexicon defines them as 'divine properties enabling cosmic activity', and further translates them as ritualistic 'office' and 'cultic ordinance'. [8] A popular understanding of the sun-disk's name may therefore be something like 'the sole power'.

---

[6] Left, Collon 1987, fig 463 on page 106. Right, Frankfort 1939, text fig 9, on page 26.
[7] PSD: AŠME [radiance]
[8] PSD: ME [being]

The Fertile Skies

As our next illustration shows, the fertility aspects of the solar cross are also very much apparent in its alternative form, known as the swastika or rotating cross.

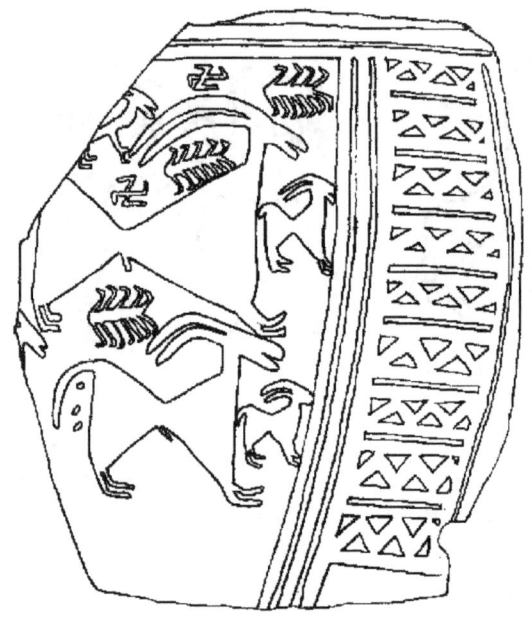

98 The rotating cross as fertility symbol [9]

This particular design places a special emphasis on the horns of the wild beasts. As can be seen, they are adorned with swastikas and what looks like millipedes (which are probably equivalent to scorpions), both symbols show that these animal's horns are endowed with the fertile power of the skies.

From the foregoing survey, we can see that all the principal forms of the radiant sun can be cast in the role of bringing fertility to the herds, and thus by implication to man.

As with so much art, ancient and modern, the simplest designs are often the most beautiful in conception. This is certainly true of the design seen below, which expresses the very same ideas about the fertile heavens by the exquisite image of the radiant star set above the mother beast.

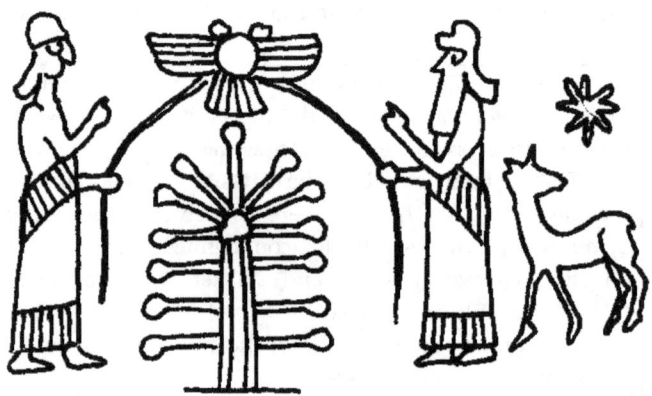

99 A hind and star icon alongside a sacred tree [10]

---

[9] MIT libraries under 'Samarra pottery' even if the style of the animals points to the Sialk II period of Iran.
[10] Assyrian seal, reference lost.

The Fertile Skies

This icon, very eloquently, expresses the idea that the mother beast is carrying her sacred child within her. We can be pretty certain of this interpretation because our next image very helpfully places this simple icon in a much more intelligible context:

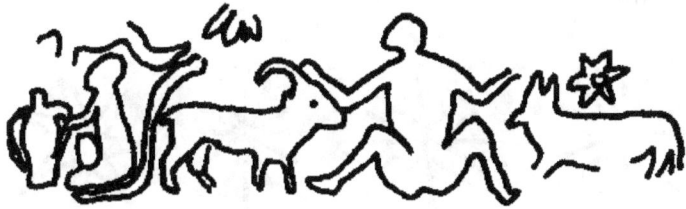

100 The fertility of the herds [11]

The human figure in the middle is indicating the salient features of the design with their outstretched hands. With one hand they touch the fertile horn of the ram and with the other they touch the head of the ewe, which, to judge by the radiant sun placed above her, is now pregnant with a new life. The horny ram has done his job!

The basic icon of the mother beast with a radiant sun-disk expresses the idea that the pregnant mother is like the whole of heaven as she too has become a macrocosm within which her own microcosmic child forms.

The image of the mother beast with a radiant sun set above her is one of the commonest icons in the artworks of the Halaf period (6th & 5th millennia BCE). In addition, a variant form of this icon is sometimes seen – instead of the radiant disk of the sun, some mother beasts are adorned with the goddess' sacred rosette (*below right*):

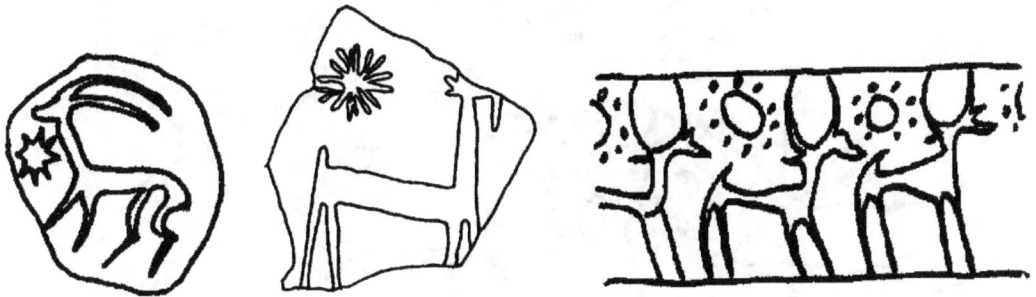

101- 103 Icons of the mother with the radiant suns and rosettes, Halaf period [12]

Taken together, these images indicate that the rosette can be identified with the luminous sun, making it another symbol of the fertile heavens. It is remarkable to see the very same connection, thousands of years later, in the cuneiform writing system. As we saw earlier, the written sign for 'heaven' and 'god' is commonly described as an eight-

[11] Amiet 1961, plate 15, fig 258.
[12] Left, Amiet 1961, plate 1, fig 20. Middle, Goff 1963, fig 86. Right, Goff 1963, fig 85.

rayed star, called the **An**-sign. Whilst the vast majority of written texts from later times represent this sign as a simple star-form composed of four crossed strokes (*below, far left*), some very early forms of the **An**-sign reveal its true nature as a fiery orb and, crucially for our study, as a beautiful rosette:

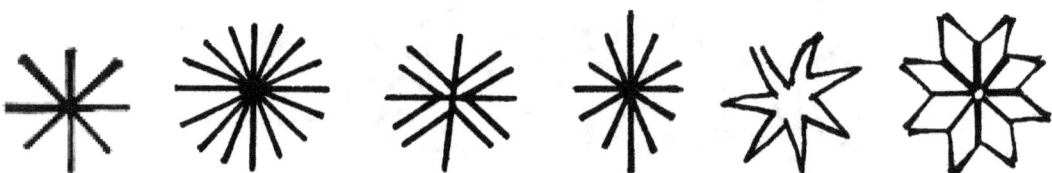

104 The standard form of the **An**-sign (*top row, far left*) and various earlier examples[13]

As well as proving the eminently fertile nature of the heavens, the varied ways of writing the **An**-sign show that its star-like form is another glyph of the sun with its rays of light pervading the heavenly worlds. The three designs of the mother beast seen in figures 101-103 also show that some of the basic elements of the cuneiform writing system were an intrinsic part of the artistic tradition thousands of years before the invention of writing (circa 3400 BCE).

In much later times, the same idea is commonly expressed by setting both the radiant sun and the rosette above the backs of the mother beast. Such a direct mirroring of these icons shows that the artists were effectively using the two symbols as interchangeable terms:

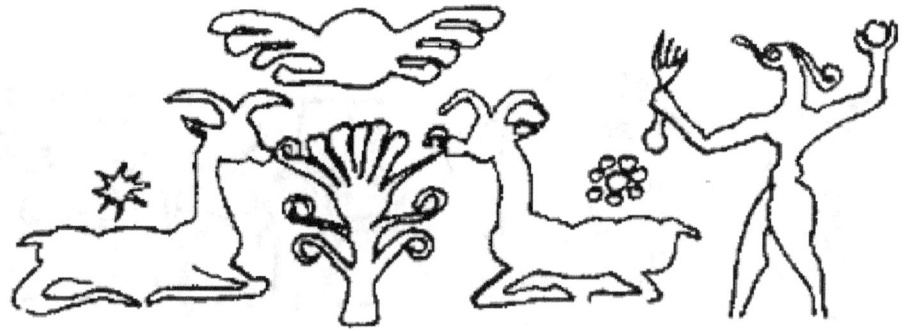

105 The rosette and sun as equivalent symbols set above the mother [14]

The way that these mother animals are portrayed has another very direct parallel in the Sumerian writing system, where the concept of 'mother' (**Ama**) was formulated by placing a single eight-rayed star within a box-like container:

---

[13] Redrawn from Labat 1988, pages 48-9, #13; Falkenstein 1936, sign numbers 192 & 193; and the Jemdet Nasr sign list, sign number 33, available on the CDLI website.

[14] Stein 1993, fig 405.

The Fertile Skies

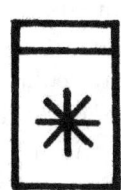 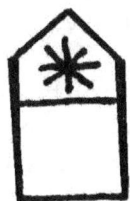 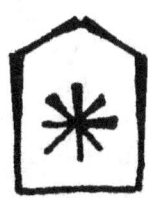

106 Three early versions of the **Ama**-sign, meaning 'mother'

I believe that this sign can be understood as the body of the pregnant mother with her sacred child within her. The outer box or container can rightly be understood as a living being, even the mother of what is depicted within her. Proof of this is seen in the similarly formed **U₈**-sign meaning 'ewe' (*right*), which depicts two bovine heads within another such 'container'.

The way these motherly signs are formulated supports the idea that the star within her body represents her microcosmic child who is naturally formed in the image of heaven.

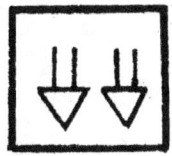 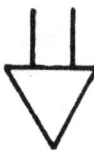

Left, the **U₈**-sign, meaning 'ewe', and right, the **Gud**-sign, meaning 'bull, ox and cattle' [15]

The most convincing manifestation of this idea is seen in our final image, in the strange decoration found of a Greek pot:

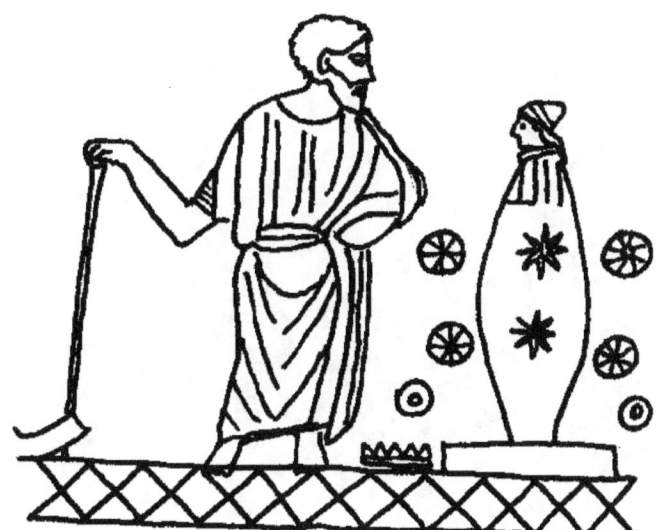

107 Detail of a Greek design of a woman-pot with stars and rosette-flowers [16]

---

[15] PSD: U [ewe] & GUD [ox]
[16] Harrison 1962, detail from fig 70 on page 280.

The Fertile Skies

The curious vase seen on the right-hand side of this illustration is seemingly shaped in the form of a pregnant woman. Outside her body we see the sacred symbols of the goddess strewn around in the form of the rosettes and their circular seeds; and within her body we see two radiant stars, which quite purposefully point to the fact that she is the Mother. Here, in this unique Greek design, we have a surprisingly archaic vision of the celestial mother goddess with her heaven-born embryos living and growing within her.

The Waters of the Sun

The fundamental conclusion drawn from the last chapter was to identify sunlight as the heavenly matrix that brought the child to birth. This idea is but one of a number of ways to understand the role of the sun in the creation of life on earth. Another way of approaching the same paradigm of humanity's heavenly origins uses the symbolism of the celestial waters rather than radiant sunlight. It is the purpose of the present chapter to explore this imagery and see how it fits in with the bigger picture of the fertile heavens.

In the archaic worldview, the heavens are full of circulating waters. At the very centre of this system lies its powerhouse, the sun, which acts like a heart pumping the ever-flowing waters between heaven and earth.

The 'solar-water cycle', as it may be called, operates over the course of a year. During the hot and dry summer months, the sun was thought to suck up water from the earth and then, over the cool and wet winter months, it released those same waters as rain. By circulating the waters in this way, the sun drives the annual cycle of the seasons, which is chiefly defined by the seasonal patterns of temperature and rainfall.[1]

By far the clearest and commonest formulation of this arcane idea is the way that the sun-disk itself is portrayed. For much of its long history, the sun has been envisioned as a radiant star with very distinct streams of water flowing from its heart:

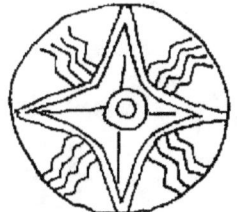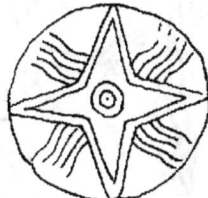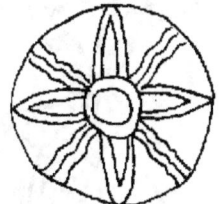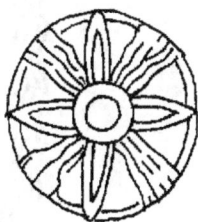

108 Examples of the solar disk from entitlement stones [2]

These four examples are quite typical of those found on entitlement stones.[3] They all share the common features of a central circle, four-fold light rays and four watery outflows. At the most fundamental level, this way of representing the sun defines it as the source of light and life-giving water.

Some atypical examples of the solar disk are also worth looking at as they place even greater emphasis on the waters:

---

[1] The theory of the 'solar-water' cycle is explicit in the Rig Veda, see O'Flaherty 1981, page 174, note 3; and page 81, verses 51-52.

[2] Left, Seidl 1989, Abb 7, Nr 61. Left-centre, Seidl 1989, Abb 13, Nr 79. Right-centre, Seidl 1989, Abb 19, Nr 97. Right, Seidl 1989, Abb 21, Nr 100.

[3] Large stone monuments, often decorated with astral symbols, which record the grating of privileges. Black & Green 1992, pages 113-114 under Kudurrus.

The Waters of the Sun

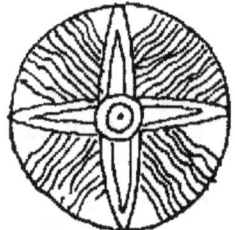 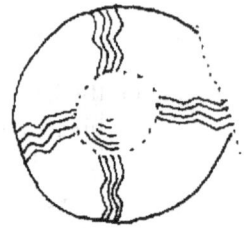 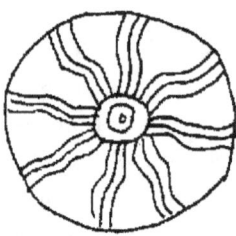

109 The waters as defining features of the sun-disk [4]

The first disk (*left*) depicts a veritable flood of waters emanating from the sun. The remaining two designs take the idea even further, as they omit the star-like rays of the sun altogether and just represent the sun-disk in terms of its flowing waters.

One of the most intriguing depictions of the heavenly waters comes from Assyria:

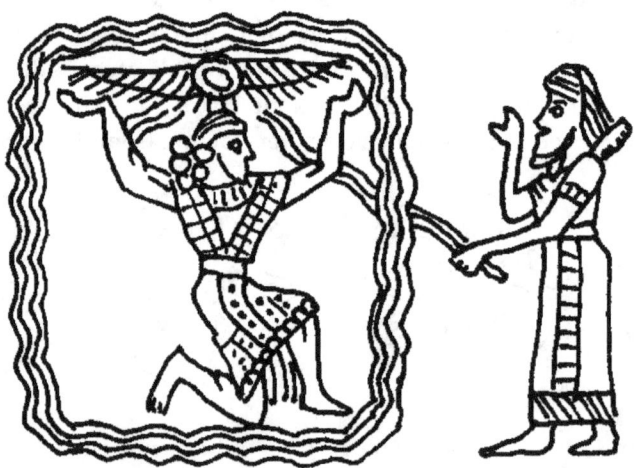

110 The waters circulate through the heavens, driven by the winged disk [5]

I believe this design depicts the whole cycle in action. The waters of the ocean are first lifted into the upper skies by the action of the sun, thereby becoming clouds. Then the waters are returned, purified, in the form of rain. This is represented by the two streams of water that fall from the winged disk. The solar-water cycle is complete. The original waters of the ocean, full of salt and inimical to all earth-based life, are purified by the sun and turned into the waters of life. Driven by the sun and the winds, this design is arguably an early recognition of the dynamic water cycle that unites heaven and earth.

---

[4] Left, Seidl 1989, Abb 23, Nr 108. Centre, Seidl 1989, Abb 2, Nr 9. Right, Ornan 2005, fig 5.

[5] Frankfort 1939, text fig 67.

The Waters of the Sun

On this evidence alone, you could redefine the celestial waters as solar in character. The seeming paradox that fire and water, the two most antithetical elements, should be united in the solar disk is a vivid way of expressing the dynamic nature the solar-water cycle and the tumultuous forces driving the whole system.

This interpretation of the sun-disk forces us to look at it in a new light. What everyone calls a solar disk is, by this measure, not actually an image of the sun but of the whole realm of heaven. The sun is only the small central circle; its rays of light and watery outflows are depicted traversing the open skies. I would further argue that the outer rim of the 'sun-disk' actually represents the horizon, where heaven and earth embrace. The 'sun-disk' is thus a complete glyph of the heavens with its circulating waters, but for ease of reference I will continue to use the terms 'sun-disk' and suchlike.

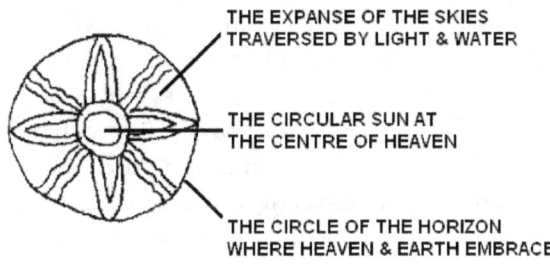

THE EXPANSE OF THE SKIES
TRAVERSED BY LIGHT & WATER

THE CIRCULAR SUN AT
THE CENTRE OF HEAVEN

THE CIRCLE OF THE HORIZON
WHERE HEAVEN & EARTH EMBRACE

The 'Sun-disk' as glyph of the whole of heaven

What we call the sun-disk is but one symbol for the fertile heavens. It is a naturalistic symbol, in that it portrays the sun amidst the heavens, however as we have already seen, the sun and its waters can also be represented by animal symbols.

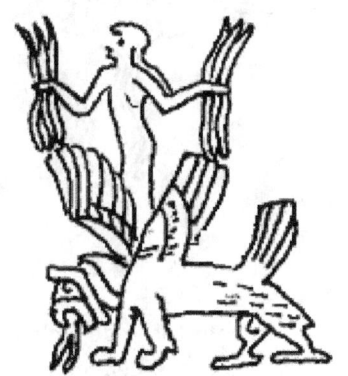

Now that we have the basic idea of the sun emanating its waters firmly in our minds, we can recognise that the goddess' storm griffin (*right*) must also be another part of the same jigsaw puzzle. It is commonly thought that the griffin represents the storm clouds but by spewing forth the celestial waters it is actually functioning like the sun.[6]

The griffin is the animal embodiment of Inanna in her aspect as goddess of the storms. It was a composite creature made up of the various parts of an eagle and a lion. And it is the lion-like head that, like the sun, disgorges the waters of heaven. While the icon of the spewing griffin may not be a familiar image to a modern Western audience – its disembodied head certainly is.

Detail of fig 70

---

[6] The identity between the sun and the storm-griffin is also confirmed in the Sumerian writing system as 'storm-demon' and 'storm' can both be written with the Sun-sign (**Ud**), which depicts the rising sun. See PSD: UD [storm]

The Waters of the Sun

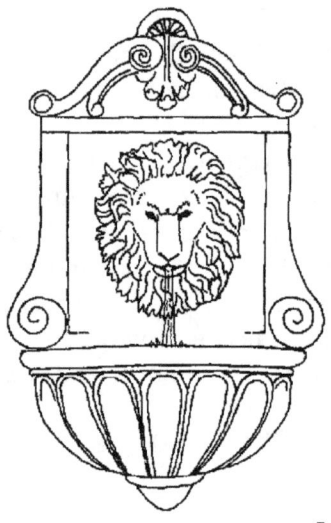

111 A Lion-headed fountain [7]

In the form of the lion-headed fountain (*left*), the archaic idea of the sun issuing its sweet waters is still very much a part of the West's classical heritage. Enlivening many a back garden and stately home, the image is such a commonplace that we hardly give it a second thought.

If you think about it for a moment, it is easy to understand that the lion's head is another glyph of the whole of heaven. Its face is the sun and its radiant mane is the sunlight pervading the skies. Now we know why the storm-bringing Anzu-bird is fashioned with a lion's head.

The symbols of the solar heavens that we have met with so far – the sun-disk, griffin and Anzu-bird – are only a part of a much broader system. As one of the defining characteristics of the fertile heavens, the celestial waters are also combined with other icons of the heavenly realms. We have already seen that the winged disk can drive the celestial waters through the skies but other illustrations of the winged disk make the connection even more direct:

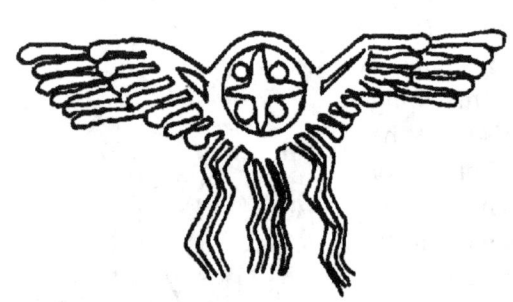
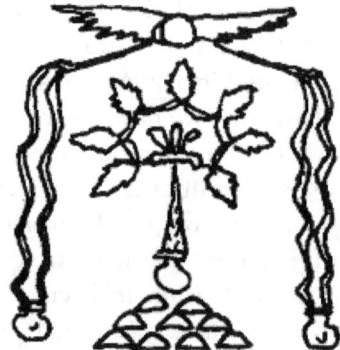

112 & 113 The celestial waters emanate from the winged disk [8]

In both these designs there can be no doubt that the winged disk dispenses the life-giving waters of heaven upon the earth. In a sense, these designs are abbreviated forms of the solar water cycle we saw earlier in figure 110. Whereas the waters are usually shown flowing directly from the body of the winged disk (*above left*), in the right-hand

---

[7] From a modern example on the internet.
[8] Left, detail from Stein 1993, detail of fig 326. Right, Frankfort 1939, text fig 65.

illustration the flying disk holds the waters in its extended legs – it thus 'carries' the waters down from heaven just as the flying bird carries its kid or calf.

Now that we have learnt that the waters of heaven flow from the sun itself, we can re-apply this knowledge and recognise further manifestations of the same idea. The illustrations rendered below show that the solar heavens can also be represented by the equal-armed cross in Mesopotamian art:

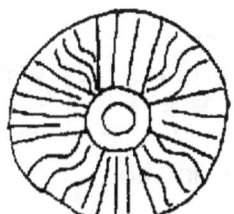 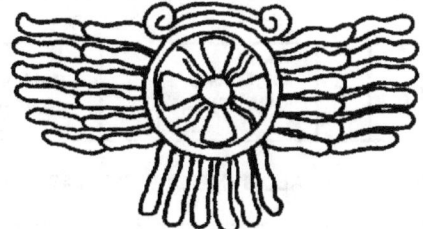

114 & 115 The solar cross with watery outflows [9]

In light of the way that the heavens are symbolised by the sun-disk, we would have to conclude that the four arms of the cross actually represent rays of sunlight pervading the skies. Just like the various forms of the sun-disk, the waters still emanate from the circular sun set at the very heart of the glyph.

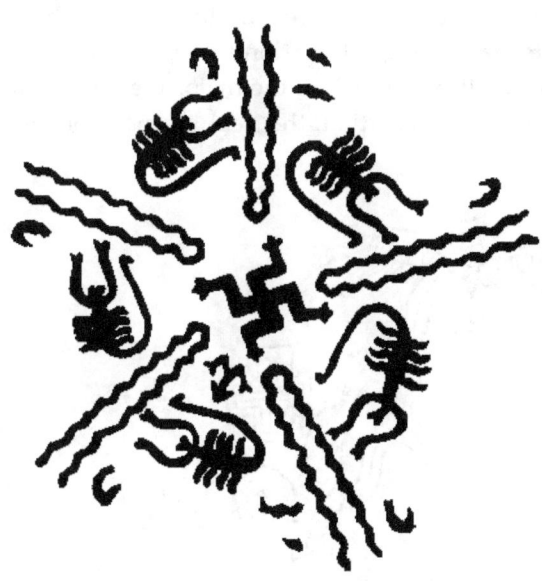

116 Decoration from a Samarran plate [10]

While most of the images seen so far in this section date to the 2nd millennium BCE, we can be assured that the essential symbolism of the solar waters is much older. In fact it goes right back to the very beginnings of Mesopotamian art. The Samarran design seen in figure 116 (left) is testament to this fact; it is conventionally dated to the middle of the 6th millennium BCE.

We can immediately see that the central swastika or 'rotating cross' represents the radiant sun and that the sets of wavy lines emanating from it are streams of water falling from the skies. The scorpions arrayed around the design are, I believe, a reference to the sexual potency within the waters. Here at

---

[9] Left, Seidl 1989, Abb 22, Nr 103. Right, Ornan 2005, detail of fig 173.
[10] Goff 1963, fig 35.

The Waters of the Sun

the dawn of the Mesopotamian tradition, thousands of years before the invention of writing, we can see that the waters borne of the sun are already a central element of religious and ritual art.

The designs we have explored in this chapter show just how inter-changeable the basic symbols of the solar heavens are. Whatever the form of the sun, it can be depicted with its life-giving waters flowing forth. This allows us to make a simple chain of identifications between all the symbols that emanate the solar waters:

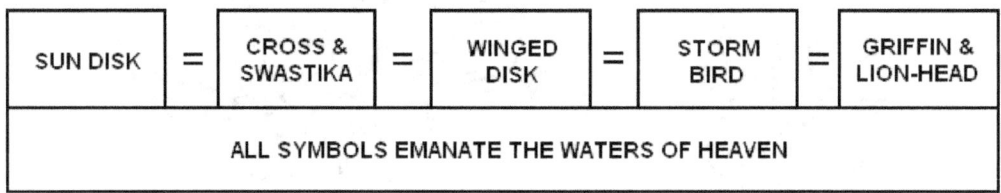

SUN DISK	=	CROSS & SWASTIKA	=	WINGED DISK	=	STORM BIRD	=	GRIFFIN & LION-HEAD
ALL SYMBOLS EMANATE THE WATERS OF HEAVEN								

Symbols of the solar waters

All these images show that the solar heavens are the source of the celestial waters. They ultimately fall as rain bringing fertility to the earth. But there is more to the solar waters than an ancient recognition of the sun driving the weather and the rain. Ultimately, the waters disgorged by the sun are the same waters of life that bear the seed of the human child (*see fig 9*).

All of the icons we have met with in this chapter only give a limited view of things as they only represent the sun emanating its waters. What they don't do is explicitly define the nature of the waters as the carrier of life. It is only when the major metaphors of the waters and the calf are combined into one image that the real purport of all this symbolism is actually made plain:

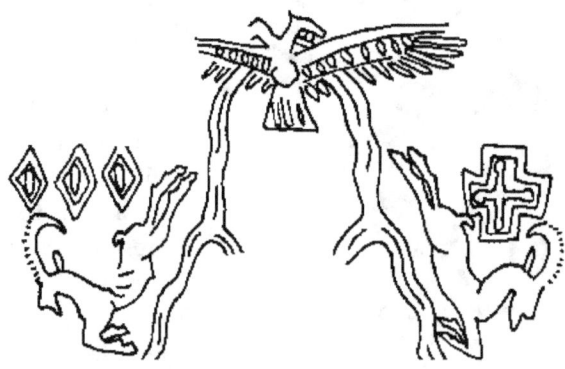

The waters of life, detail from figure 77

Here we see that the waters do indeed flow forth from the heavenly bird just as they do from the winged disk but now the waters are definitively characterised as the 'carrier' of the descending calf-child. Images such as this prove that the solar waters carry the seed of life from heaven in the form of the rains. By combining the two child metaphors

The Waters of the Sun

in one icon we have a kind of 'master-image', that gives us the all-important bigger picture.

All this material shows that the celestial waters were regarded as the source of all life; they emanate from the sun, which can be regarded as the crucible of earthly life. Now, in the final section of this chapter, we need to prove the essentially feminine nature of the sun and the waters in archaic art.

All this imagery is defining the sun and the solar heavens as a vast reservoir of water. And this is why the vase or jug is another symbol of the fertile heavens. It is easy enough to understand that the vase and its waters represents the rain-bringing aspects of the skies but it takes a further logical step to see that the vase itself must be a symbol equivalent to the sun disgorging its waters. These ideas are beautifully realised in the ritual jug seen in figure 117 (*right*). Decorated with the goddess' sacred flowers and pairs of solar eyes this spouted jug epitomises the nature of the fertile heavens.

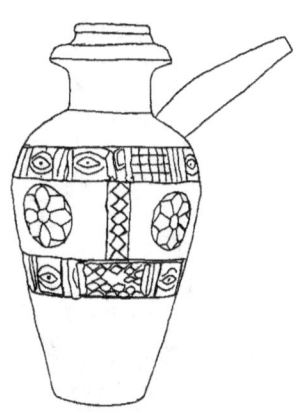

117 A Sumerian ritual jug [11]

The feminine nature of the watery heavens is equally clear in the pair of anthropomorphic vases seen below:

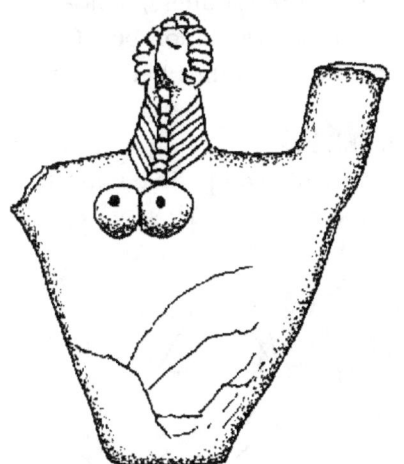

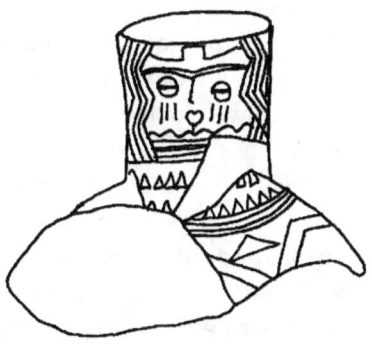

118 & 119 An Iranian water pot in the form of a woman; and part of a Samarran vase.[12]

---

[11] Goff 1963, fig 479. Jemdet Nasr period.
[12] Left, Godard 1965, fig 1. Right, Oates & Oates 1976, page 43. See also Goff 1963, fig 42.

The Waters of the Sun

These two vases, one seemingly with a bird's head and the other with wave-like hair, are both expressions of the same fundamental idea that the heavens are a reservoir of life-giving waters. How one vase is embellished with breasts can only point to the maternal aspects of the sky goddess. Nearly all the individual features seen in these two vessels are combined in the figure of our next goddess, which dates back to the Halaf period:

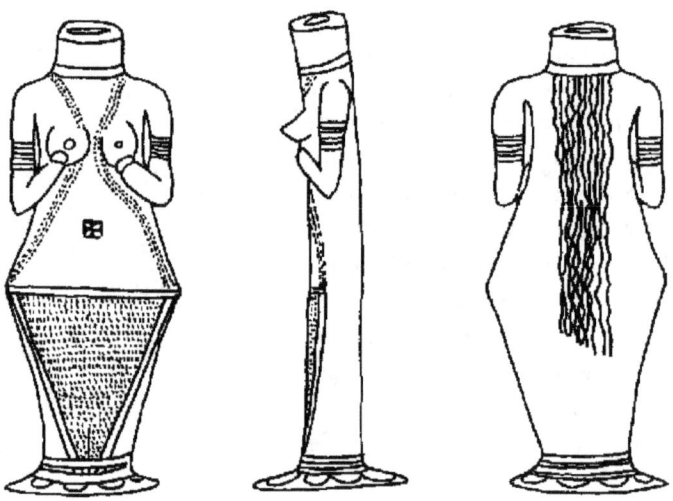

120 A vase in the form of the goddess [13]

This figure is another water vase shaped in the form of the goddess, hence her absent head. The frontal view leaves no doubt as to her 'fertility' orientation but it is the back view, showing her long hair flowing down her back, that identifies her as a goddess of the watery skies.

This figure of the goddess, so abstract in form, still has intriguing details especially the four-petalled flower at her navel. This detail is certainly compatible with the mythic notion of the navel in the sky that succours the foetal child. When you add in the geometric qualities of her figure, which are reminiscent of some fundamental creative principles in geometry (*right*), it is easy to suspect that this lady has some particularly dense symbolism embedded in her figure. I believe she is a little masterpiece of archaic art, and testament to the greater symbolic faculty of pre-literate cultures.

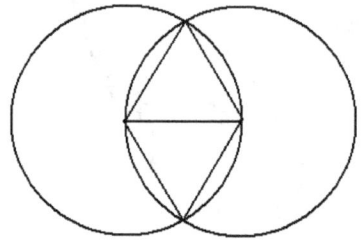

In many systems of sacred geometry the Vesica Pisces has a feminine creatrix role [14]

---

[13] Halaf period, 6th millennium BCE. Huot 2004, page 61.
[14] Schneider 1994, chapter 2.

The Waters of the Sun

The symbolism of the sun and the celestial waters finds its most elegant and economical expression in the pair of Samarran designs seen below:

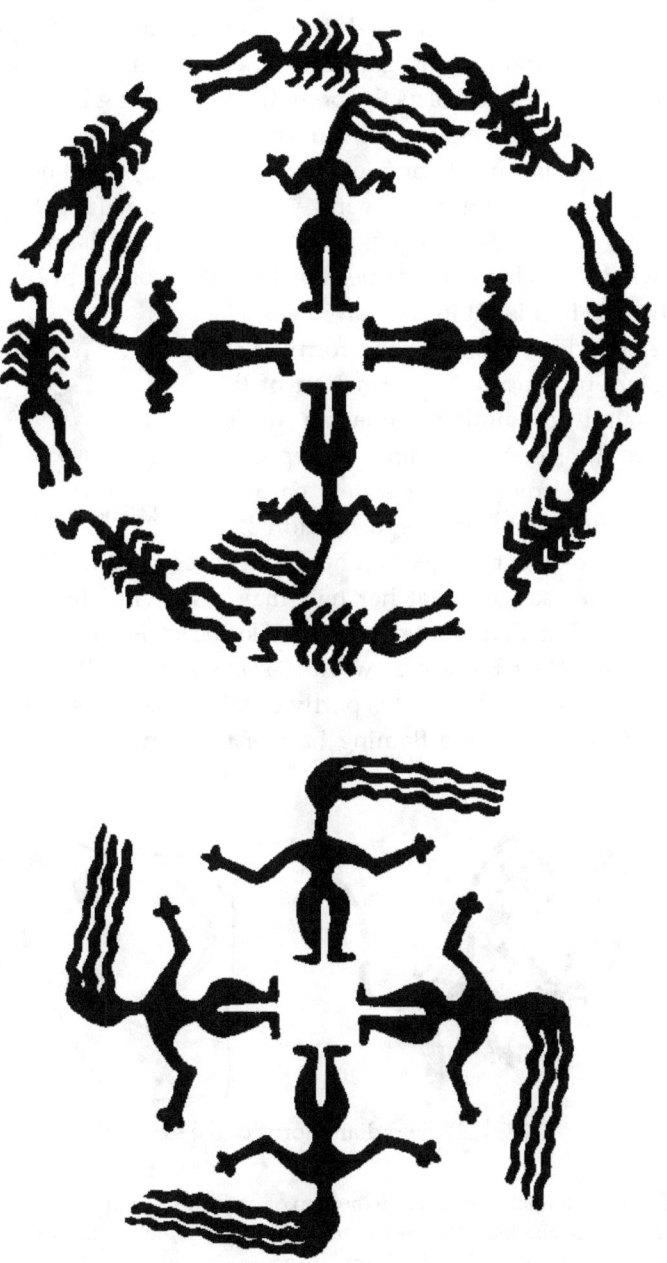

121 & 122 The decoration from two reconstructed Samarran bowls [15]

---

[15] Above, Northern Iraq, 6th millennium BCE, Goff 1963, fig 33. Below, Goff 1963, fig 32.

The Waters of the Sun

These wonderfully simple images of women with wind-swept hair are overflowing with symbolic significance. The way in which both designs are laid out on the pattern of the rotating cross defines her as the embodiment of the fertile heavens full of light.

Detail of fig 45

Her stylised legs and curvaceous thighs are surely the origin of the goddess' omega'-symbol (*left*), which now defines the symbol as the potentiality of giving birth.

The flowing hair of these goddesses is, I believe, the central and most complex symbol. At face value, her hair appears to be blowing in the wind – this is no fanciful interpretation as much later figures (*figs 59 & 156*), which can be positively identified as the personified winds, also have this same stylistic feature of swept-back hair.

The way that her hair is set in regular waves, like the hair of other goddesses, echoes the form of the ever-flowing waters of heaven. Confirmation of this proposition is found in another Samarran design (*right*), which uses the same wavy lines to represent the horns of a deer. The proof of their watery nature is seen in the four fish jumping from the deer's horns.

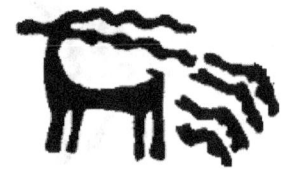

123 The watery horns of the deer [16]

So there is good reason to think that her hair represents the celestial waters and the winds. I would further suggest that her hair may also symbolise the sunlight. This is largely based on the fact that the horn of the sky-beast is thought to radiate light in roughly contemporary Near Eastern artworks (*below*) and is still accorded this nature in much later mythical literature;[17] and it is partly based on parallels to Vedic traditions that equate the rays of the sun to the flaming hair of the sun god and to the mane of his horse.[18]

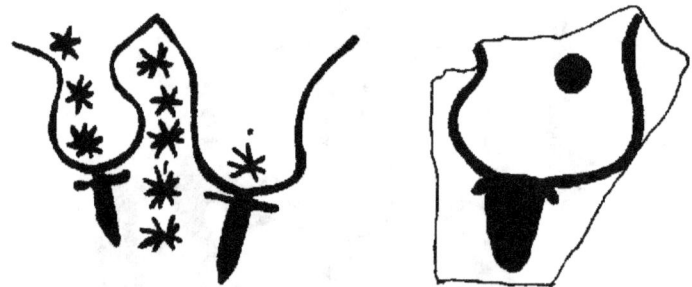

124 & 125 The radiant horns of the sky-bull [19]

---

[16] Mellaart 1965, fig 40 I; also Roaf 1965, page 39 (bottom of page) for a photo.

[17] Cattle with 'shining horns' abound in Sumerian literature – search the ETCSL website. One reference in particular associates the bull whose 'shining horns are aggressive, holy and lustrous' with the sun god, see ETCSL: Temple Hymns 169-177.

[18] O'Flaherty 1981, page 87, verse 9 & note 12 on page 89 for the sun god's hair (Rig Veda 1:163) . Page 190, verse 9 for his horse's mane (Rig Veda 1:50).

The Waters of the Sun

There are even more details that we can pick up upon. As a modern academic has already pointed out,[20] the hands of our Samarran goddesses also appear attached to the arms of the rotating cross (*right*). This not only identifies the figure of the goddess with the archaic form of the solar cross but also gives us a clue as to how to interpret the symbol of the rotating cross.

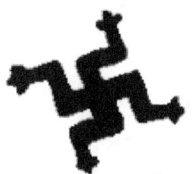

Detail of fig 116

I would suggest that the central part of the swastika – the equal-armed cross – represents the central sun with rays of light emanating to the quarters, and that the extra arms, that transform this figure into the rotating cross, are equated to the winds and waters that ceaselessly flow through the heavens. The reason why the goddess' hands have been adjoined to the cross must surely rely on the affinity between the goddess' arms and the wings of the storm-bird (*see the A₂-sign on page 58*). It adds a new level of meaning to the way that the heavenly bird 'touches' the mother beasts to make them pregnant (*see figs 48-50 and the discussion*)

All in all, we have here a fecund mother goddess whose nature is of the sunlight and the life-bearing waters of heaven. She is the womb of heaven and her sacred scorpions show that she is pregnant with the seed of the archetypal child. In the final analysis, the whole complex of ideas about the fertile heavens is compressed into this seemingly simple image of the goddess.

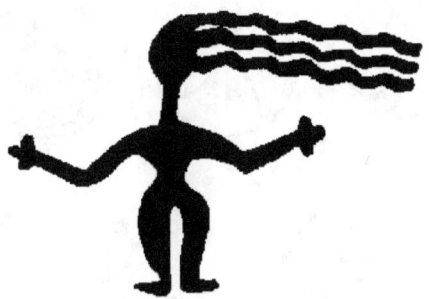

---

[19] Left, Mellaart 1975, fig 150, lower left on page 233. Right, Goff 1963, fig 88.
[20] Laura Goff 1963, in her discussion of this icon – figure 33 in her book.

The Flower of Heaven

Flowers and rosettes are perhaps the most evocative and meaningful symbols of the fertile goddess. Since time immemorial rosette ornaments have decorated the temples of the goddess and in the form of jewelry, they have also adorned the body of the goddess herself.

More than any other symbol, flowers express the radiant beauty of the sky goddess and the potentiality of the seeds that the flower holds within it is a profound image of the nascent life that resides in the skies.

Flowers are probably one of the oldest symbols of the fertile heavens. As such, they come in all shapes, sizes and styles. From almost naturalistic flowers with distinct petals to highly very geometric forms, the goddess' flower has endured the ages as one of the primary symbols of the feminine:

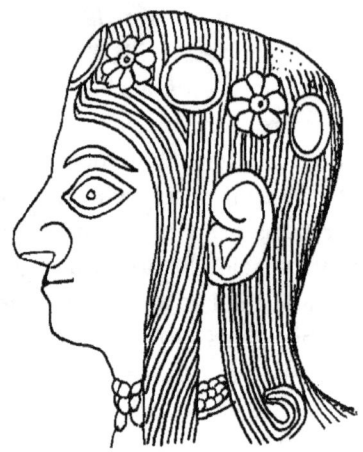

126 Head of an Assyrian goddess [1]

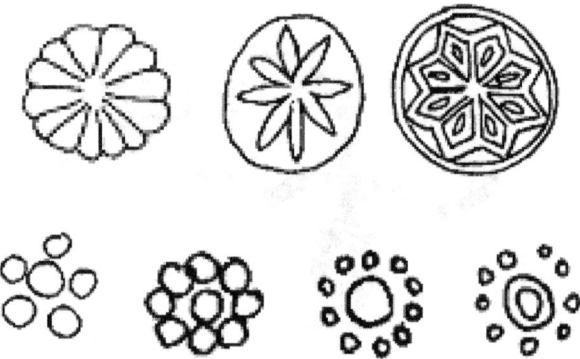

127 Varied examples of the rosette drawn from various seal designs

The differences in appearance, from recognisable flowers to clusters of circles, might be due to a difference in emphasis on the flower or its circular seeds. As we will see a little later, the cluster forms are almost identical to the date-clusters of the palm. In either case, it is the seed or fruit developing high in the tree that is the essential element as they represent the germinal forms of the goddess' children forming in the heights of heaven.

---

[1] Neo-Assyrian. Metropolitan Art Museum, gallery 400, ascension # 52:23.3

The Flower of Heaven

The flower is present as a major symbol in the earliest Mesopotamian art. Way back in the 6th millennium BCE, it appears on painted plates and bowls, with its all-important seeds arrayed around it:

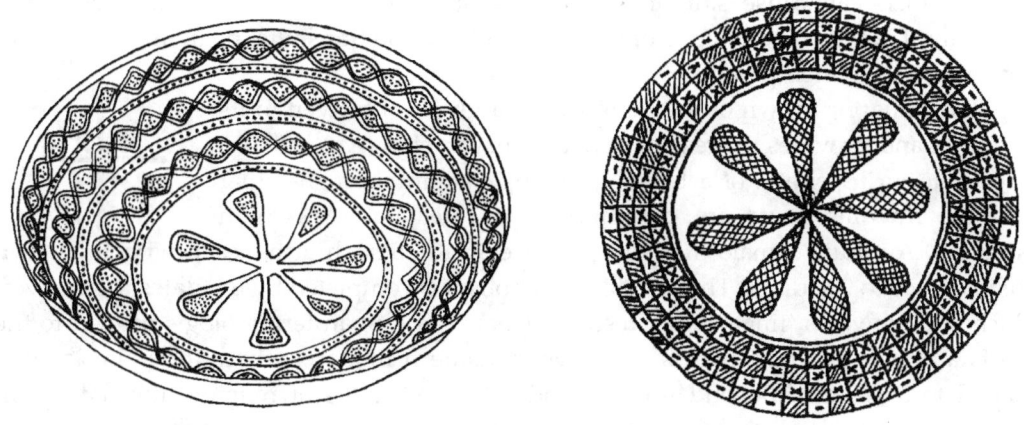

128 & 129 A Samarran Rosette and a Halaf period example [2]

These geometric flowers are, I believe, set in the frame of their seeds. To judge from later evidence, the chequerboard border seen in one plate is an image of the farmer's cereal fields laden with their freshly sown seed, and the same idea of seeded fields is probably conveyed by the rows of lozenges in the other design. The rise of farming, and its impact on symbolic art in Mesopotamia, deserves a study in its own right. For now, we need to return to the reproductive cycle of the flowers instead.

As I mentioned before, the cluster form of the flower can represent a bunch of dates hanging in the heavens:

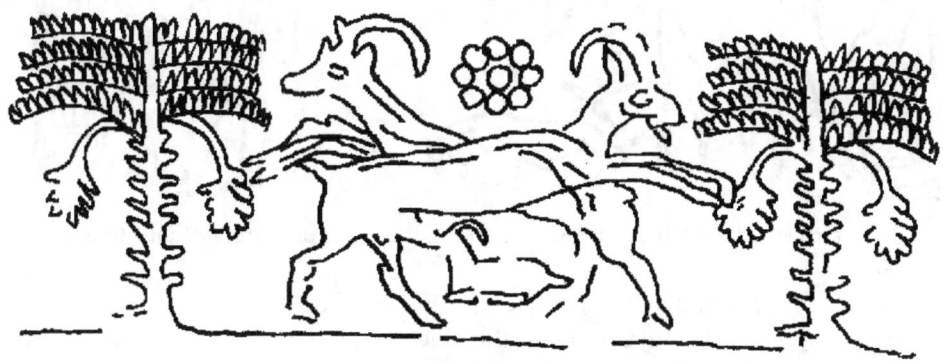

130 Goats with a kid beneath the palms [3]

---

[2] Left, internet source for search term 'Samarran pottery', see also Mallowan & Cruikshank, 1935, fig 53:2.
  Right, Goff 1963, fig 67
[3] Ornan 2005, fig 171.

The Flower of Heaven

The clusters of dates, often glowing red, bright yellow or vibrant orange in colour, are fitting symbols for the fertile sun shining down from heaven. The solar nature of dates is well-known, the 'fiery' effects of eating too many fresh dates is called 'heating the blood', which can cause skin inflammations and weak eye-sight – both very solar symptoms. Like the other glyphs of the fertile skies, it too transmits the living offspring of man and beast to their parents.

The radiating crown of the palm tree is a glyph of heaven in its own right and provides the reason why the heaven-sign (**An**) can also be used to write 'crown of a tree'.[4] The long hanging branches that hold the ripening dates are called 'Arms of Heaven' (**A₂-An**) in

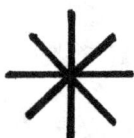

Sumerian. An adult female tree will produce 15 to 25 such arms, each with their own cluster of 150 to 200 dates. The arm-like symbolism is completed by the dates themselves, which are known as 'fingers' in Greek (*dactylis*). The human terminology applied to the tree is a relic of the past that is still alive in modern folklore, where the palm is often likened to a woman. Beyond folklore and into the realms of religion, the date palm represents the celestial mother goddess nurturing her abundant harvest of children in the high heavens. The seeds of humanity are contained in her sun-like clusters of dates.

The same ideas are applied to the flowers, which are set in the crown of the tree or atop the stalk. As the next illustrations show, the heavenly seeds formed within the flower finally fall to earth as the calf or child.

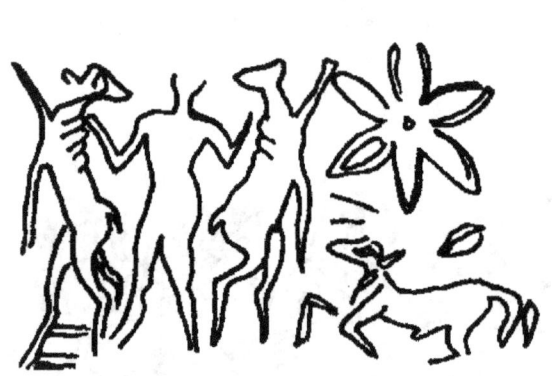
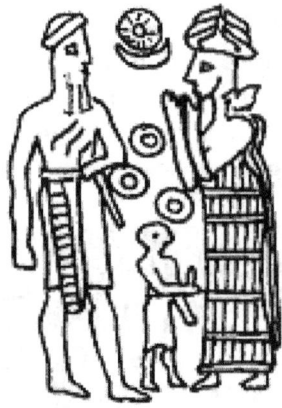

131 Left, the seed falls from the flower. Right, the 'Seed of Mankind' falls to earth [5]

The eminently natural symbol of the seed falling from heaven is, of course, akin to the imagery of the calf descending from the skies in the talons of the mother bird. This demonstrates that the same basic narrative is followed in all the principal metaphors of the child's creation.

---

[4] PSD: AN [heaven]

[5] Amiet 1961, plate 70, fig 936. Detail from Collon 1987, fig 570 on page 136.

The Flower of Heaven

A few seal designs, like the next one excavated from the city of Ur, get very explicit about the sexual symbolism of the flower:

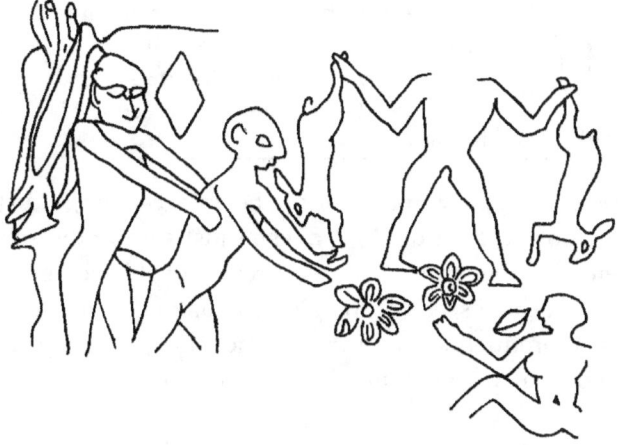

132 The symbolism of human impregnation [6]

This design (*like figure 52*) is all about impregnation. Like the wild goats that eat of the seed-laden tree, the women here are 'eating' the seed of the rosettes. That means they have the seed of mankind in their bellies and in accordance with the turning seasons, that seed, if correctly nurtured, will eventually 'fall to earth' as her children.

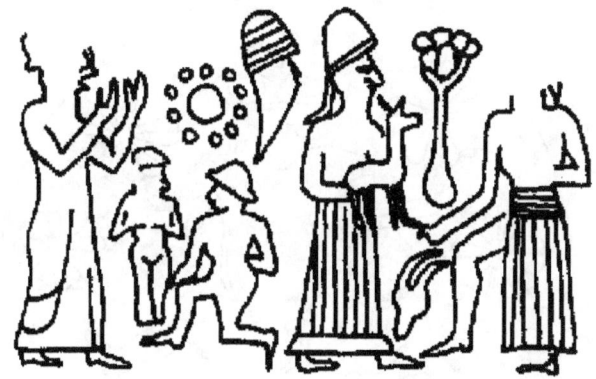

133 The seed of mankind falls from the heavenly flower [7]

These last few designs show the flower to be the heavenly source of life on earth. However, the meaning of the flower symbol doesn't have to be inferred from artwork as it is very clearly conveyed in the Sumerian writing system, where the flower appears in the form of the **Gurun**-sign:

[6] Fig from Tom ('Ur Excavations', Archaic Seal Impressions 370) & Amiet 1961, plate 63, fig 846.
[7] Collon 1975, fig 197.

The Flower of Heaven

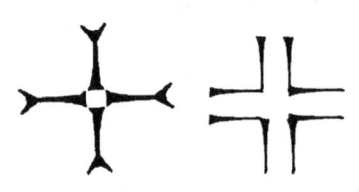

Two versions of the **Gurun**-sign

Only the earliest known examples of the Flower-sign (**Gurun**) convey its essence as a cross-like form. This is presumably a simplified figure of the radiating lines of the rosette, which immediately relates it to the name of the sun-disk, **Ašme** (see page 110)

The lexical meanings of this sign extend from 'flower' to 'fruit'; and in a more abstract sense it is used to signify 'sex appeal'.[8]

The meanings of the **Gurun**-sign turn out to be an excellent guide to the symbolism of the goddess' sacred flower. First of all, it doesn't just signify the self-evident 'flower' but also explicitly refers to the 'fruit' – the end result of the flower's generative cycle, which contains the fully formed seeds of the plant. Thus the meanings of the Flower-sign encompass the whole reproduction cycle from conception, through formation to birth. This shows the flower to be a true symbol – it represents the potentiality of the seed coming into being.

As well as being a primary symbol of the fertile heavens the rosette is also an indelibly feminine symbol, closely associated with the whole process of human conception and birth. The quality of 'sex appeal' or allure, assigned to **Gurun**, bespeaks of the flower's age-old association to womankind and to the goddesses of love and fertility. This defining quality is most clearly manifest in the symbolism of the maiden, who is as much the goddess as every fertile woman:

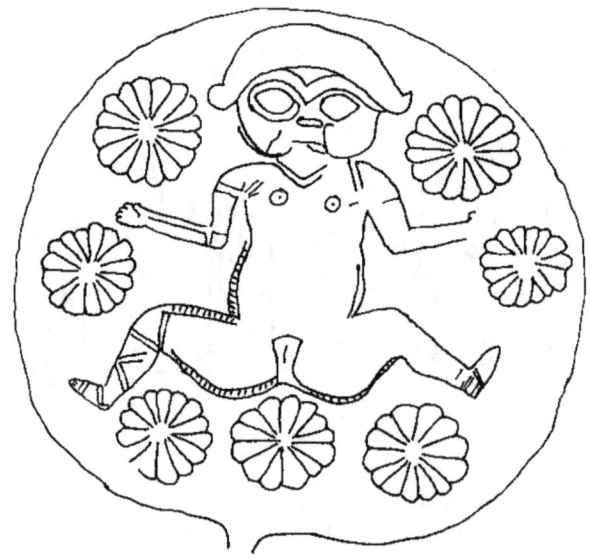

134 The flowery maiden [9]

---

[8] PSD: GURUN [flower] For early forms of the sign, search the CDLI website for OB forms of **Gurun**.
[9] Godard 1965, fig 61.

The Flower of Heaven

This design, from an Iranian clothing pin, is the first of three that very explicitly map out the whole cycle of female reproduction around the sacred flower. The woman among the flowers is the 'maiden', the sexually mature young lady, whose allure is likened to the scent of the flowers. Like bees, young men desire her, for like the radiant flower, she is ready and ripe for fertilisation. The modern romantic use of 'flower' to designate young ladies is implicitly present in the term 'deflowering' used to refer to a maiden losing her virginity. The flower analogy continues as the seeds develop and the pod starts to swell up just like the mother's belly.

The pregnancy itself is the subject of the second Iranian pinhead in our little series. Here we see the pregnant mother with her tiny foetus curled up beside her:

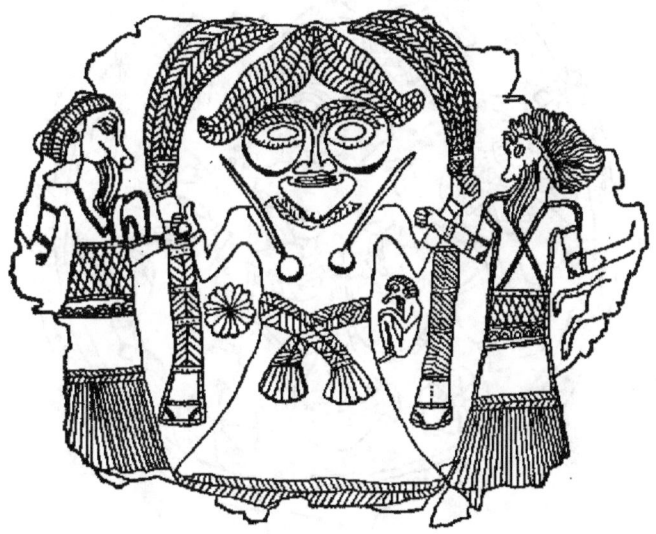

135 The pregnant mother with her embryo [10]

The rather grotesque faces of the foetus and the male attendants are characteristic of these Iranian designs; I don't believe it has any particular significance. Although the pinhead has suffered damage and has lost its periphery, there is enough to show that one of the male attendants is carrying a descending calf (*on the right-hand side*).

Another aspect of this design that stands out for me are the details of the woman's clothing. It only struck me quite late on in the writing of this book and only after reading a description of the Roman goddess Juno.

Under the name Lucina,[11] Juno was the goddess who watched over childbirth. Offerings were made to her to petition an easy birth, and no one making those offerings

---

[10] Porada 1965, fig 60. See also Godard 1965, plate 21 (photo).

[11] Ovid derived her name from Latin lux – 'light'. In another version Lucina was Juno's daughter and she was delivered without pain and was therefore prayed to by mothers in labour. Lampriere's Classical Dictionary under Lucina, page 367.

The Flower of Heaven

was allowed to have any sort of knot upon them. All belts, ties and fastenings had to be undone as their 'binding magic' might hinder the delivery of the child.[12] And that could well explain why the clothes-pins of our Iranian lady above don't actually bind any clothing together but just seem to be floating in mid-air above her shoulders. More convincing still is the depiction of her belt: its ends, rather than being tied, are just laid one on top of the other. So we may conclude that this lady, with all her ties loosened, is ready to bear her child.

Her term of pregnancy comes to fruition in the third and final pinhead of the series:

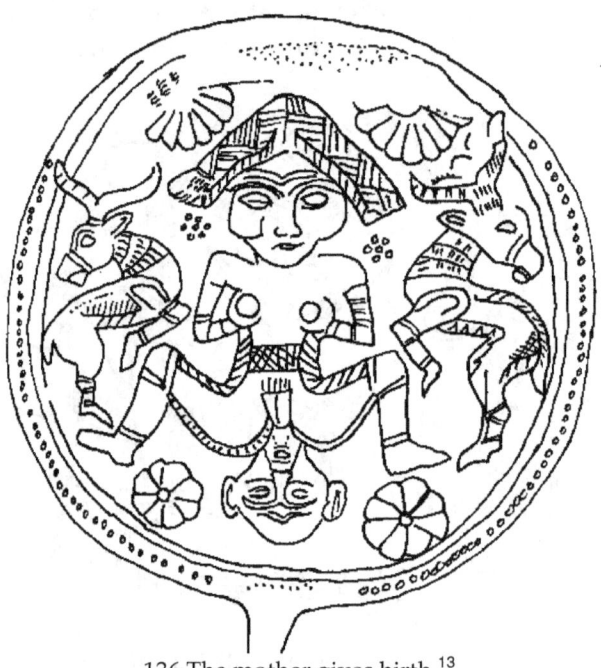

136 The mother gives birth [13]

The mother finally gives birth to her child. Descending headfirst, the wrinkled face of the baby emerges into the light of day and the start of his own independent existence. His mother has rightly adopted the breast-cupping attitude (*see figs 54 & 55*) illustrating that beyond the moment of birth, the woman and goddess are still united in the divine function of feeding and nurturing the new-born child.

All in all, the flower is the most appropriate and enduring symbol of motherhood. But we should not forget the heavenly nature of the flower. Afterall, it has been a symbol of the sky goddess, alongside the heavenly birds and celestial waters, for untold millennia.

Our next series of images elucidates this concept of the heavenly flower.

---

[12] Grimal 1990, page 231 under Juno.
[13] Godard 1965, fig 62.

The Flower of Heaven

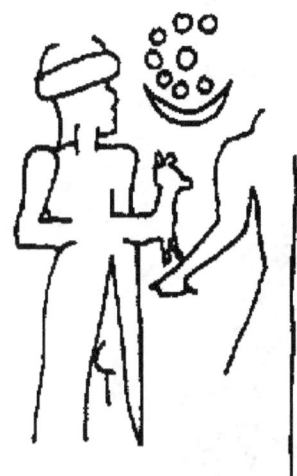

137 The rosette-sun [14]

The simplest and most convincing proof that the heavens were thought to be full of seed is seen in figure 137(*left*). This design makes it obvious that the sun and the rosette are interchangeable terms. Could there be a simpler and more elegant way of identifying the radiant flower with the fertile heart of the heavens?

The rosette is evidently another symbol of the fertile skies full of light. This means that the circular centre of the flower is considered to be the radiant disk of the sun, and its petals represent its rays of light that illuminate all heaven. By placing the seeds within the petals of the flower, the solar rosette is expressing the idea that the seed of mankind is contained within and transmitted by the rays of the sun.

The solar nature of the flower is made manifest in our next design from a Neo-Assyrian stone carving, which places the flower within the frame of the winged disk:

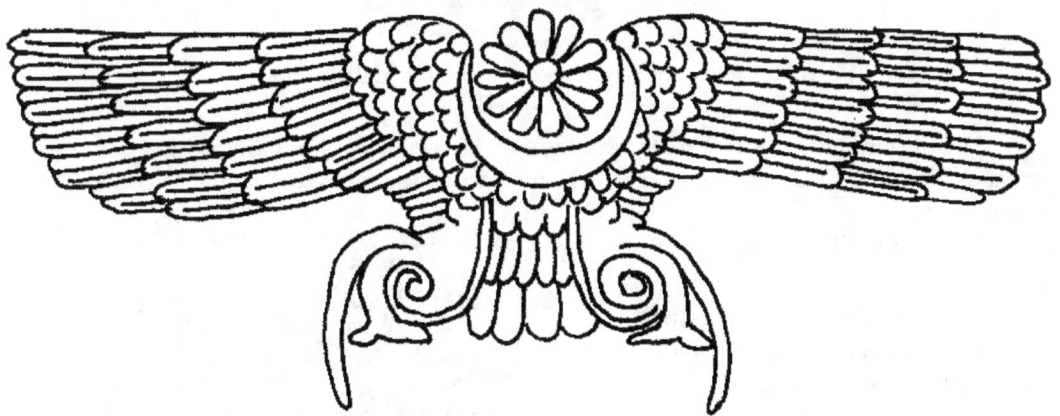

138 A winged disk with a rosette representing the sun-disk [15]

This design is one of the most elegant depictions of the fertile skies. The seed of mankind may form in the solar heart of the flower but it falls to earth in the celestial waters that spring from the body of the winged disk. The powers of the sun and the circulating waters of the skies are hereby combined into a wonderful glyph of the heavenly realms that bring all life to birth upon the earth.

---

[14] Collon 1975, fig 128.
[15] Winter 2010, chap 6, detail of fig 19. page 268.

The Flower of Heaven

The basic idea that the fertile seed of all life is transmitted in the rays of the sun is most eloquently expressed in our next image. Dating back to the Halaf period (circa 5500 BCE) it is testament to the antiquity of the idea and its central place in the art traditions of Mesopotamia.

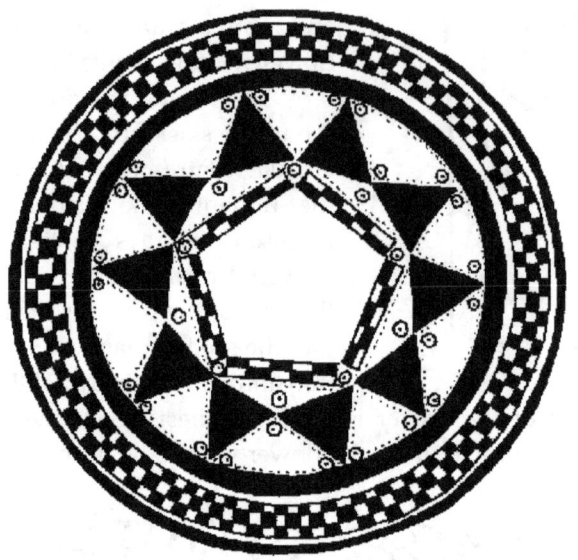

139 A geometric solar rosette from the Halaf period [16]

This elegant image proves that the seed of all life is nurtured within the light of the sun. It leads us on to our final series of images, which return to the figure of Inanna, as goddess of the sunlit skies.

Given the life-engendering nature of sunlight, the strange symbolism applied to the rays of Inanna's massive sun-disk (*right*) now makes perfect sense.

As the image clearly shows, the circular forms placed upon the tips of the sun's rays are none other than the seeds of life. What could be a more graphic way of saying that all life originates in the ethereal realms of the sunlit heavens.

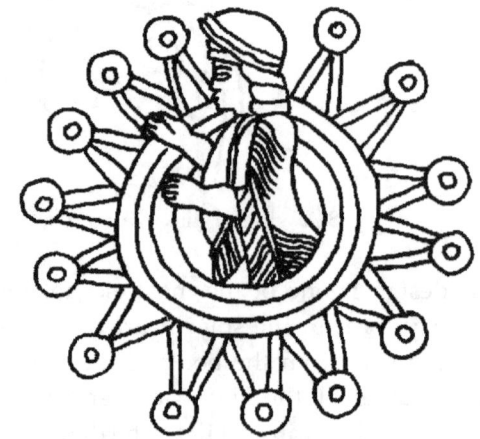

140 The goddess in her seed-laden sun-disk [17]

---

[16] Goff 1963, fig 69.
[17] Ornan 2005, fig 115.

The Flower of Heaven

This design formulates the concept of the pregnant sky goddess by the eminently simple devise of combining the form of the solar disk with the imagery of the seed-bearing flower. The solar heavens may act like the matrix within which this seed evolves, but we should not assume that the seeds are necessarily an inherent quality of sunlight. One has to ask the question: Are these seeds an inherent quality of sunlight or are they an independent entity, in their own right, that is merely carried by the rays of the sun? What then is the real nature of the celestial seed that engenders mankind?

The answer to this question is found in the icons of Inanna in her celestial shrine:

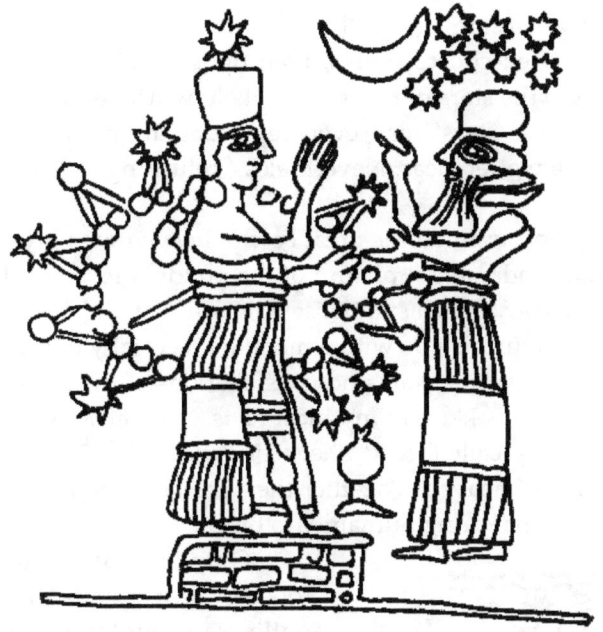

141 Celestial Inanna in her shrine [18]

The goddess' sun-disk gives us an answer – the seed of mankind is the light of the stars. This is the seed that the mother of humanity gestates in her heavenly womb.

It is difficult to be more specific about the 'starlight' in Inanna's solar rays as cuneiform doesn't have separate signs for star, constellation or planet. Instead, all such objects, along with meteors and comets, were categorised under the cuneiform sign known as **Mul** (*right*).[19] From an overly intellectual perspective, this sign may appear a bit vague as it doesn't distinguish the classes of celestial object we recognise today. But that misses the

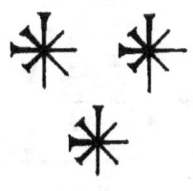

The **Mul**-sign

---

[18] Ornan 2005, detail of fig 162. See also Black & Green 1992, fig 87 for another version of the same design, which places crescent shapes upon the solar rays rather than circlets as in Ornan's image.

[19] PSD: MUL [shine]

point. Rather than being a vague term, I would argue that the **Mul**-sign, like so many Sumerian signs with a range of meanings, is an 'integral' symbolic term. The sun and the moon, the stars and the planets are all part of the same picture in Sumerian thought. The ultimate meaning of the **Mul**-sign is really seen in its 'action state' where it signifies the verb 'to shine or radiate'. Once again, the symbolic trail leads us back to the ineffable lights of the heavens.

Taking stock of figure 141, which is arguably an icon of the whole of heaven, leads me to think that all the major astral bodies that adorn the firmament are directly present or are at least implied here. Beyond the great sun-disk and the lunar crescent, the heavens are adorned with the seven stars of the Pleiades. And if the Pleiades are here representing the class of stars and fixed constellations, then the stars shining in Inanna's solar rays might then be related to the stars of the zodiacal belt, which all the celestial bodies travel. On the other hand, these 'stars' may even represent the planets. Unfortunately these designs don't make the matter clear. Nevertheless, returning to the metaphor of celestial cattle can help us out.

We have already encountered the great cow of heaven who gives birth to her sacred calf. This gives us the fundamental picture of the goddess forming the child in her own image. But beyond the cow, which symbolises the unity of all heaven, we also find other sets of celestial cattle that furnish us with a more detailed tally of the heavenly powers. It is of utmost significance that the stars and constellations of the night-time skies could be referred to as the Cattle of Šakkan in mythical texts.[20] Equally significant is the fact that the planets are commonly called Wild Sheep or Wild Cattle.[21] All these celestial cattle roamed the high plains of heaven. Together they present a much more detailed account of the formative powers that bring humanity to birth.

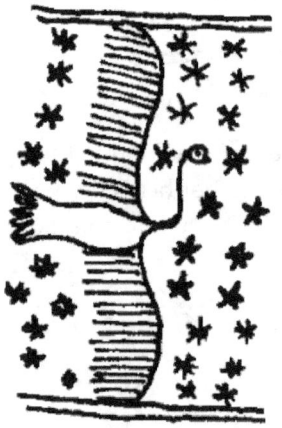

Detail of fig 60

Only by drawing these various strands together is it possible to formulate the bare outlines of a profound philosophy that places mankind's ultimate origins among the stars.

From images like the mother-bird flying through the night (*left*), we can infer that the cosmic journey of human embodiment does indeed start among the stars of the firmament.

The next stage of the journey brings the descending child into the realm of the solar heavens with all its winds and weather, until it finally alights upon the sacred tree and lays its precious brood of eggs. That mythical

---

[20] Dalley 1989, page 296 (Tablet II of the Akkadian Erra Epic) where the Fox-star (a star in Ursa major) is counted as one of the Cattle of Šakkan.

[21] I will explore this topic in greater depth in a future publication.

The Flower of Heaven

Tree, in which Anzu built her nest,[22] is of course, the family tree of the human parents that the child will be born to.

All these themes are implicit within our final image. Here the inter-related metaphors of sunlight, starlight and the flowers of heaven finally collide to produce a cosmic vision of radiant Inanna:

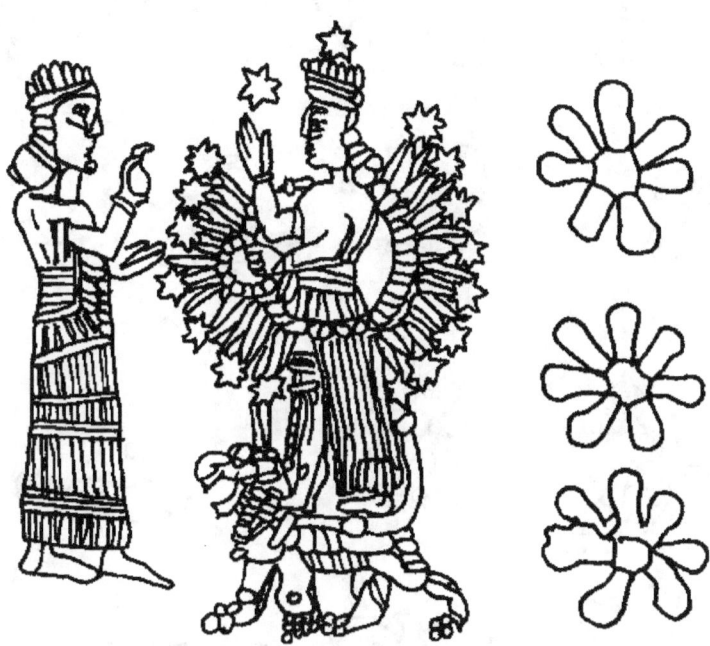

142 Inanna, the goddess of heavenly light [23]

This icon of the goddess portrays her as the whole of heaven, which, day and night, is resplendent with her divine light. Her massive sun-disk is adorned with a myriad of stars. Their light, which is ultimately identified as the 'seed of mankind', is transmitted in the lustrous rays of the sun. This was how the ancients conceived of their origins.

We will have to leave any further exploration of the stellar and planetary realms for another time and another title. For now, this concludes Part Two of the book and our investigation into the essential nature of the goddess in the artistic traditions of the Ancient Near East.

On the next page, I have presented a summary of the principal symbols of the fertile skies that we have encountered in the last few chapters. After that, in Part Three, we will trace out the historical demise of the goddess and the break-up of her age-old symbol system.

---

[22] There are two mythical narratives concerning Anzu and her nest. ETCSL: Lugalbanda & the Anzu-bird, lines 28ff; & the Akkadian *Etana Epic*: Dalley 1989, pages 191-192.

[23] Ornan 2005, fig 124.

The Flower of Heaven

Symbols of the Fertile Skies

By way of a simple summary and a useful reference, all the main symbols of the fertile skies can be set out together.

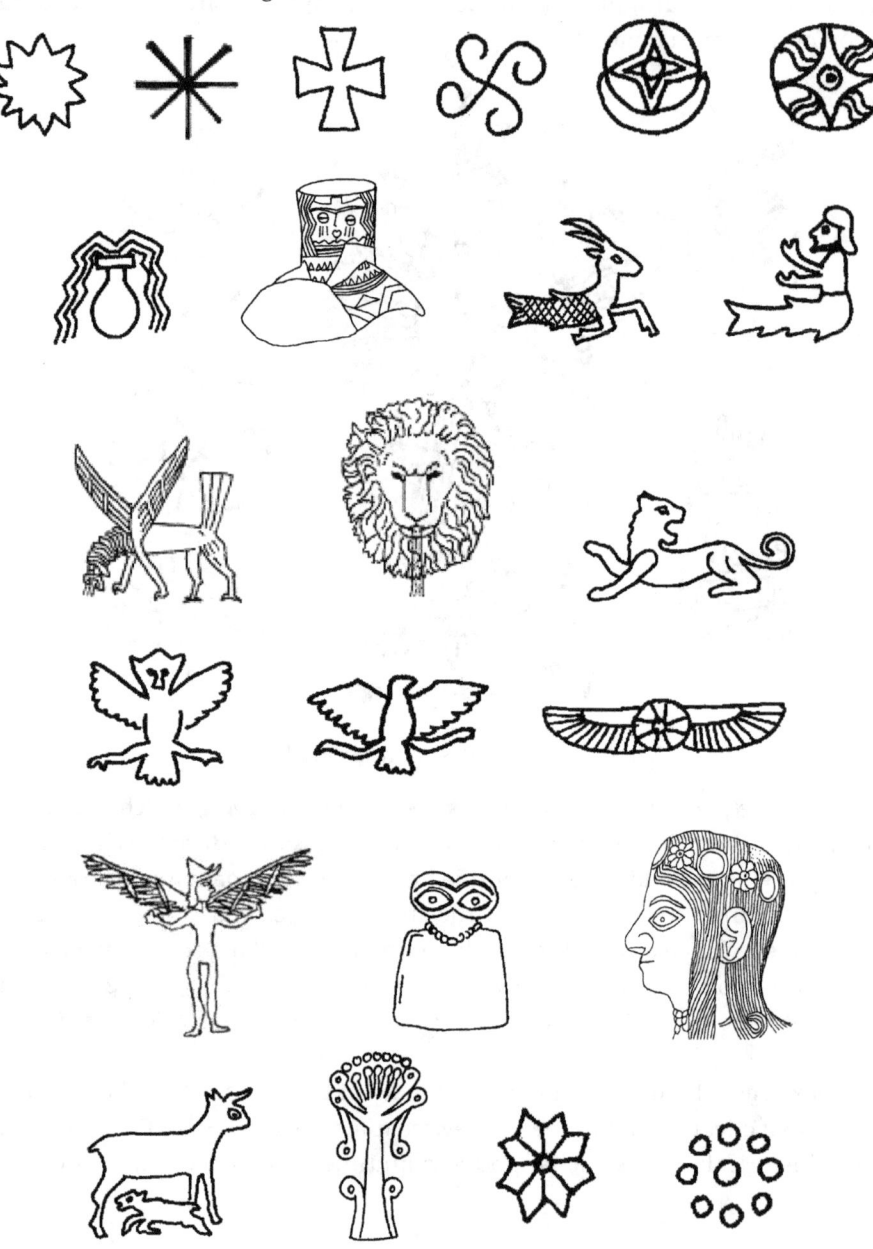

PART THREE
The Fall of the Goddess

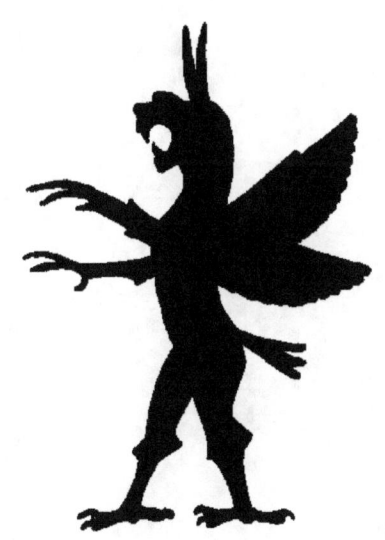

The Battle of the Gods

Many modern scholars of the Ancient Near East hold the opioion that the goddesses held sway in the earliest times and, by implication, that the well-known gods of written myth were interlopers of a later age.[2] In Mesopotamia, we can detect the arrival of a male dominated pantheon, headed by the Akkadian god Enlil, in the Early Dynastic period (3100-2390 BCE). For several centuries the two traditions appear to have co-existed side-by-side, but the uneasy peace would not last for long. It is fair to say that in this mythic era, the heavens were over-populated, and over-populated by a host of very diverse beings. Exactly this situation is portrayed in our first design, half of which we are already familiar with:

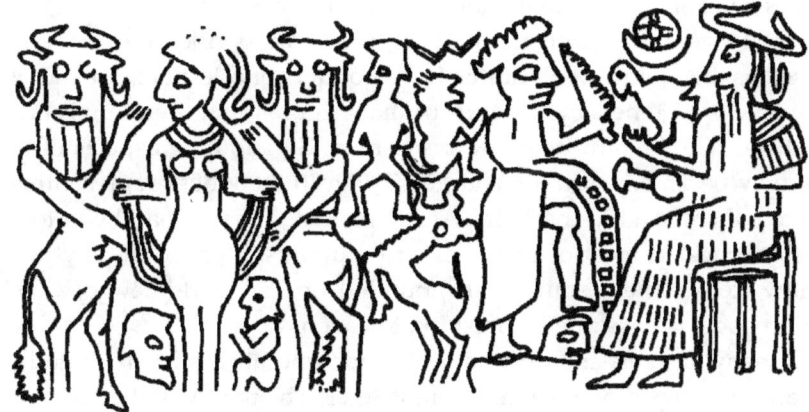

143 The goddess and the high gods of Akkad [1]

The unfamiliar half of this design portrays the new order of gods. Enlil, the leader of the pantheon sits enthroned and his warrior son, Ninurta, the conqueror of the foreign lands, enters his august presence.

This design encapsulates the religious world of the Early Dynastic period when kingship and Akkadian culture were rising to the fore. The tipping point came around the middle of the 3rd millennium when images of warrior gods slaying monstrous creatures (*overleaf*) start to appear in the artistic record. It is the first indication that the new Akkadian gods are turning upon their older animalian compatriots. A century or so later, the Akkadians seized outright control of Sumeria and the cultural clash came to its climax. Enlil decreed that the old order should fall and that the mother goddess and her animal-kin should be cast out of heaven. The warrior god, Ninurta 'hero of Enlil', was charged with defeating the old powers and his battles against these archaic beings form

---

[1] Early 2nd millennium seal design, Frankfort 1939, text fig 75.

[2] Leick 1991, pages 119-121 under Mother Goddess. Steinkeller 1999, page 113.

The Battle of the Gods

the backbone of the myths of the so-called 'Slain Heroes' known in late 3rd millennium sources.[3]

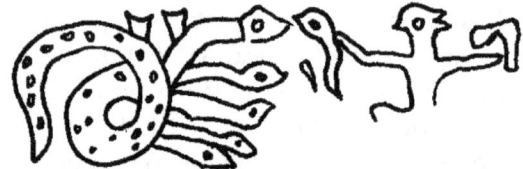

144 A hero battling against a Seven-headed serpent [4]

The profound changes in the religious world that culminated in the war of the gods can be best summarised as three succeeding ages – the Age of the Goddess, the Age of Transition, and the Age of the High Gods. Understanding the basic nature of the Three Ages provides a major key to understanding ancient art and myth.

In the First Age, the Age of the Goddess, the goddess ruled the heavens alone. She was portrayed as the mother of all humanity, a goddess of celestial light and water. In the Second Age, she was joined by a group of male figures that were envisioned as semi-human creatures like the bird-man and bison-man. By adopting aspects of the goddess' symbolism, they became masculine counterparts to the goddess representing the fertile powers of the fathers. And in the Third Age, a male dominated pantheon took control of the heavens and ousted most of their former occupants. Most of the myths and hymns that we know from written sources are founded on the worldview of this Third Age when the high gods had assumed rulership of heaven.

A great many designs, and written myths, incorporate a mixture of gods, goddesses and supernatural beings drawn from different Ages. The theory of the Three Ages tries to make sense out this diverse data by dividing the various mythical beings and motifs into different cultural and historical strata. The theory tries to map the various belief-systems that have successively held sway over humanity in its pre-literate past.

The theory of the Three Ages is very necessary for an understanding of the overall evolution of ideas in prehistoric times. Many significant images and motifs found in ancient art only start to make sense when viewed through its threefold prism. Once you get used to its principles and application, the theory becomes another tool that helps to clarify the thought-patterns and philosophies underpinning the traditional visual arts.

Returning to our main storyline. By far the clearest articulation of the 'war of the gods' is seen in a new genre of art, in which one set of divine beings fight against another. Many of the animalian figures are captured and bound and brought to judgement before the high gods. Several of the ancient deities are found wanting and are brutally slain with their arms still bound behind their backs (*fig 81*). And alongside these doomed deities we also see the demise of the sky goddess.

---

[3] Annus 2002, pages 109ff, Ninurta's myths have long been recognised as the basis of Herakles Labours.
[4] Detail from Frankfort 1939, text fig 27.

The Battle of the Gods

The artistic sources tell a compelling story of how a great cultural age came to an end and how a new world-order came to dominate the religious mind-set of the Ancient Near East.

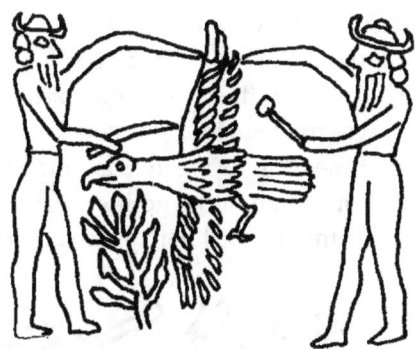

145 Two gods battle with Anzu [5]

The narrative concerning the end of the goddess' sacred bird is the easiest to reconstruct from ancient art. In figure 145 (*right*) we see two warrior gods battling with an eagle; they have plucked the heavenly bird from the skies, and under force of weapons they take it into captivity.

If we read the design more imaginatively, this image tells the tale of the goddess' demise and the fall of her cult. The actions depicted here have to be understood as taking place in the physical and spiritual realms simultaneously. A very similar battle took place in ancient China in 1122 BCE, in which many ancient gods and spirits were killed off including several archaic stellar deities. In more earthly terms, this Chinese battle also marked the transition between the ruling dynasties of the Shang and Chou.[6] Just like the Mesopotamian battle of the gods, the Chinese 'battleground' comprised the ideological realms of religion and power politics.

As the next image shows, the sacking of temples and shrines involved the physical removal of its cultic icons. Here we see the Assyrian army looting the temples of Babylon's goddesses. Here the sacred bird and tree of the goddess are being taken away as war-booty; they could almost treated as prisoners of war, being displayed in victory parades alongside vanquished kings.

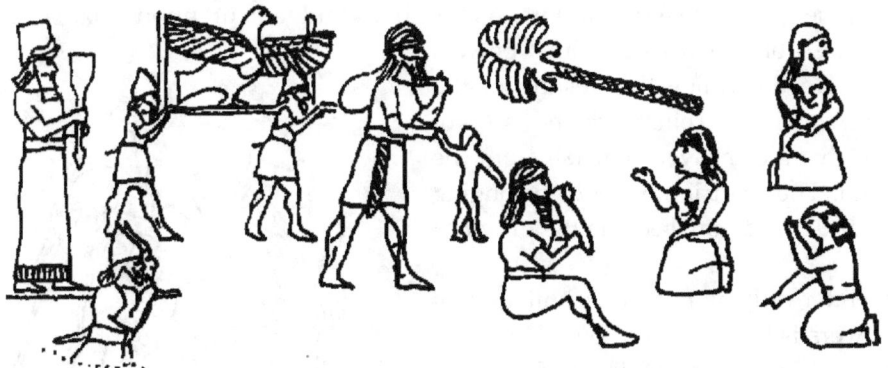

146 Assyrian troops strip the temples of Babylon [7]

---

[5] Boehmer 1965, Tafel XXVIII, fig 334. Goff 1963, fig 722
[6] Walters 1992, pages 123-125, under Battle of Mu.
[7] Ornan 2005, fig 120.

The Battle of the Gods

Ultimately, I believe that the battle of the gods seen in the Akkadian age was an attempt to eradicate the goddess' ancient cult and its place in Sumerian society. Her sacred bird and tree wouldn't just be removed from the temples; they would have been utterly destroyed. A parallel case is found in the bible where the destruction of the Asherah (a treelike goddess) was part of the 'smashing of idols' and the 'tearing down of altars' prescribed by the jealous god of the Israelites.[8]

Our two previous images actually place as much emphasis on the tree as they do on the eagle. These designs are just as much about the demise of the bird symbol, as they are about the destruction of the goddess' sacred tree. This is made clearer, in the next design, where the birdman and the holy tree are together brought to their judgement:

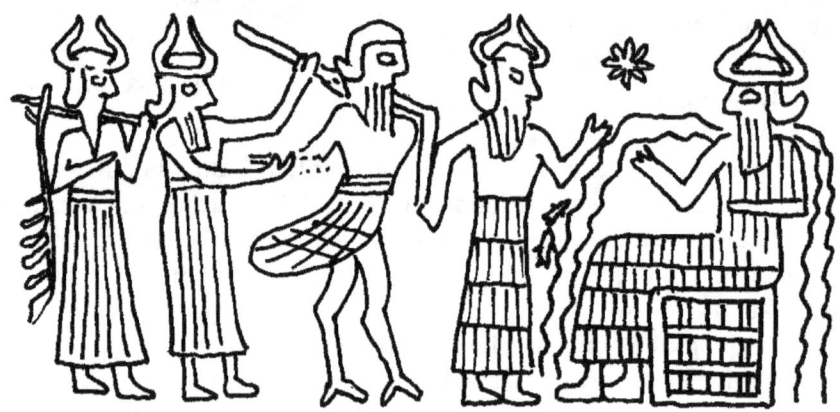

147 The judgement of Anzu & the tree, from an Akkadian seal [9]

The bird-man with his arms bound behind his back is forcibly brought to judgement before Enki, the god of the fertile waters. As for Enki's 'judgement' upon Anzu, it is really about Enki absorbing Anzu's ordained powers – the power to determine the destiny of the rolling rivers. These 'rolling rivers' are, of course, the rivers of heaven that fall from the skies as rain. These attributes, once belonging to the sky-bird, have now become the province of Enki.

The end result of Enki's assimilation of Anzu's powers is better seen in our 'Mountain of Sunrise' design (*right*). Here Enki has acquired the flying bird as an attribute. The image is saying that Enki, once the male

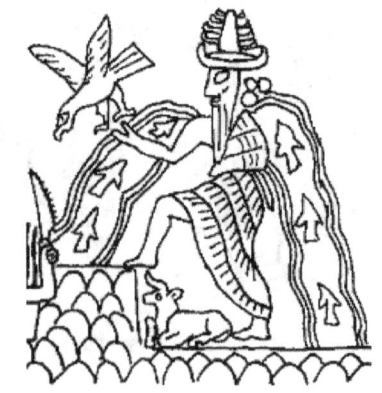

Detail of fig 84

---

[8] Deuteronomy 7:5.
[9] Boehmer 1965, Tafel XLIII, fig 510.

counterpart of the feminine waters, has now usurped his place and has become the sole controller of the heavenly rains.

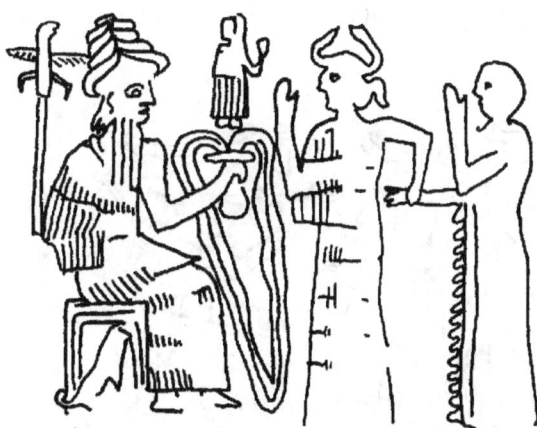

148 Enki, the water god, now holds the power to grant progeny to man [10]

It is important to stress that Enki took over the goddess' symbols along with all their accrued meanings. This is confirmed in fig 148 (*left*) where a Lama goddess plays out her more usual role of introducing the Lord into the presence of the high gods. Like the previous illustrations, this design shows that Enki has assumed patronage of the life-engendering waters and has adopted the bird of the skies as his sacred emblems.

Nor is this the end of the matter. In the annals of literature, Ninurta is named as slayer of Anzu.

Beyond his aspect as a warrior god, Ninurta was also the god of the farmers and the controller of rain and thunder. And in the same way that Enki absorbed the fertile aspects of Anzu's waters, so Ninurta assimilated Anzu's thunderous nature and adopted the eagle as one of his emblematic beasts:

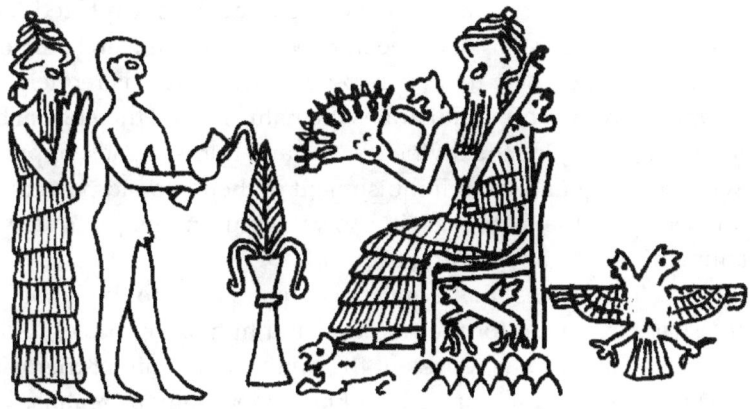

149 The enthroned god Ninurta with Anzu as one of his emblems [11]

The conquerors are dividing up the ancient powers and symbols, and are sharing them out between themselves! The 'judgement' that the high gods impose on their captured foes redefines their fate, their nature and function in the new world-order. The

---

[10] From an internet source via Tom, captioned as Heuzey Rev d'Assyria V page 139. Decouvertes page 307.
[11] Frankfort 1939, text fig 38.

The Battle of the Gods

animalian powers are now conceived of as raw elemental forces, which the heroic gods have conquered and controlled for the benefit of mankind.

We will have to catch up on the fate of the sacred tree elsewhere. For now we shall follow the fate of the bison-man, whose capture is another favourite theme in Akkadian art:

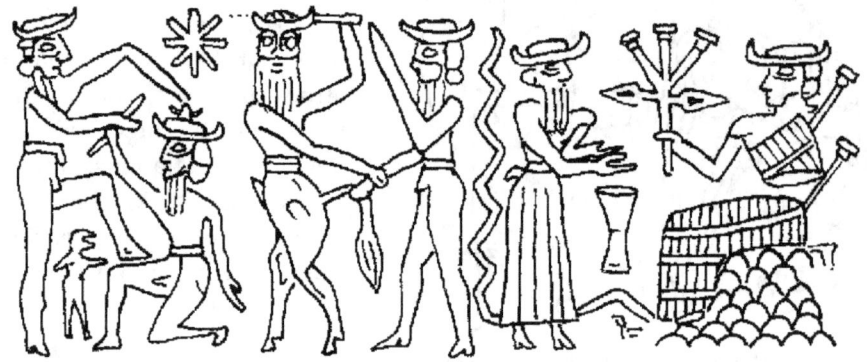

150 Ninurta as conqueror of the mountains [12]

In this image we see the warrior god, Ninurta, in all his military might enthroned upon the mountainous lands he has conquered.[13] He is rightly known as the 'weapon god' of Mesopotamia,[14] and his martial powers are represented by the multiple-headed weapon he holds in his hand and the twin battle maces set to his left and right.[15]

In the field before Ninurta, the phallic Bison-man is captured and another unidentifiable god is overpowered. This kneeling god is one of the archaic powers as can be seen from the old-fashioned way that his two-tiered headdress is rendered.[16] The way that the gods grapple with each other illustrates the nature of the theological battle taking place – the conquering gods seize the divine crowns and horns of their opponents, which at once signifies their taming and the relinquishment of their age-old powers. This design depicts the end result of the battle as it shows Ninurta, the conqueror, sitting in judgement, granting his boons and issuing decrees.[17]

At one level, the 'mountains' that Ninurta conquers refer to the lands surrounding Mesopotamia that were exploited for their natural and human resources, but on another more symbolic level, the mountains represent the mythical domain of the rising sun. The bison and bison-man were natural inhabitants of both mountainous realms.

---

[12] Boehmer 1965, Tafel XXVI, fig 299.

[13] PSD: KUR [mountain]

[14] See Cooper 1978, pages 154-162.

[15] Ninurta's twin maces are known as Šarur & Šargaz. See Babylonian Star-lore under Scorpion's Sting.

[16] Fischer 'Twilight of the Sun-god' (Iraq LXIV – 2002) page 125 & 127. Such details can help in identifying one set of gods from another but it is not a consistent feature in these images.

[17] The myth of Ninurta and the Stones contains the story of how Ninurta judged the rocks and minerals of the mountains. See Leick 1991, page 136; & ETCSL: Ninurta's Exploits, lines 416-644.

The Battle of the Gods

Our next illustration (*below*) depicts another version of the battle, which confirms that the mountains where the Bison-man roams are indeed the 'Mountains of Sunrise' but instead of the Akkadian gods we saw earlier (*fig 84*) here we see the archaic powers of sunrise in the form of our luminous goddess:

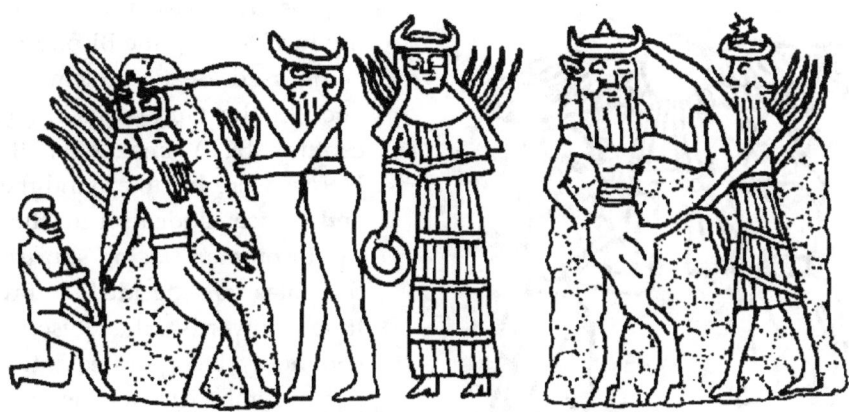

151 The archaic mountain of sunrise with the radiant goddess [18]

The radiant goddess stands between the twin peaks of the eastern mountains – she can be none other than the rising sun shedding her divine light upon the lands. This very scene is described in hymnal praise: 'All the countries are building a house for you as for the risen sun, a shining torch is assigned to you, the light of the land'.[20] The circlet that she holds in her hand identifies her with the celestial goddess we have already met (*see figs 141 & 142*). She was the original solar deity before the male sun gods, Utu and Šamaš, took over her divine offices and her symbolic creatures. The proof of this is seen in the next illustration, which shows that it was the sun god that assimilated the defeated bison-man into his cultus and iconography:

152 The rising of the Sun god from an Akkadian seal [19]

[18] Boehmer 1965, Tafel XXVI, fig 300. Goff 1963, fig 716.
[19] Boehmer 1965, Tafel XXXIII, fig 397. Also Amiet 1961, plate 112, fig 1488.
[20] ETCSL: Inana D, lines 1-8.

The Battle of the Gods

Here we see an attendant throwing open the gates of the east for the sun god to rise into heaven. But instead of the sun rising between twin mountains, the god seems to climb upon two recumbent bison-men. The sun god's hunching posture is probably due to him grasping the bison-man's horns, which are a timeless symbol of animal fertility.

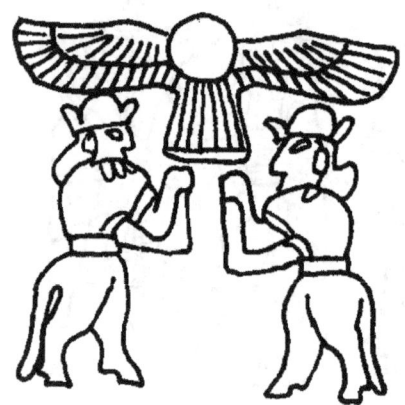

153 Bison-men and the winged disk [21]

Many centuries after his mythical slaying the Bison-man is still being used as an emblem of the sun god. In the Gudea inscriptions (21st century BCE) images of the Slain Heroes were set up around the temple and palace; Gudea set up the head of the Bison-man 'facing sunrise, where the fates are decided'.[22] From this time onwards the bison-man is commonly incorporated into the sun god's symbolism. He is most often seen in pairs, either supporting the sun god's throne or holding aloft the winged disk (*left*).

Earlier, we saw the radiant goddess between the twin mountains of sunrise (*fig 151*). In the midst of the divine battle, she stands aloof, untouched by any foe. Yet her fate is also awaiting her. Alongside the Bison-man and the other Slain Heroes, the enigmatic figure of the solar goddess is also captured and brought to her judgement. So far, only one clear depiction of her judgement has been discovered:

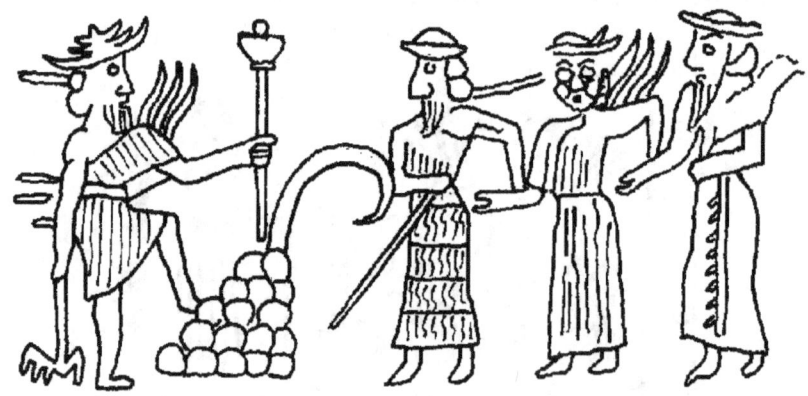

154 The radiant goddess is brought for judgement [23]

---

[21] 9th century BCE stone relief from Tell Halaf. Source lost.
[22] Ellis 1989, page 130, note 66.
[23] Boehmer 1965, Tafel XXXI, fig 376.

The Battle of the Gods

Even though not bound, the goddess is forcibly brought before a warrior god who wields an enormous battle-mace and scimitar. To judge from his rays and the way he steps up upon the mountain this warrior god is Šamaš, the Akkadian sun god.

The judgement passed down upon the solar goddess was severe: she was stripped of her time-honoured attributes and effectively cast out of heaven. As far as the new national pantheon was concerned, she died a theological death. Her pictorial symbol system was dismantled and divided up as war-booty among the new gods of Akkad. What remained of the great goddess was finally combined and utterly confounded with the Akkadian divinity Ištar.

The destruction of the ancient goddess and her reformulation as Inanna-Ištar was quite successful in the sphere of literature, which could be controlled by a small but powerful elite. Indeed, the earliest hymns to the goddess, which show her as the complex fusion of Inanna and Ištar, were reputedly written by the high-priestess Enheduana.[24] If she really was the author, then the political dimension of her works may be judged by the fact that she was installed as a high priestess by her father, king Sargon, founder of the Akkadian empire and conqueror of all Sumeria.[25]

However, in the artwork of the largely illiterate populace the visual icons of the celestial goddess continued to thrive. In reality, the old sky goddess never died, she lived on for thousands of years and much of her symbolism is still with us today in the designs and motifs of the traditional arts.

While the solar aspects of Inanna were evidently suppressed after the battle of the gods, her stormy aspects were endorsed in the new order. Thus Inanna continued to act out the role of storm goddess, even though she lost her wings and was invariably set alongside images of her masculine counterpart (*see figs 70-75.*).

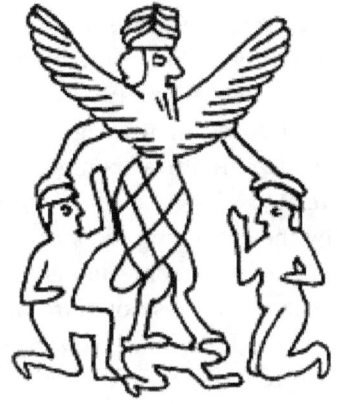

155 The male form of Anzu [26]

During the course of the 3rd millennium BCE, the symbolism of the heavenly bird underwent a series of transformations. The first tangible evidence for a reformulation of the bird symbol is found in the early 3rd millennium, when we see the masculine form of the bird-man appearing (*right*). It was this male symbol of the fertile skies that was killed off by the Akkadian gods (*see fig 147*).

---

[24] There is some doubt about Enheduana's authorship of the hymns as the earliest copies so far discovered only date back to the late 3rd millennium. See also Leick 1991, page 61.

[25] Steinkeller 1999, page 124.

[26] Boehmer 1965, Tafel XXIX, fig 340. Amiet 1961, plate 96, fig 1264.

The Battle of the Gods

The masculine reformulation of the heavenly bird was only a part of a broader process of iconic transformation. Towards the end of the 3rd millennium, we see the first appearance of a set of new figures that personify the winds; and by the early 2nd millennium all four winds start to appear together in seal designs:

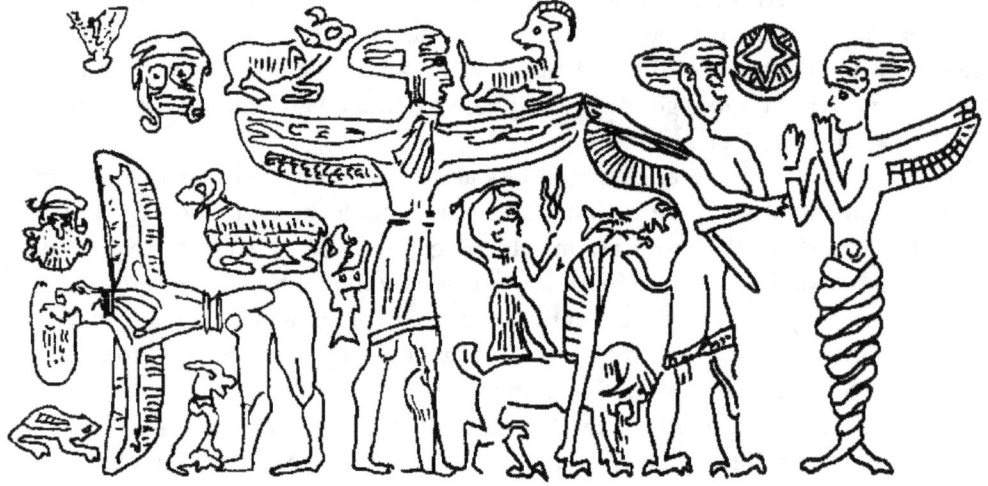

156 The Four Winds with the storm god [28]

This illustration shows some of the common characteristics of the winds. Their chief defining feature is naturally their outspread wings, but their aerial nature is also conveyed by their hair, which is swept back in the wind. More variable details, such as bird's feet or scorpions tails, are only sometimes present. In truth, the appearance of the winds is pretty variable, some being entirely animalian in character (*see fig 69*), which in itself suggests they are relatively new creations of the mythic imagination.

These figures, neither gods nor demons, don't quite fit into the conventional schemes of supernatural beings. Even though literate sources tend to emphasise the weather-related aspects of the winds, in artworks they still retain their fertile nature as evinced by the crouching kids, calves and lambs that are strewn around this image. This would explain why some images of the female South Wind do sometimes show her carrying a pair of calves down from the skies (*see fig 56*).

The basic form of the winged goddess also appears under another name and another nature in the form of the *Lilu*. Closely related to the winds, these male and female creatures were classified among the demons of Mesopotamia. Later tradition has it that they were meant to be the unhappy ghosts of people who died unmarried virgins. Their fate, after death, was to become wind-like demons that came back to earth to seduce men in their sleep and rob them of their seed.[29] That, at least, is the Akkadian version of the *Lilu*-demon.

---

[28] Wiggermann 2007, fig 7 on page 142. From left to right, we have the west, east, north and south winds.
[29] Wiggermann 2007, page 227.

The Battle of the Gods

However, there is more than a hint that the *Lilu*-maid's lovemaking could actually result in progeny – one version of the Sumerian King List plainly states that a *Lilu*-demon, the male form of the creature, was counted as the father of Gilgamesh.[30] Given their fertility aspects we would be right in being suspicious about the demonic gloss applied to the *Lilu*-maid, and rightly so, for a very plausible depiction of her appears on a Greek stone-cut relief, where a wayfarer, perhaps to avoid the midday sun, has fallen asleep under a shady tree.

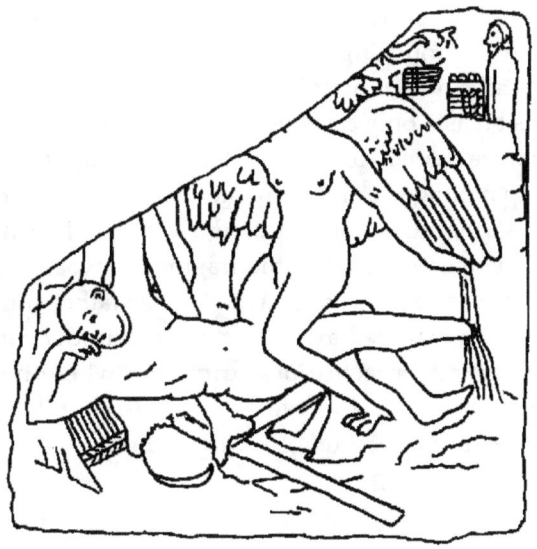

157 A Greek stone carved in relief [31]

The wayfarer is seduced by a beautiful naked goddess who is not only decked out with a full set of wings but even has the same bird-like feet seen on some of our Near Eastern figures. Now we can see beneath the demonic gloss of the *Lilu* and see her true origins. The significance of her name, is once again embedded within the cuneiform writing system. The **Lil₂**-sign, with which her name is written (*right*) probably depicts a mat woven of reeds; it is chiefly used to write 'wind and breeze' but its secondary meanings of 'ghost or phantom' [32] harkens back to her origins as the winged goddess. Ultimately she is the mother of all souls. This sense of *Lilu* appears in Ninlil's name. Ninlil, the highest-ranking goddess of Mesopotamia and wife to Enlil, was not simply the 'Lady of the Winds' as her name is often understood, but the 'Queen of the *Lilu*-maids'.

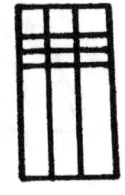

The **Lil**-sign

The process of demonisation brought to bear on the winged goddess reached its logical conclusion by transforming the archaic animal forms of the goddess (*such as those*

---

[30] ETCSL: Sumerian King List, lines 112-115.
[31] Harrison 1962, fig 38 on page 203.
[32] PSD: LIL [Ghost] and CDA: *zīqīqu*.

seen in figs 38 & 174) into full-blown demonic figures, whose evil hearts were set against the fortunes of mankind.

Thus was Lamaštu created; she was the vilest of demons – a baby-snatcher and killer. Miscarriages and cot deaths were attributed to her baleful influence. Even before the baby was born, she watched and waited, counting out the months and then blocking the 'gate' of the baby to cause extended periods of labour. Like the winds and breezes, to whom she is closely related, Lamaštu is said to glide through men's houses like a serpent. She 'sweeps over' men bringing disease and infirmity to his limbs, but more often she preys on pregnant women by touching their bellies to make them miscarry their unborn children. Other texts describe her kidnapping young babies and taking on the role of wet-nurse but her pendulous breasts only dispense poisonous milk to the innocent babe.[33]

Despite her evil nature, Lamaštu was counted as a daughter of Anu and a sister to Inanna. Although her parentage and her name, marked with the star-like sign for divinity, single her out as a significant mythical figure, her archaic nature was deemed an abomination to Akkadian sensibilities. Mythic fragments expand upon this idea where they tell us that Lamaštu was cast out of heaven by her father for asking to eat human flesh for her dinner.[34] From what we have learnt, we can understand that this trait very likely derives from the funerary practice of excarnation where human corpses are left exposed on a platform for the birds to devour (*see fig 64*).[35] Like the Harpies of Greek myth, Lamaštu was the deathly 'Snatcher' of young and old.

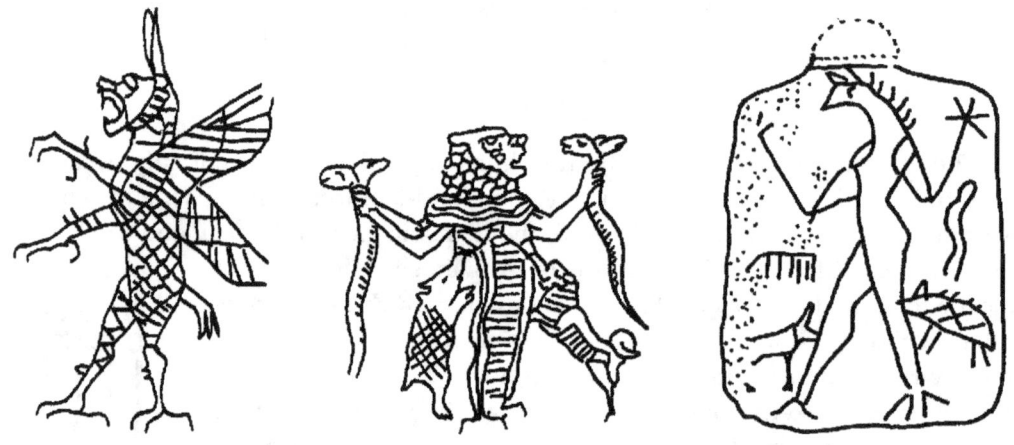

158-160 Three images of the baby-killing demoness Lamaštu [36]

---

[33] The profile of Lamaštu is built up from Leick 1991, page 110, Black & Green 1992, pages 115-116, and Wiggermann 2000.

[34] Wiggermann 2000, page 225.

[35] A similar charge of abomination (eating *asakku*-food) is also made concerning the eagle in the *Etana Epic*, see Dalley 1989, page 191 & note 10 on page 201.

[36] Left, Wiggermann 2000, fig 4, Middle, Pritchard 1969, plate 657, fig 215, Right, Wiggermann 2000, fig 1.

The Battle of the Gods

Although her name probably only means something like 'figure' or 'figurine'– a reference to the protective amulets engraved with her image that were worn by pregnant women to keep evil away (*above right*) – Lamaštu was always depicted in totally animalian form. In earlier depictions she has a tendency to retain her aerial wings but as time goes by, she progressively loses these vestiges of her long lost past.

Even though Lamaštu is portrayed in the most grotesque of forms she still retains something of her motherly character in the way she suckles a piglet and a whelp (*above centre*). Another image of the demoness (*below*) makes a more symbolic connection to children.

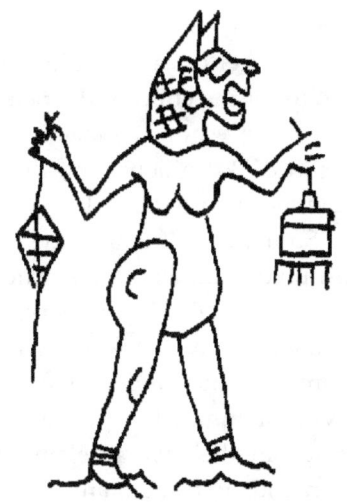

161 Lamaštu with her spindle & comb [37]

The symbolic attributes that Lamaštu holds – a spindle and comb – are typically feminine symbols in Mesopotamia where they appear in birth incantations denoting that a baby girl will be born to the pregnant mother (boys are likewise symbolised by weapons).[38] In the hands of an evil-working demoness such devices may be thought as of charms to spirit away the child to its destruction, but the use of these very same symbols in birth incantations makes it more likely that they another remembrance of Lamaštu's more benevolent past. Similarly, the evil touch of Lamaštu, which later ages twisted to be the proximate cause of miscarriages, would originally been her divine touch that made the mother pregnant.

Even within the Akkadian milieu a set of literate attributes tells another two-sided tale. As a disease-bringing demoness, Lamaštu could be characterised by the two terms 'fever' (*ummu*) and 'bile' (*martu*). However, as the lexicon shows, another interpretation is not only possible but has to be regarded as inherently plausible – as the Akkadian word *ummu* is more commonly used to signify the 'mother' , while the term *mārtu* represents her 'daughter'.[39]

---

[37] Wiggermann 2000, fig 4.

[38] Cunningham 1997, page 72, lines 46-48 of text.

[39] CDA: *ummu* I is 'mother', *ummu* II is 'heat or fever'. *Mārtu* refers to a 'daughter or girl' and *martu* to the 'gall-bladder or bile'. See Wiggermann 2000, page 238.

The Sun & the Child

The various symbols of the fertile heavens that we have explored in the course of this book all place the sun at the very heart of the fertile heavens. If the sun is indeed central to the whole system, then we should be able to find traces of the life-engendering sun in the myths and symbolism of Utu, the Sumerian sun god. According to our reconstruction of prehistory, the Sumerian sun god is little more than a male counterpart to Inanna. We have already seen that he shared many of Inanna's symbolic attributes, like the torch and eye, but above all else, the Sumerian sun god should have a strong fertile element and ultimately be progenitor of the child or the peoples.

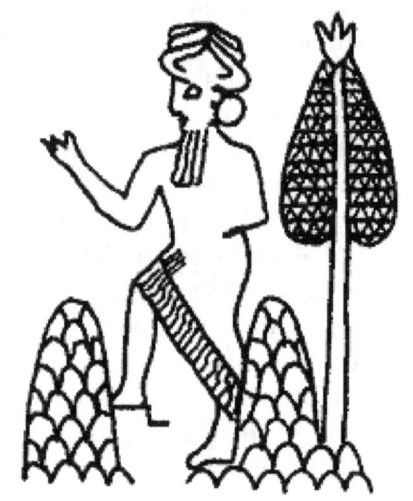

162 The sun god and below, the Sun-sign (**Ud**) depicting the rising sun [1]

In the new male dominated pantheon of 3rd millennium, the sun was represented by a fusion of two male gods – the Sumerian Utu and the Akkadian Šamaš. Like Inanna and Ištar, the two sun gods are actually two very different mythological characters with very different attributes and symbolism. As we did with Inanna-Ištar, we will have to separate out the diverse elements of the two sun gods to understand them and the historical processes that have influenced the way that the sun was perceived in ancient times.

As was the case with the dual goddess Inanna-Ištar, it is much easier to create a personality profile for the Akkadian sun god as he has direct parallels in other Semitic cultures. Like his feminine counterpart Šapaš,[2] the symbolism of the Akkadian sun god falls into two neat categories: day and night. The Semitic solar deities are the masters of two realms, the light and the dark, the resplendent heavens filled with light and the subterranean land of the shades.

The daytime eye of the sun sees all that happens on earth. The gaze of Šamaš is the heavenly witness to all men's acts. That is why he and the sun gods of many lands are lords of 'truth and justice'. The sacred saw that he holds, may have had its origins as a horticultural tool used in palm tree cultivation,[3] but in the hands of Šamaš it became a

---

[1] Boehmer 1965, Tafel XXXVI, fig 432.

[2] Leick 1991, page 149.

[3] Black & Green 1992, page 184.

symbol of retributive justice. According to one ancient source, the saw of the sun god was 'imposed' on crooks, presumably to cut off their hands.[4]

All this symbolism makes the sun god a perfect model for the king whose justice extends throughout the realm; conversely, it also explains why Šamaš has a strong warrior aspect to his mythic character. Like the sun god, the king oversees his realm and judges the people according to the law. Indeed, the king can be directly identified with the sun god – in several royal inscriptions he is simply referred to as 'the sun god of the land'.[5] All in all, the daylight aspects of the Akkadian sun god boil down to an image of the king judiciously overseeing his realm.

The night-time symbolism of Semitic deities like Šamaš and Šapaš often comes as a surprise to modern readers as they are intimately connected to the underworld and the governance of the ghosts.

At night, Šamaš is 'lord of the dead' (*bel miti*) and 'king of the ghosts' (*šar eṭimmi*).[6] He is the chief judge in the underworld and alongside the moon and the other infernal powers he pronounces the second great fate of mankind – his place and status in the underworld. The second fate of mankind is so decreed: "the sun god, the great lord of the netherworld, after turning the dark places to light, will judge your case. May the moon god decree your fate on the day of sleep ... May the god of the underworld utter prayers for you".[7]

The Akkadian sun god, as lord and judge of the underworld, governs the interactions between the living and the dead. Listening to the appeals of men haunted by ghosts or afflicted with ill from their ancestral kin, the sun god and his deputies enquire and examine, they pass judgement and set things aright.[8]

Šamaš is actually thought to transport souls between the realms of the living and the dead. The idea is clearest in some idioms from the ancient city of Ugaritic where 'to reach the sunset' and 'to enter the host of the sun' are both polite euphemisms for death.[9] These idioms reveal that the setting sun, descending below the horizon, was thought to take the ghosts of the dead down to the underworld. This must be why Nergal and Eriškigal, the traditional regents of the underworld in mythical sources, are called the lord and mistress of 'the land of the setting sun'.[10] The same idea, in negative form, is particularly common in curses where the sun god is implored to punish a wrong-doer: 'May Šamaš uproot him from the land of the living and leave his ghost to thirst for water in the world below'.[11]

It appears that all transactions between the underworld and the land of the living were overseen, even enacted, by the sun god. At funerals, the gifts for the underworld

---

[4] Sumerian gods and their Representations. page 5.

[5] Fischer 2002, page 132.

[6] CAD: *eṭemmu*

[7] An elegy on the death of Nannaya, lines 88-98.

[8] Lambert 1960, page 40. Said of Gilgamesh in his role as judge of the dead alongside the sun god.

[9] Ugaritic Texts, page 37.

[10] For Eriškigal see Lambert 1980, page 56. For Nergal see ETCSL: The Temple Hymn, line 464.

[11] CAD, under *eṭemmu*, section 1b, on page 399.

The Sun & the Child

gods, to be buried with the corpse, were first ceremoniously presented to the sun god.[12] Similarly, it is Šamaš who ensures that the all-important libations and offerings for the dead reach the underworld: 'Without you (Šamaš) the gods of the underworld do not receive funerary offerings'.[13] In both cases, it is tempting to think that it is the sun god himself who actually takes them down to the underworld. The idea that the sun god transports souls between the worlds is encapsulated in the pithy formula: 'O Šamaš, the Judge. You carry those from Above down to Below, and those from Below up to Above'.[14]

What Šamaš transports 'below' are the spirits of the recently deceased, and what he brings back 'above' are the ghosts of the dead that necromancers have called forth from the land of shades. Šamaš is not just lord of the dead he is also the god of necromancy.[15]

This is why Šamaš is so prominent in the magical lore of the necromancer. The essential elements of raising the dead are laid bare in an Akkadian incantation designed to evoke a ghost from the underworld and compel it to communicate: '... May he (Šamaš) bring up a ghost from the darkness for me. May he put life back (?) into the dead man's limbs'. The ghost is then conjured into a skull and the necromancer declares: 'I call upon you, O skull of skulls: may he who is within the skull answer me. O Šamaš who brings light in the darkness'.[16]

The Semitic sun goddess Šapaš, who sees all that happens on earth also travels the underworld at night and rules over the ghosts, whom she judges. And in parallel to Šamaš' involvement in necromancy, her presence is considered essential when invoking the dead.[17]

The varied aspects of Šamaš and Šapaš follow almost identical lines. This helps to confirm that these traits are the essential features of the Semitic conception of the sun. It is also important to take note of what solar traits are missing from Šamaš' profile. He is not a god of fertility, nor is he a progenitor of man or beast. On the contrary, the light of the Akkadian sun deities, although it may illuminate the upper and lower worlds, appears to be entirely sterile with no life-engendering aspect at all.

In contrast to the sterile light of the Akkadian sun god, the Sumerian solar deities are portrayed as the primary source of animal and plant life. Although Inanna-Ištar is widely recognised as the embodiment of Venus in the mythical traditions of later times, the older Sumerian form of Inanna was the goddess of all heaven and, according to my interpretations, she has a very pronounced solar aspect to her character.

I would advocate the idea that the Sumerian sun god Utu is little more than a masculine form of Inanna – both deities fully incorporate the symbolism of the life-giving

---

[12] George 1999, page 67 (Tablet VIII lines 136, 145 etc)

[13] CAD: *Kispu* section 2 on page 426.

[14] Finkel 1983, page 11, lines 13-14 of translated text.

[15] Finkel 1983, pages 1-17.

[16] Finkel 1983, page 9, lines 1-6 of translated text.

[17] Leick 1992, page 149 under Šapaš; also Astour 1980, page 232 and Healy 1980, page 240.

solar powers within their fundamental natures. Just as the Akkadian Šamaš appears to have had feminine roots in the Semitic traditions, so too was Utu created, probably in the latter half of the 4th millennium, as the male equivalent to his sister Inanna.

We have already seen that Utu and Inanna hold some major symbols in common. Both carry the light-bringing torch, and both are symbolised by the eyes of the sky. If it can be shown that all the major symbolism typically applied to Utu also has close parallels in Inanna's lore we will have demonstrated their affinity through proxy – in effect showing that the sun gods were later creations, masculine caricatures of the goddess' archaic solar aspects.

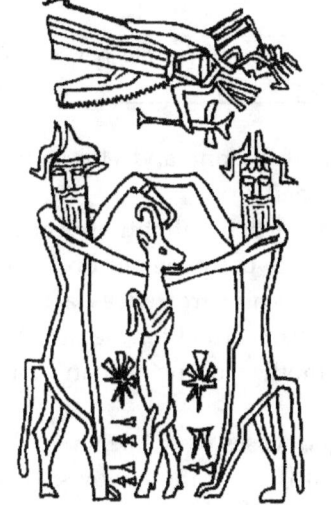

163 The sun god with bison-men [18]

The Sumerian god Utu shares many of the animal symbols associated with Inanna. He is likened to a 'bison running over the mountains', he is a flying eagle and sometimes a lion. But his most salient quality is the power of his gaze, which brings calves and lambs to the fold. Utu is the 'bright-eyed youth', a would-be lover of the goddess, rather than a warrior. Utu is all about life, unlike Šamaš who is all about death, the ghosts and the underworld. The life-bringing aspects of Utu are reflected in one of his standard titles, where he is known as the 'father of the black-headed peoples' – that is, he is 'father' of the Sumerian peoples. And if Utu engenders cattle to the fold and fathers the people of earth – he too embodies the essential nature of the fertile skies.

These generative aspects of Utu show how utterly different he was from Šamaš. More significantly they mark the Sumerian sun god as the male equivalent to Inanna, the heavenly mother of mankind.

The essential features shared by Inanna and Utu can be summarised in tabular form:

UTU	INANNA
Holder of a light-bringing torch, also identified with the torch.	Holder of a light-bringing torch, also identified with the torch
Identified as the brilliant light [19]	Identified as the brilliant light
Symbolised by the eye	Symbolised by the eye goddess
The sunlight is his fertile gaze bringing cattle to the fold	Her sunlight is fertile as the solar rays of her disk have seed symbols upon them
Progenitor of the Sumerian peoples [20]	Progenitor of humanity

[18] Frankfort 1939, text fig 41
[19] ETCSL: Šulgi Q, lines 1-11.
[20] ETCSL: Utu B, lines 1-6

The Sun & the Child

This table stresses just how many fundamental traits they share. And the similarities don't end there. Largely for those a bit more familiar with Near Eastern mythology, I have constructed a further table of shared attributes. This concentrates on the more specific solar traits shared by the divine siblings.[21]

UTU	INANNA
Patron of justice, [22] and of good over evil [23]	Patron of justice, and of good over evil [24]
Patron of travellers [25]	Patron of travellers [26]
Close association to the storms [27]	Close association to the storms
Commonly identified with calves,[28] bulls, lions,[29] bison and eagles [30]	Commonly identified with cows, lionesses, bison and eagles
His rising awakens the people, his setting brings on sleep [31]	Her rising awakens the people, her setting brings on sleep [32]

All in all, these very specific attributes shared by both Inanna and Utu show that they are really male and female versions of the same basic deity.

There is one final quality associated with Utu that is worth highlighting. Another of his well-attested, if somewhat unexpected, attributes was his patronage of orphans and widows. In surviving Sumerian literature this trait is typically treated as a feminine attribute. A hymn to the goddess Nanše, states that she is 'concerned for the orphan and concerned for the widow', and more specifically she is 'a mother for the orphan … a carer for the widow'.[33]

These compassionate traits naturally attributed to goddesses were taken over by the sun god in a Sumerian hymn: 'Utu, as for the orphans. Utu, as for the widows. Utu, the orphans look to you as their father. Utu, you succour the widows as their mother'.[34] Although it may be argued that the sun god, as lord of justice would protect the weak and innocent, it does not explain why he should act as 'mother' for the widow. This isn't a casual term of reference. As we will see a little later, Utu was also the 'father and mother' of another orphaned child. Little oddities like these show that the Sumerian sun god acquired his character traits from the goddesses and not the other way round.

---

[21] All the footnotes refer to the ETCSL website which can be searched for English words.

[22] ETCSL: Gudea A & B, lines 271-276.

[23] ETCSL: Išme-Dagan A + V, lines 90-99.

[24] ETCSL: Iddin-Dagan A, lines 89-105.

[25] Tigay 2002, page 169-170. See also George 1999, page 114 lines Y 259-261.

[26] ETCSL: Inana (C), lines 243-253.

[27] ETCSL: Šulgi Q, lines 1-11.

[28] ETCSL: Utu F, line 18.

[29] ETCSL: Šulgi A, lines 7-15. Šulgi Q, lines 1-11.

[30] ETCSL: Utu B, lines 27-32.

[31] ETCSL: Temple Hymns, lines 479-488.

[32] ETCSL: Iddin-Dagan A, lines 89-105.

[33] ETCSL: Hymn to Nanše, lines 20-31.

[34] ETCSL: Utu F, lines 50-56.

The Sun & the Child

We have been able to identify both Utu and Inanna as the progenitors of mankind. But to get closer to the generative natures of the solar deities we need to go back to the visual imagery of the heaven-born child. As a starting point we shall return to one of our earlier designs:

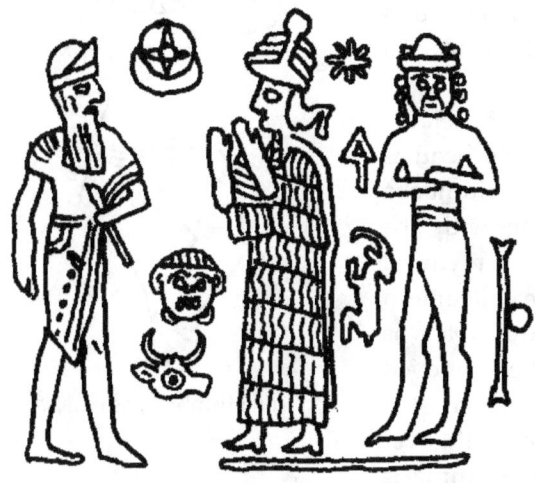

164 The metaphor of the calf-child [35]

We have already seen most of this design in Part One of the book. The child that the Lama goddess prays for is represented by the human and bovine heads. The child's head is actually a rather ugly-looking visage that is often called 'Humbaba's head'. Such heads (*below*) often appear in an architectural setting, where they are placed above doorways like gargoyles to keep evil at bay.

In the background of fig 164, we also see another one of our curly-haired men or 'lineage figures' as I prefer to call them. We have already seen how his curly hair expresses his sexual maturity and virility (*fig 30*), I further suggested that he represented the potency of the fertile fathers and therefore also contained the seed of the child.

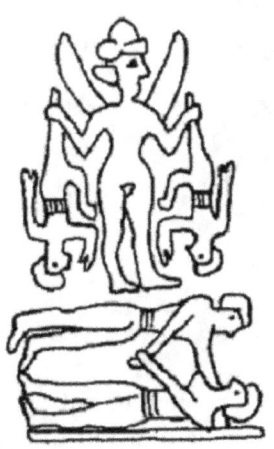

Detail of fig 52

His hat and belt also point in the same direction. His hat directly relates him to the innumerable images of children all in their own characteristic hats (*figs 1 & 46*). And his belt, I believe, links him to the idea of family lineage. Another of our previous images (*left*) helps us out. It depicts all the members of the human family wearing the same type of belt around their middles. This gives us a clue as to the belt's significance. Whatever else it may be (I'd suspect a link to the umbilicus), it is a sign of a familial bond.

165 The head of Humbaba [36]

---

[35] Mid to late 2nd millennium seal from Alalakh (modern Turkey) Collon 1987, fig 185 on page 49.
[36] Reconstructed from Iraq 29 (1967) plate 31b.

The Sun & the Child

The varied strands of symbolism concerning the child and the lineage figure are drawn together in figure 166 (*right*) where we see a human infant naked but for his belt. This image of a bow-legged baby also proves that the motif called Humbaba's head is ultimately based on the wrinkled up face of a newly born baby.

The fact that so many of our birth related designs render the child with Humbaba's head is another surprise. In the *Epic of Gilgamesh* Humbaba is portrayed as an evil ogre-like being with the ferocious nature of the storm god. He is the mythical enemy, an embodiment of evil, whom Gilgamesh righteously captures and kills. Humbaba, as portrayed in the *Epic* couldn't be further removed from the innocent child. Yet ancient artists persisted in using Humbaba's head to represent the child over hundreds of years. A most instructive example is seen in our next illustration:

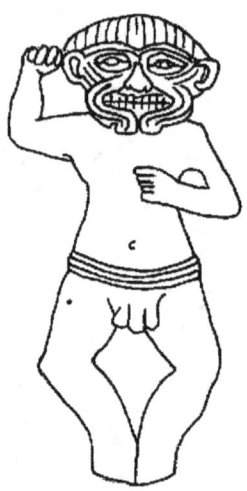

166 Humbaba as child [37]

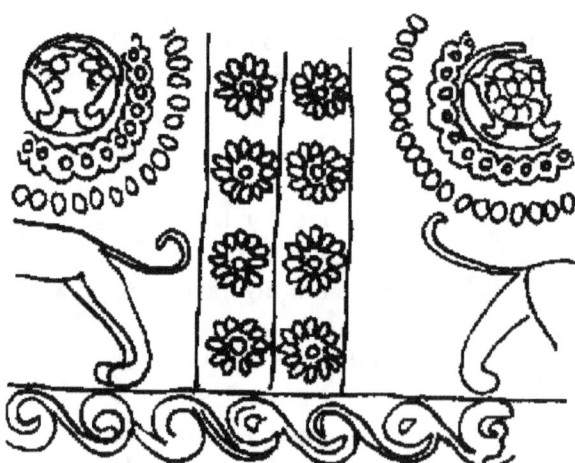

167 The head of Humbaba within a solar flower [38]

This design unquestionably places Humbaba's head in the context of our symbol system. Residing at the centre of Inanna's solar rosette, the wrinkled face of the baby represents the abiding spirit of life within the sacred flower. He is the 'seed' that the flower has produced and will bring to birth.

---

[37] Parrot 1960, fig 369 page 302.
[38] Collon 1975, fig 106.

The Sun & the Child

To resolve the seeming dilemma of using an ogre's head as a symbol for the baby, we need to explore the mythical deeds of Gilgamesh, who was renown in the ancient world as the slayer of the monstrous Humbaba. From a human perspective, Gilgamesh's exploits are motivated by a desire for enduring fame, even immortality of a sort, and killing a renown monster could impart just that. But beyond the human hubris, there are another set of motivations – in the realm of the gods. Behind the heroic scenes the Akkadian sun god is always at work. Even from birth, Šamaš had given Gilgamesh a restless heart, and it appears that it is he that inspired Gilgamesh to slay the ogre Humbaba in the first place. For reasons never stated in the *Epic* 'Šamaš abhors' Humbaba, and Gilgamesh promises to 'annihilate from the land the Evil Thing that Šamaš abhors'.[39]

Images of the heroes slaying the monster were a popular subject among seal-engravers. In nearly all the renditions of his slaying, Humbaba is forced into submission and the heroes trample him down as they go in for the kill.

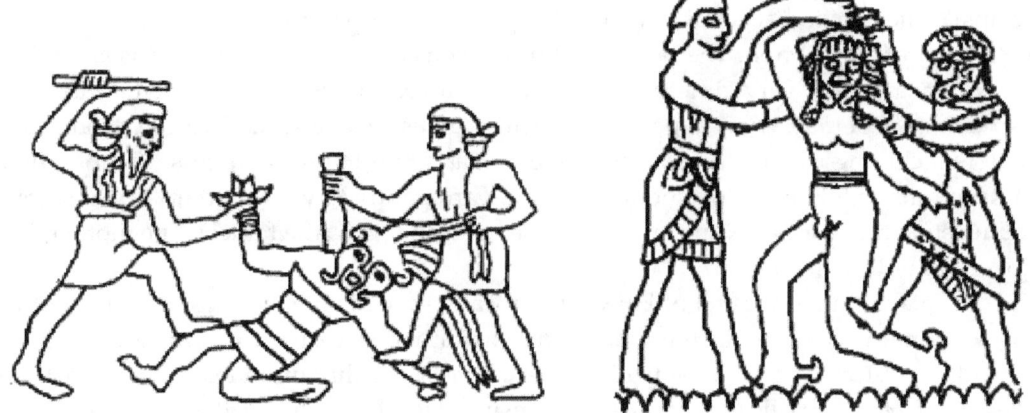

168 & 169 Two versions of the slaying of an ogre-like Humbaba [40]

In the characterful design on the left, the otherness, and therefore evilness, of the ogre is conveyed by his grotesque face and claw-like hands. However, the example seen on the right, is much more interesting from our perspective. Here Humbaba is rendered with distinctly curly hair and he is naked except for his belt. If this Humbaba wore a hat he would be almost identical to our 'lineage figure' see in figure 164.

This is the first hint that Humbaba may not be the fearsome ogre found in Akkadian literature. To learn why Šamaš so abhors Humbaba requires us to examine the earlier Sumerian traditions concerning Gilgamesh. In the poem called *Gilgamesh and the Cedar Forest*, we have a very different account of his battle with Humbaba or, as he is called in Sumerian, Huwawa.

---

[39] George 1999, page 28 (Tablet III, line 205)
[40] Left, George 1999 fig 22 on page 160. Right, Lambert 1987, fig 9.

The Sun & the Child

The heroic clash of fearsome ogre and god-like king recounted in the *Epic* is replaced by a much more sober account of how Gilgamesh first tricked, and then overpowered his opponent. In the Sumerian account, Huwawa is still part storm-god but he is also very clearly a man of noble descent, and Gilgamesh falsely offers him friendship and even goes so far as to offer him his sisters in marriage. But it is all a ruse.

After working Huwawa off his guard with false promises, Gilgamesh unceremoniously 'punched him on the ear'. By these ignoble means Gilgamesh takes his dazed host captive. As the heroes discuss what to do with their captured foe, Huwawa starts to plead for his life. Addressing Utu, who takes the place of Akkadian Šamaš in the Sumerian sources, Huwawa makes a remarkable statement: 'O Utu, I never knew a mother to bear me, I never knew a father to rear me. I was born in the mountains, it was you (Utu) who reared me'.[41]

Utu, the Sumerian sun god, evidently acts as father and mother to Huwawa, the orphaned child, just as he is 'father and mother' to the orphans and widows in his hymns.[42] The sun god acts this way to the orphans out of paternal love and because he is the mother of all children. The fact that Utu was considered to be 'a mother' is also made explicit in another, very different, Sumerian source. In the ancient poem called the *Instructions of Suruppag,* an experienced farmer gives wise advise to his son on many matters including the filial piety and respect that is due to one's parents. The pertinent passage runs as follows: 'You should not speak arrogantly to your mother … you should not question the words of your mother or your personal god (the father). The mother, like Utu, gives birth to the man …'.[43]

In an alternative version of Huwawa's plea to save his life, he says that 'the mother who bore me was a cave in the mountains, the father who sired me was a cave in the uplands'.[44] Putting these pieces together we can now see that underneath the monstrous persona of Humbaba lies the previously unsuspected character of the orphaned child. That he is unknown to human mother or father shows he is the child of the heavens rather than any biological parents; that he was born in a mountain cave and was fostered by the sun god simply identifies him as the solar child. Mythically speaking, the mountain cave is where the sun god rises from the netherworld, and, it should go without saying, that the cave is also a very basic metaphor for the womb. Here at last, we see that a sun god, the Sumerian Utu, is indeed acting as a mother and father to the sacred child.[45]

This is why Šamaš so abhors Humbaba. What he hates is the idea that Utu, his antique counterpart, should be a male god who bears offspring in the same way that a woman gives birth to a child.

---

[41] George 1999, page 159, lines 155-6. Bilgamesh & Huwawa, Version A.

[42] ETCSL: A hymn to Utu (F), lines 50-56.

[43] ETCSL: Instructions of Suruppag, lines 255-260.

[44] George 1999, page 166, lines 152-3. Bilgamesh & Huwawa, Version B.

[45] This may explain why the Sumerian word for 'sun' (**Utu**) is so similar to the verb 'to give birth' (**Utud**).

The Sun & the Child

Other depictions of Humbaba's demise tell a very different story to the monster-slaying images we saw above. Many such designs, like the one seen below, actually place Humbaba within a recognisable fertility context:

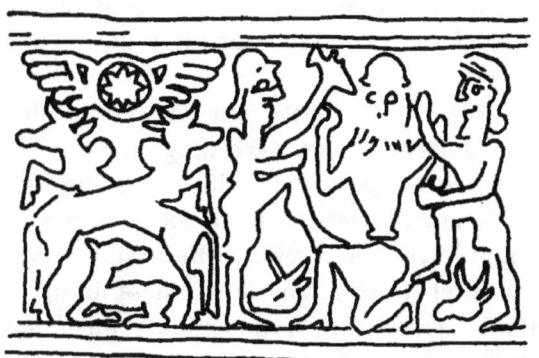

170 Celestial cattle alongside the Slaying of Humbaba [46]

The background motifs seen in this design confirm our contention. The pair of bull-heads set around Humbaba and the independent icon of the heavenly cattle giving birth to their sacred calf, place Humbaba firmly within the fold of the birthing metaphors.

This image further confirms that Humbaba is the one of our lineage figures, complete with his domed hat and traces of his curling beard. This image, and others of a similar nature, opens up a whole new dimension concerning the nature of Humbaba. Behind the monstrous visage promoted by the literary account of the *Gilgamesh Epic* we see a completely different picture emerging. Humbaba has to be another one of the archaic fertility figures that were destroyed by the new gods and their kingly counterparts in the battle of the gods.

The next image of Humbaba is much clearer; it also incorporates another major birthing metaphor in the form of the sacred flower and its seed.

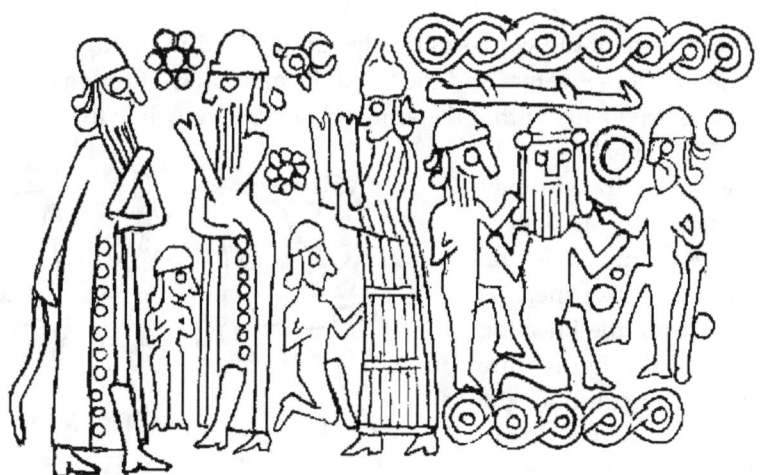

171 The slaying of Humbaba alongside the Flower metaphor [47]

---

[46] Frankfort 1939, text fig 53.
[47] Collon 1987, fig 855 on page 180

The Sun & the Child

Here Humbaba is most definitely depicted as the curly-haired man of virility. This figure represents the potency of the ancestral lineage that was considered to be the ultimate source of the child in the Second Age of myth. Like some of our other designs (*below*) this lineage figure also embodies the nature of the child. This is apparent in his kneeling posture and in the large circlet next to his head that identifies him as the 'seed' of the sacred flower.

In light of these defining characteristics, Humbaba has to be viewed as a fusion of the sacred child and the sexually mature lineage figure. Accordingly, Humbaba must represent something akin to an ancestral collective from which all children are born. And the fertility motifs like the celestial bulls and flowers that are found alongside him indicate that this ancestral collective would have been located in the sunlit heavens, not in any kind of underworld. In fact, as a number of designs show, these lineage figures were portrayed as the abiding life within the waters of heaven in mid 3rd millennium art:

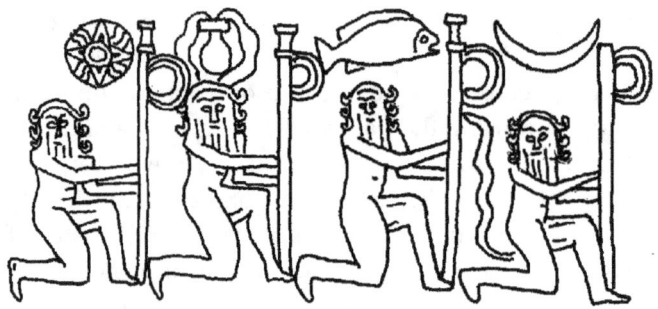

172 Design from an Akkadian seal [48]

The celestial nature of the waters is neatly summarised in the upper register of this design but the nature of the waters and the 'seed' it carries have fundamentally changed. Once the 'seed' was the foetus within the amniotic waters, now it is the invisible potency within semen. The kneeling child appears to have been transformed into the virile man with his watery seed. Nevertheless, the postural language of these virile men is obviously derived from the kneeling child. Even though the figures are now grown men, they still hold the seed of future children within them.

The truth of this statement is seen in figure 173 (*right*) where these

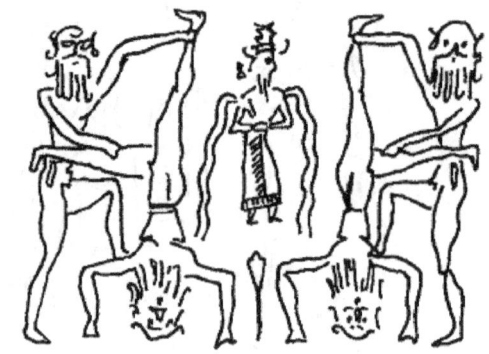

173 The dual nature of the lineage figures [49]

---

[48] Boehmer 1965, Tafel XLIV, fig 525.
[49] Boehmer 1965, Tafel XXIV, fig 279; and Amiet 1961, plate 111, fig 1470.

same men play out the dual roles of heavenly progenitor and descending child under the auspicious gaze of the water god, Enki-Ea.

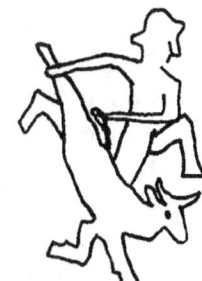

In summary, these 'lineage figures' by partaking of the nature of the male 'seed' ultimately blur the boundaries between the newborn child and the virile ancestors. In practical terms, this lineage figure can play out the role of the progenitor and the child. And this finally explains one of our earlier template designs (*left*), where a lineage figure, representing the fertile ancestors, brings the descending calf down from heaven. The conclusion is obvious, the concept of the male lineage is now taking the place of the goddess as the heavenly progenitor of human life.

Detail of fig 3

Another obscure, but most intriguing fact, that supports a heavenly locale for Humbaba, is that he was once represented among the stars and constellations of ancient Mesopotamia.[51] The heavenly nature of Humbaba and the lineage figures are finally revealed in the pivotal Iranian design seen below:

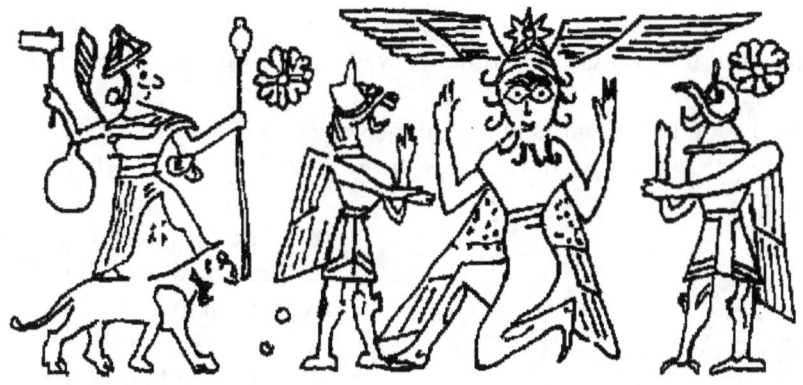

174 The celestial lineage figure [50]

Here we see the real Humbaba that lies behind the propaganda of later ages. He is a true denizen of the starry heavens. He is the ancestral potency that resides in the skies; he is the spirit of life that descends on the winds and alights upon the earth in the form of the kneeling child. At heart, he is a symbolic union of the two aspects of the male seed – he is simultaneously the potency of the fathers and the essence of the child.

The icon of sacred rosettes with their falling seeds ultimately identifies Humbaba as the child of the fertile heavens. He is the child born to Utu, and before that he was the

---

[50] Ornan 2005, fig 37.

[51] See Babylonian Star-lore under Slain Heroes. Gossmann 1950, section 188, on page 74; see also De Santillana & von Dechend 1977, page 403.

The Sun & the Child

child born of Inanna, who rightfully presides over this design. She is present in her human form as the storm goddess riding her griffin, and she is also present in her animalian aspect as the lion-headed demons that stand either side of the kneeling child (*see also fig 38*). They appear to be intimately connected with the descent of the 'seed of mankind' through the heavenly realms.

Now, we can give a fuller answer to our original question concerning why Šamaš so abhors Humbaba. Beyond the abhorrence that Šamaš felt towards the Sumerian sun god giving birth to children, he is also utterly averse to the whole notion of the fertile heavens, especially the idea that human life originated and ended in the heavenly realms.

At the very heart of this theological conflict is the basic nature of heavens and its relationship to mankind. For the Akkadians, the heavens were the realm of the all-powerful gods who ruled the affairs of the world like earthly kings. Men were confined to the surface of the earth and the underworld. Šamaš had a huge vested interest in these ideas because one of his primary roles was to transport the remnants of man – his ghost – to the underworld below.

In stark contrast to this, Sumerian culture viewed the heavens as the source of all life and fertility, the matrix from which mankind originated and to which he returned after his death. As the theology of the fertile skies lost favour, its symbols and cult were destroyed. Humbaba was slain because he didn't fit in with the new ways of religious thought. And Utu, the sun god of Sumeria, was likewise reformed of his mythological 'character defects'.

Fortunately for us, the artistic record provides us with some fascinating images relating to this process. The first comes from a votive plaque, dating to the Old Babylonian era:

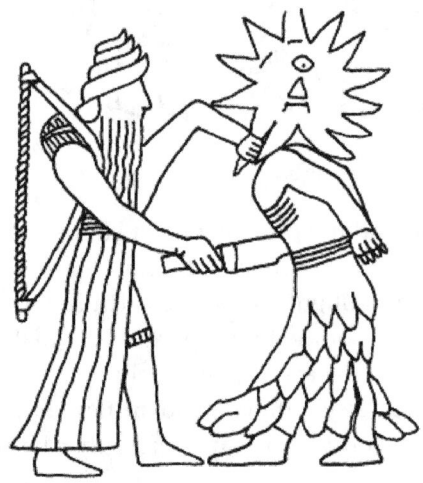

175 A warrior god slays a one-eyed solar deity [52]

The plaque shows what can only be described as the death of an archaic solar deity. The warrior god executes his captive without mercy, his arms still bound behind his back. With a radiant solar disk for its head and a single Cyclops-like eye, the slain god is evidently a 'primitive' icon of the sun; we could justifiably call him a 'solar titan'. The designer of the plaque has purposefully contrasted the wholly human form of the warrior god with the highly symbolic form of the slain god whose head – the most human part of a man – is replaced by the solar disk.

---

[52] Old Babylonian. Roaf 1966, page 77.

The Sun & the Child

If the single eye can be treated as a defining characteristic of the solar titan, then we can trace his image back to much earlier periods. The Cyclops figure, without any solar rays, is certainly an ancient figure as he appears in the artwork of much earlier periods:

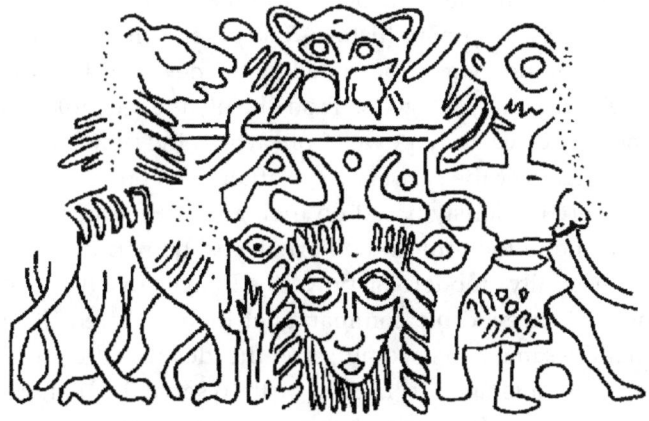

176 The Cyclops with bison-man and lions [53]

The fact that he appears in the company of lions and bison-men suggests that he is related to our slain sun god. This suspicion is confirmed in our final design:

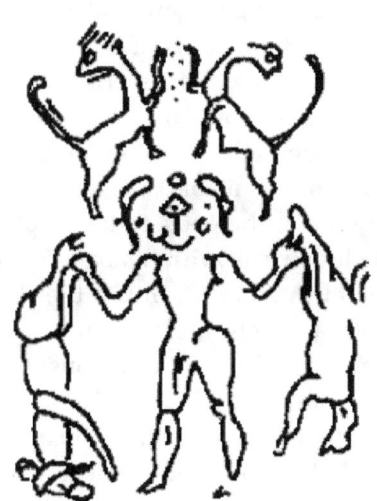

177 The solar Cyclops as carrier of the calf [54]

This Cyclops is portrayed bringing down the newborn calves from heaven. He is acting out the role of the heavenly mother and, as such, has to be thought of as giving birth to the children of mankind. He must be an aspect of the Sumerian sun god Utu, who acted as father and mother to the child.

From the perspective of this book, this single image is of the utmost importance. In fact, it can be regarded as a veritable 'missing link' between the archaic goddess and the sun gods we know from later times. Above all else, it proves that archaic solar deities, male and female, were considered to be the bearers of the sacred child.

---

[53] Jemdet Nasr period (3100-2900 BCE) Amiet 1961, plate 73, detail of fig 964.

[54] Jemdet Nasr period. Amiet 1961, plate 40, detail of fig 615; and Goff 1963, fig 283 (photo).

Death Enters the World

As we have already seen, the centuries round the middle of the 3rd millennium BCE were a pivotal time in Mesopotamian history. The older Sumerian culture, based on the concept of the celestial mother, was superseded by the new idea that the skies were home to a male dominated hierarchy of gods. From being the birthplace of humanity, the heavens became the seat of worldly power from which the new gods, headed by Enlil – the 'god of gods'[1] – ruled over the earth and the affairs of men.

The new gods were obviously based on their earthly counterparts the first kings of Mesopotamia, who came to the fore in the Early Dynastic period. As such, the principal Akkadian gods are basically 'models of power' – images of an authoritarian father in heaven thundering their irrevocable commands at their children. It will not come as a surprise to learn that the same gods promulgated the idea that the great mass of mankind were little more than servants fated from their birth to serve the higher powers.[2]

Alongside these far-reaching societal changes, the nature of mankind also had to be redefined to fit the pattern of the new world order. From being an aerial soul, a denizen of the light-filled heavens, the very concept of 'man' was also reformulated to make him a creature born of the earth rather than the skies. In simplistic terms, a spiritual cosmology gave way to a political cosmology where man was defined as a predominantly material being with but a spark of the divine within him. Accordingly, new Akkadian myths about the creation of mankind revolve around the idea that the gods moulded man's body from earthly clay, which they had enlivened with the blood of a sacrificed god. The many versions and variants of this mythic form attest to its popularity and widespread distribution. The following version of the story is based on Tablet 1 of the *Atrahasis Epic*,[3] which is the most detailed and complete Akkadian account available.

Under the divine auspices of the water god, Enki-Ea, the gods gathered pure clay from the watery Abyss. The water god kneaded the lowly clay with his bare feet just as country potters do to this day, and then Nintur, the birth goddess, mixed the clay with the flesh and blood of the sacrificed god.[4] This god, a purely literary figure, is called **Geštue**, which means 'intelligence or understanding'. His divine 'flesh' constitutes the ghost of man [5] – the living, thinking person within their corporeal frame. Thus the basic material from which mankind would be made was prepared. That inchoate matter, already fermenting with life, now needed to be divided and shaped – this is where the goddesses stepped in and took over.

---

[1] Steinkeller 1999, page 114 note 36. The older understanding of Enlil's name was 'Lord of the winds'.

[2] Dalley 1989, pages 1-38.

[3] Dalley 1989, pages 1-38; and also Lambert & Millard 1999 for a more comprehensive presentation.

[4] The idea that human life was due to the sacrifice of a god is an Akkadian idea. Jacobsen 1976, page 167.

[5] This may involve a play on words as the Akkadian the words for 'ghost' (*eṭemmu*) and 'intelligence' (*ṭēmu*) are so similar. See Dalley 1989, page 36, note 11.

Death Enters the World

Mami, the great 'midwife of the gods', pinched off 14 separate pieces of the kneaded clay, and setting seven pieces to the left and seven to the right, she placed the brick of birth between them. Mami then called up 'seven and seven wise and knowledgeable womb-goddesses' who are described as 'creators of fate', and it is they that actually fashioned the bodies of seven men and seven women from the 14 pieces of clay.[6]

The story of how the prototypes of mankind were originally created in the mythical foretime ends here but its magical purpose is to act as a symbolic template for the birth of real children in the here and now. Just as the seven and seven wise womb-goddesses shaped the forms of primal man so too were they thought to shape the foetus of every child within its mother's womb. Accordingly, the same text continues its narrative in relation to a pregnant mother about to give birth : 'the womb-goddesses were assembled and Nintur was present. They counted the months, and called up the tenth month as the term of fates. When the tenth month came, the 'elapse of the period opened the womb' [7] and Mami acted as mid-wife for the birth of the child.

Although the goddesses – Mami, Nintur and the womb-goddesses – still play the essential part in the shaping and formation of the child, the addition of Enki and his clay is a new element. And this changes everything. This Akkadian myth is founded upon the idea that the child is a manikin fashioned from clay; and the gods, by shaping the clay, are cast in the role of divine potters. In remembrance of Enki's newly acquired role in the creation of mankind he was henceforth known as Nudimmud – 'the one who created mankind',[9] and 'the Potter'.[10] In tune with these new ideas, the metaphor of the potter and the pottery was simultaneously introduced into Akkadian depictions of the mother goddess:

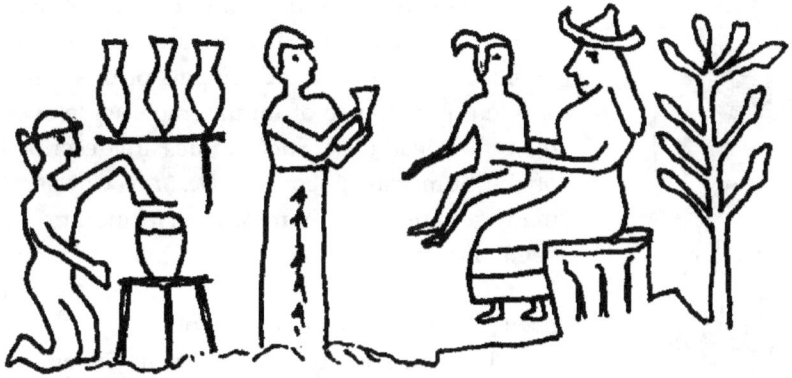

178 The icon of mother & child set alongside a potter [8]

[6] Dalley 1989, pages 16-17.

[7] Dalley 1989, page 17. Also Lambert & Millard 1999, page 63, line 282.

[8] Akkadian seal, Boehmer 1965, Tafel XLVII, fig 555.

[9] Jacobsen, 1976, page 111.

[10] PSD: BAHAR [pot] & [potter] The potter is Bahar2 with divine determinative it is a by-name for Enki.
    Labat 1988, # 309 on pages 140-141 & page 292 under Ea.

Death Enters the World

The metaphor that defines man as being fashioned from lifeless clay, necessarily predicts he will return to clay after his demise. He will reside again within the cold earth that bore him and his insubstantial ghost will linger on in the gloomy underworld, at the very bottom of the cosmic order. This metaphor of mankind has to be placed within the broader setting of the Akkadian conception of the 'world as polity', which may be graphically tabulated as follows:

HEAVEN

The gods rule over the earth from on high

EARTH

Man is born upon earth where he acts as servant to the gods

UNDERWORLD

Man's ghost descends to the underworld after his death

The Akkadian model of the universe as polity

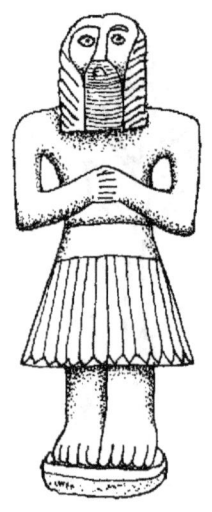

179 An ancestor statue [11]

In the early 3rd millennium, the cult of the dead as we know it appears in Mesopotamia alongside its telltale artefacts. In temples and chapels of this time we see the sudden appearance of innumerable wide-eyed statues of the pious dead (*left*). Such statues are described at the end of the Sumerian poem *The Death of Gilgamesh*: 'Men, as many as are given names, their (funerary) statues have been fashioned since days of old, and stationed in chapels in the temples of the gods: how their names are pronounced will never be forgotten'.[12]

Literate sources indicate that Gilgamesh was very much involved in the introduction of the underworld and its rites into the Mesopotamian world. In the Sumerian poem *Gilgamesh and the Netherworld*, Enkidu, the friend and companion of Gilgamesh, was trapped in the underworld and Gilgamesh, wishing to bring him back,

---

[11] Parrot 1960, fig 130 B, on page 102.
[12] George 1999, page 207, *Death of Bilgamesh,* lines M 298-301.

Death Enters the World

petitions the high gods to intervene. Only the wise and knowledgeable Enki helps; he asks the sun god to bring back the ghost of Enkidu as he rises from the Netherworld. The sun god duly obliges, and temporarily the friends reunite. There is more to this necromantic act than a sentimental reunion; Gilgamesh's true purpose in raising the ghost of his dead friend is to learn about the conditions of the dead in the land below.[13] And this reveals the real objective of the poem – to popularise the new vision of the underworld and set out the laws and regulations binding its citizens.

Later in the same poem, we learn that it is Gilgamesh himself who actually introduces the new rites for the dead. During his necromantic episode with the ghost of Enkidu, his dead friend painted a dire picture of the underworld, including the sad fate of Gilgamesh's own parents who 'drink water from a dirty place, the place of a massacre'. This prompted Gilgamesh to instigate new water-pouring rites to his forebears. Making funerary statues of his parents, Gilgamesh lifted his head to the sun god and declared 'O my father and mother, I will have you drink clear water', for nine days he performed the rites and the people of Uruk wept with him. The cult practice seems to have caught on as the poem continues 'the citizens of Girsu matched his actions'.[14]

The redefinition of man as a creature made of earthly clay, whose ghost sank to the underworld after his death, had dire consequences for the heavenly mother and the belief that man originated in heaven and returned there after his demise. The *Atrahasis Epic*, from which the myth of man's creation from clay was drawn, also describes the fate of the mother goddess. The text records that an assembly of gods rendered a 'judgement' upon Mami. The *Epic* recounts that the great goddess was renamed, and thus redefined, by the great assembly: 'We used to call you Mami (the baby-word for 'mother')[15] but now your name shall be Mistress of all the Gods'.[16] In other words, Mami, the great midwife and womb-goddess[17] of heaven was transformed into the childless hierodule, the embodiment of sexual allure and eroticism. The ancient Sumerian title of the goddess 'Mother Inanna' (**Ama Inanna**)[18] became little more than a literary relic, a memory of former times.

The worldviews of the Sumerians and Akkadians couldn't be more different. They reflect completely different spiritualities and even different cosmological systems. In the old system, mankind was intimately related to the whole cosmos but in the new world order he is relegated to the status of a servant to the gods and is confined to the environs of the earth and the underworld. Ultimately, I believe that the idea that man was made of clay gave rise to the conception of the earth goddess being the mother of mankind. In the

---

[13] George 1999, Bilgames and the Netherworld, page 187, lines 238-43.

[14] George 1999, pages 190-191, *Bilgamesh & the Netherworld*. Girsu was a city aprox 50 miles (75 km) to the north-east of Uruk.

[15] Leick 1992, page 114 under Mamma.

[16] Dalley 1989, page 16.

[17] Dalley 1989, page 15.

[18] PSD: AMA'INANAK [goddess]

Death Enters the World

bigger picture, however, mankind and the celestial goddess who gave him birth have both been utterly banished from the heavens.

In tune with these wholesale changes, man's spiritual constitution was also redefined as a material being endowed with a ghost rather than a heavenly soul. The difference between the ghost and soul is most clearly expressed in terms of their characteristic domains – the aerial soul naturally has its true home in the shining heavens whereas the ghost of man resides at the other end of the cosmic order, in the darkest recesses of the underworld. In reality, the ghost and soul belong to different worldviews - one borne of burial within the earth, and the other ultimately borne from the practices of exhumation and cremation.

In much later times, the conflicting ideologies of the underworld ghost and the heavenly soul were reconciled and became the basis for a tripartite division of man into body, soul and ghost. In a similar way, the divergent destinations for the dead were united in the idea that the faithful ascend to the pearly gates of heaven while the wicked fall to endless torment in a subterranean realm below.

The introduction of concepts like the 'ghost' and 'dead person' are best traced in their written forms. Originally, writing had evolved as an accounting tool. It was pretty basic, more of a notation system that recorded a wide range of goods, who sent them and who received them. The earliest 'texts' are really invoices for goods received and disbursed. With the rise of kingship, at the start of the 3rd millennium, all this changed.

The royal houses of Sumer recognised the power of the written word – that it could speak far and wide and for untold centuries. Royal inscriptions are among the earliest 'proper texts', which have a basic grammar and a regular sign order. These inscriptions typically declare that such and such a king built this temple or dedicated a certain object to a shrine. However, the old writing system was specialised for accounting goods; it was not well suited to the task of transcribing actions and events. So the whole sign system was revised – hundreds of old signs were cast out and many new signs created. They are evidence of a semantic revolution.

The new signs created in this era are indicative of the changes taking place in society and their associated beliefs. From our perspective, the most interesting new signs are the ones like 'ghost' and 'dead man'. But before looking at them we need to have a quick look at the underlying sign for 'man'. This was called the **Lu₂**-sign (*right*), which represents 'man or person'. The sign is a simplified figure of a man's head and torso; the lines upon his body probably represent his ribs.

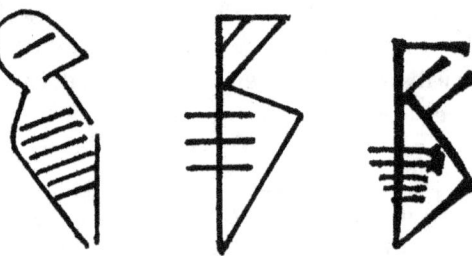

Different versions of the **Lu₂**-sign [19]

---

[19] Redrawn from various sign lists such as Labat 1988, & the sources published on the CDLI website.

Death Enters the World

A separate sign for a 'dead man' was created by simply crossing through the figure of the man, thus creating the sign known as **Adda** (*right*), which signifies a 'corpse' and the 'wreck' of a boat – the ribs of the man probably being likened to the arching timbers of the ship's bracings. The extra arrow-like sign etched onto the man's chest can signify the verb 'to die' (Sumerian **Uš₂**)

While our first **Adda**-sign can be understood as the body of a man that is simply 'struck through' with the sign of death, the second example is more interesting as it adds several extra pairs of lines to the man's body. I believe they represent the wings and tail of a bird and thus point to the image of the winged ghost or soul. The description of ghosts as winged beings is found in Enkidu's vision of the underworld, where the ghosts are described as clad in coats of feathers like birds.[20] The next sign adds some weight to this idea.

Very similar appendages appear on the **Dim₃**-sign (*right*), which is obviously very closely related. This fact may explain why it is used to write both 'corpse' and 'demon'. Referring to demons, this sign is the principal character used in writing the name of Lamaštu.

The seemingly feathered forms of the dead and the demons bespeak their ancient past as heavenly beings, as only aerial creatures should be fitted out with outstretched wings. However, the descent of the dead into the realm of the ghoulish is only completed with the last two signs (*right*), which represent the 'ghost' and 'evil demon'.

The only real difference between these two signs is that the evil demon is differentiated from the lurking ghost by the addition of the **Kud**-sign upon his body, which may allude to the demon's power to 'cut' the thread of fate, thereby causing death.

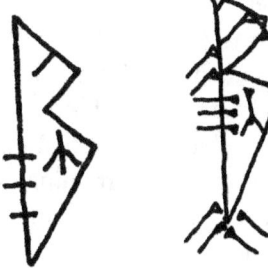

Two versions of the **Adda**-sign meaning 'corpse' or 'dead man'

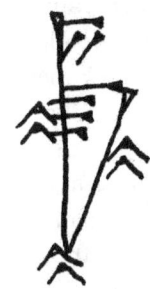

The sign for 'demon' (**Dim₃**)

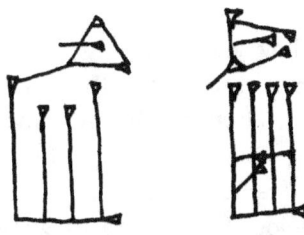

The signs for 'ghost' (**Gidim**) and 'evil demon' (**Udug**) [21]

---

[20] George 1999, page 61 (Tablet 7, line 189)

[21] Redrawn from the sign lists and texts published on the CDLI website.

Death Enters the World

To judge by these last few signs, the dead and their lifeless corpses were considered to be sources of contamination akin to the demons. This is especially true in the case of the restless ghosts, who were feared like the evil **udug**-demons that brought death, pestilence and disease to mankind.

The insubstantial existence of the ghost still needed the sustenance of funerary offerings to keep it alive and content in the underworld. This belief had some quite bizarre correlates in the realm of ghost magic. The most well-known case concerned the Assyrian king, Assurbanipal, who, after raiding the land of Elam, opened up the ancestral tombs of the Elamite kings and removed their bones to Assur, his capital city. The stated purpose of this rather sinister act was to 'inflict restlessness on their ghosts' and to deprive them of their funerary offerings.[22] The idea behind this act of desecration was that the starving ghosts would sooner or later return to earth and start haunting their lineal descendants, afflicting them with all manner of disease and distress from beyond the grave.

In order to accommodate the ghosts of the dead it was needful to create a new cosmic domain – the Underworld, the fabled 'House of No Return'. Set deep in the bowls of the earth, this realm was seen as a dismal copy of life on earth. It was dominated by the citadel of the dead, and was ruled over by a ghostly hierarchy of kings and linen-clad priests. It was the grave writ large, the earthly end of man where his body rotted away to dust. Akin to the Christian sentiment of 'dust to dust and ashes to ashes', dry lifeless earth and endless dust are emblematic of this sterile world.

It may sound a little strange, but it's as if the underworld suddenly appeared out of nowhere sometime around the middle of the 3rd millennium BCE as far as Mesopotamia was concerned. Although the belief had probably been an intrinsic part of the Akkadian and Semitic worldview for centuries past, it was not part of the established Sumerian religion based as it was on heavenly Inanna. The royal establishment of Mesopotamia, dominated as it was by Akkadians,[23] decided to change all that. They so thoroughly embedded the notion of the underworld in the minds of the populace that it is still with us today.

They achieved this true act of magic by instituting the most macabre of state rituals – the mass sacrifice of the king's servants and staff upon his death and their communal burial in a richly endowed tomb. Just such a scene is described in the Sumerian poem *The Death of Gilgamesh*.[24] Very few western scholars took this account seriously until royal graves, replete with the bodies of courtly attendants, were actually discovered by archaeologists at the Early Dynastic cemetery of Ur.[25] The bodies of up to 80 attendants, courtiers, soldiers and cart-drivers could accompany their masters and mistresses to the

---

[22] CAD: *eṭemmu* section 1b on page 399 of volume E.

[23] ETCSL: Sumerian King List, lines 40-94. Of the varied kings of Kiš, which formed the first historical royal dynasty of Mesopotamia, roughly half have Akkadian or foreign-sounding names.

[24] George 1999, pages 206-207; see also pages 67-69 for the funeral rites of Enkidu (Tablet 7, lines 128-188).

[25] Black & Green 1992, pages 104-105. For an in-depth analysis see Cohen 2005.

Death Enters the World

underworld. The world had not seen anything like it before. Just imagine the scene. A seemingly endless procession of all the great and good of the land, all bitterly lamenting the loss of their beloved lord as they trudge through the streets towards his final resting place. Then at the graveside, the endless ceremonial offerings and precious gifts dedicated to the infernal powers were ritualistically displayed before the sun god before being placed in the grave. The story of the king's funeral and the sacrifice of his devoted courtiers established a most potent paradigm for the rest of mankind. Through their untimely deaths they created the underworld we know today.

Then, just as suddenly as it had arisen, the practice of mass human sacrifice ceased, never to be seen again. Why? Because its fundamental purpose had been achieved: the doom of man had been reset, his spiritual constitution recast and the very structure of the world reformed upon a new model. Now, the ghosts of men would follow the path set out by the kings of yore, they too would descend to the gloom-ridden underworld at the end of their days. Thus did death finally enter the world.

Bibliography & Indexes

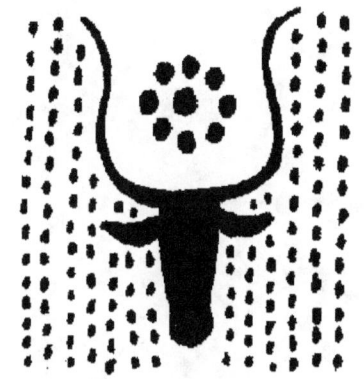

Bibliography

Amiet 1961. La Glyptique Mesopotamienne Archaique. Centre National de la Recherche Scientifique.

Annus 2002. The God Ninurta. Neo-Assyrian Text Corpus Project.

Astour 1980, The Netherworld and its Denizens at Ugarit (Death in Mesopotamia pages 227-38)

Atac 2010. The Mythology of Kingship in Neo-Assyrian Art. Cambridge University Press.

Ayatollahi 2002. The Book of Iran. The History of Iranian Art. Centre for International Studies.

Babylonian Star-lore. Gavin White. Solaria Publications 2008.

Black & Green 1992. Gods, Demons & Symbols of Ancient Mesopotamia. British Museum Press.

Boehmer 1965. Die Entwicklung der Glyptik Wahrend der Akkad-Zeit. Walter de Gruyter & Co.

BPO2 – Babylonian Planetary Omens vol 2. Reiner & Pingree 1981. Undena.

Bunson 1995. A Dictionary of Ancient Egypt. Oxford University Press.

CAD – Chicago Assyrian Dictionary – online at the Chicago University website.

CDA – Concise Dictionary of Akkadian. Black, George & Postgate. Harrassowitz Verlag 2000.

CDLI – Cuneiform Digital Library Initiative – online archive of Sumerian texts & sign-lists.

Cohen 2005. Death Rituals, Ideology & the development of Early Mesopotamian Kingship. Brill-Styx.

Collon 1975. The Seal Impressions from Tell Atchana/Alalakh. AOAT Band 27.

Collon 1987. First Impressions. British Museum Press.

Copper 1978. The Return of Ninurta to Nippur. Pontificum Institutum Biblicum.

Cunningham 1997. Deliver Me from Evil. Editrice Pontificio Istituto Biblico.

Dalley 1989. Myths from Mesopotamia. Oxford University Press.

Dalley 1986. The God Şalmu and the Winged Disk. Pages 85-101 of Iraq, volume 48.

Death in Mesopotamia 1980. Edited by Alster. Akademisk Forlag 8/RAI 26.

Ellis 1989. An Old Babylonian Kusarikku. Pages 121-135 of DUMU E₂-DUB_BA-A: Studies in Honor of Ake Sjoberg. Ed: Behrens. University of Pennsylvania Museum.

ETCSL – Electronic Text Corpus of Sumerian Literature – online at the Oxford University website.

Falkenstein 1936. Archaische Text aus Uruk I. Online at the CDLI website.

Finkel 1983. Necromancy in Ancient Mesopotamia Pages 1-17 of Archiv fur Orientforschung XXIX.

Fischer 2002. Twilight of the Sun God Pages 125-133 of Iraq, volume 64.

Frankfort 1939. Cylinder Seals. Macmillan.

George 1999. The Epic of Gilgamesh. Penguin.

Goddard 1965. The Art of Iran. George Allen & Unwin Ltd.

Goff 1963. Symbols of Prehistoric Mesopotamia. Yale University Press.

Bibliography

Gossmann 1950. Planetarium Babyloniacum. Sumerian Lexicon part IV/2 of Deimal. Photostat.

Grimal 1990. Penguin Dictionary of Classical Mythology. Penguin.

Harcourt-Smith 1928. Babylonian Art. Frederick Stokes.

Harrison 1962. Prolegomena to the Study of Greek Religion. Merlin

Healy 1980, The Sun deity and the Underworld in Mesopotamia and Ugarit. (Death in Mesopotamia pages 239-242)

Horowitz 1998. Mesopotamian Cosmic Geography. Eisensbrauns.

Huot 2004. Une archeologie des peoples du Proche-Orient. Tome II.

IDD website – Iconography of Deities and Demons in the Ancient Near East - online.

Jacobsen 1976. Treasures of Darkness. Yale University Press.

Jones 1991. Northern Myths of the Constellations. Fenris Wolf.

Labat 1988. Manuel D'Epigraphie Akkadienne. Geuthner.

Lambert 1960. Gilgamesh in Religious, Historical & Omen texts and the Historicity of Gilgamesh. Pages 39-53 of Gilgameš et sa Legende.

Lambert 1980. Theology of Death (Death in Mesopotamia pages 47-60)

Lambert 1987. Gilgamesh in Literature and Art: the second and first millennia. Pages 37-52 of Monsters and Demons in the Ancient and Medieval Worlds, Verlag Philipp von Zabern.

Lambert & Millard 1999. Atrahasis. The Babylonian Story of the Flood. Oxford at the Clarendon Press.

Lampriere's Classical Dictionary. Bracken Books 1984.

Leichty 1970. The Omen Series Šumma Izbu. TCS 4.

Leick 1991. A Dictionary of Ancient Near Eastern Mythology. Routledge.

Mallowan 1965. Early Mesopotamia & Iran. Thames & Hudson.

Mallowan & Cruickshank 1935. Excavations at Arpachiyah. Iraq 11, pages 1-178.

Mellaart 1975. The Neolithic of the Near East. Thames & Hudson.

Metropolitan Museum of Art – online galleries.

Nemet-Nejat 1999. Women's Roles in Ancient Mesopotamia, A Reference Guide. Greenwood Press.

Oates & Oates 1976. The Rise of Civilization. Elsevier Phaidon.

O'Flaherty 1981. The Rig Veda. An Anthology. Penguin.

Ornan 2005. The Triumph of the Symbol. Academic Press Fribourg/Vandenhoeck & Ruprecht.

Parpola 1997. Assyrian Prophecies. Helsinki University Press.

Parrot 1960. Sumer. Thames & Hudson.

Porada 1965. Ancient Iran. The Art of Pre-Islamic Times. Methuen.

Price 1927, The Great Cylinder Inscriptions of Gudea. Hinrichs.

Pritchard 1969. Ancient Near Eastern Texts relating to the Old Testament. 3rd edition + supplement. Princeton University Press.

PSD – Pennsylvania Sumerian Dictionary – online.

Bibliography

Reiner 1995. Astral Magic in Babylonia. Transactions of the American Philosophical Society, volume 85, part 4.

Roaf 1966. Cultural Atlas of Mesopotamia & the Ancient Near East. Facts on File Inc.

De Santillana & von Dechend 1977. Hamlet's Mill. Godine.

Schneider 1995. A Beginner's Guide to Constructing the Universe. Harper Perennial.

Scurlock 1995. Death and the Afterlife in Ancient Mesopotamian Thought. Volume III, pages 1883-1893 of Civilisations of the Ancient Near East (4 volumes). Charles Scribner's Sons.

Seidl 1989. Die babylonischen Kudurru-Reliefs. Vandenhoeck & Ruprecht.

Stein 1993. Das Archiv des Šilwa-Teššup. Harrassowitz Verlag.

Steinkeller 1999. On Rulers, Priests and Sacred Marriage. Pages 103-137 of Priests and Officials in the Ancient Near East, ed by Watanabe.

Sumerian Gods & their Representations 1997. Ed: Finkel & Geller. Styx.

Tigay 1971. Literary-critical studies in the Gilgamesh Epic, An Assyriological contribution to biblical literary criticism. Imprint.

Tigay 2002. Evolution of the Gilgamesh Epic. Imprint.

Ugaritic Texts … unknown author & publication.

Veldhuis 1991. A Cow of Sin. Styx.

Walter's Art Museum – online.

Watanabee 2002. Animal Symbolism in Mesopotamia. Institut fur Orientalistik der Universitat Wien.

Walters 1992. Chinese Mythology. Diamond Books.

White 2008. Babylonian Star-lore. Solaria Publications.

Wiggermann 2000. Lamaštu, daughter of An, A Profile.. Available online at the Academia. Edu website.

Wiggermann 2007. The Four Winds and the Origins of Pazuzu. Available online at the Academia. Edu website.

Winter 1987. Frau und Gottin. OBO series 53. Heidelberg-Brill.

Winter 2010. On Art in the Ancient Near East. Brill.

Symbol Index

Rather than a conventional word index set out in alphabetical order, a symbol index is more appropriate to the nature of this book. By using this index, the reader will be able to reference all the designs that contain a particular icon, and thus be able to explore any particular theme in much more detail.

The listings of this index are set out in the following categories:
HUMANS – CELESTIAL – DEITIES – MYTHICAL BEINGS – ANIMALS – PLANTS – GEOGRAPHIC - GEOMETRIC & CULTIC

Humans

	Lord, the central figure in many designs, often appears alongside the **Lama** goddess who prays on his behalf. Figs: 1, 2, 3, 4, 6, 9, 11, 12, 13, 17, 19, 20, 23, 24, 31, 32, 33, 37, 38, 40, 41, 42, 47, 52, 133, 137, 141, 148,
	Nobleman, sometimes prays for the **Lord**. Figs: 17, 37, 38, 80,
	Child, usually seen kneeling down on one knee or walking. In later times, he could be closely related to the **Lineage Figure**. Figs: 1, 3, 9, 22, 24, 33, 37, 38, 46, 47, 52, 53, 62, 133, 135, 148, 155, 166, **Children**, in groups of identical siblings. Figs: 24, 47, 80, 83,
	Descending Child, about to be born, closely related to the **Descending Calf**. Figs: 18, 47, 52, 53, 136, see also 173 for a descending lineage figure
	Child's Head, an abbreviation for the child, which depicts a baby's wrinkled face. It can be identified as the Head of Humbaba. Figs: 4, 34, 46, 85?, 133, 156, 165, 166, 167,
	Girl or Daughter, very similar to figures of the **Naked Goddess**. Figs: 2, 37, 133,
	Lineage Figure represents the male potency within the waters, & the concept of ancestral lineage. Figs: 30, 42, 156, 164, 169, 170, 171, 172, 173, 174,

Symbol Index

	Water-pourers, make offerings to the gods Figs: 70, 149, 178, **Purifiers**, use a bucket & sprinkler to bless sacred objects. Figs: 33, 85,
	Potter, part of the Akkadian creation of man myth. Figs: 178,
	Sex scenes are often set alongside fertility animals. Figs: 43, 52, 132,
	Impregnated Woman, a pose adopted by the mother giving birth & an impregnated woman. Figs: 132, 134, 136,
	Drinking Ritual, women drink a brew. Figs: 52
	Dead Man, carried off to the land of the dead by a bird. Figs: 63, 64,

Celestial Orbs

	Winged Disk, the solar disk with a set of wings, representing the winds and weather. Figs: 10, 19, 24, 33, 41, 67, 78, 79, 80, 82, 95, 99, 105, 112, 113, 115, 138, 153, 174,
	Radiant Star, a common way of representing the sun and stars. Figs: 10, 13, 14, 18, 20, 38, 41, 44, 50, 52, 60, 80, 81, 83, 85, 86, 93, 94, 95, 99, 100, 101, 102, 104, 105, 106, 107, 124, 125, 141, 142, 147, 150, 164, 174,
	Solar disk, portrayed with outflows of water. Figs: 31, 68, 85, 86, 108, 109, 112, 114, 139, 140, 141, 142, 172, 175,
	Lunar Crescent, a narrow crescent with upward pointing horns. Figs: 10, 18, 36, 44, 61, 80, 85, 141, 172,

Symbol Index

	Sun & Moon, combined into a single heavenly icon. Figs: 1, 2, 3, 4, 6, 18, 23, 38, 42, 67, 74, 75, 137, 138, 143, 156,
	Celestial objects, stars & possibly planets with the sun & moon. Fig: 61,
	Pleiades, the only recognisable constellation in ancient art. Figs: 10, 85, 141,

Deities

	Winged Goddess, often seen carrying calves, kids & children. See also the **South Wind** & **Greek Gorgon** Figs: 48, 52, 55, 62, 157,
	Courtesan or Hierodule, closely related to Inanna Figs: 42, 46, 80, 83,
	Naked Goddess, granter of fertility. Figs: 20, 34, 54, 65, 120,
	Breast-cupping Goddess, symbol of motherhood. Figs: 54, 55, 120, 136,
	Mother Goddess with her child. Figs: 22, 135, 136, 178,
	Pot Goddess, symbol of the fertile skies. Figs: 107, 118, 119, 120,
	Storm Goddess, often seen riding upon her storm-griffin. Figs: 70, 71, 72, 73, 74, 75, 80, 174,

Symbol Index

	Solar-Sky Goddess, with rays of radiant light or standing before the sun-disk Figs: 78, 82, 84, 85, 86, 121, 122, 140, 141, 142, 151, 154,
	Eye Deities, the solar eyes of the sky goddess. Figs: 88, 89, 90, 91, 92, 117, 126,
	Hand of a God, a symbol of divine action. Figs: 34, 47, 116,
	Goddess of Life or Gula, Babylonian goddess of midwives & pregnant mothers. Figs: 22, 41, 42, 44, 45,
	Syrian Goddess, with her unusual hat; she sometimes grants boons to the **Lord**. Figs: 6, 24,
	Lama-goddesses, tutelary deities that pray on behalf of the **Lord**, or introduce him into the presence of the gods. Figs: 1, 2, 3, 4, 6, 9, 11, 12, 13, 19, 23, 24, 31, 32, 33, 34, 37, 38, 40, 44, 52, 83, 85, 133, 148,
	Greek Gorgon, a mother image based on Near Eastern goddesses. Figs: 15, 53,
	Sun god, known as Utu & Šamaš, often seen rising into the heavens from the eastern mountains. Figs: 81, 84, 151, 152, 154, 162, 163,
	Cyclopes, an archaic solar god. Figs: 175, 176, 177,
	Water God known as Enki or Ea, with his fertile waters. Figs: 84, 147, 148, 173,

Symbol Index

	Storm God, known as Iškur or Adad, rides in a chariot or on a storm beast. Figs: 70, 71, 72, 73, 74, 75, 151, 156,
	Syrian Thunder God, a distinct form of the **Storm God** seen in northern seals. Figs: 83,
	High God or Enlil, leader of the pantheon, represents the principles of kingship. His chief son is Ninurta, the **Warrior God**. Figs: 143,
	The Warrior God or Ninurta, fights against the mythic monsters & acts as a paragon for the all-conquering king. Figs: 84, 143, 144, 149, 150, 175,
	Battle of the Gods, one set of deities kill another. Figs: 81, 144, 145, 150, 175, **Judgement**, where one set of gods judge another. Figs: 147, 150, 154,

Mythical Beings

	Anzu, lion-headed eagle, symbol of the sky goddess, often seen carrying calves in its long legs. Figs: 14, 49, 51, 61, 63, 66,
	Man-headed bird, male equivalent to Anzu. Figs: 147, 155,
	Bird-man, a genie of the fertile skies. Figs: 41,

Symbol Index

	Lion-demoness, animal symbol of the sky goddess who brings humanity to birth. Figs: 38, 174, **Lamaštu**, a demoness. Figs: 158, 159, 160, 161,
	Demon, without wings. Figs: 81, 105, 168,
	Storm Griffin, unleashing the storm-waters from its mouth. Figs: 70, 71, 72, 73, 74, 75, 156,
	Sphinx, combine elements of lion, human & bird. Figs: 31, 32, 33, 34, 41, 42, 80,
	Bison-man, symbol of the fertile fathers. Figs: 41, 46, 150, 151, 152, 153, 163, 176,
	Goat-fish, symbol of the celestial waters. Figs: 11, 18, 47,
	Fish-human, symbol of the celestial waters. Figs: 9, 52, 77,
	7-headed Dragon, an archaic monster killed by the **Warrior God**. Fig: 144,
	Winged Genie, may be the eagle-form of the Seven Sages. Figs: 21, 85, **Carriers of the calf** without wings. Figs: 132, 135,

Symbol Index

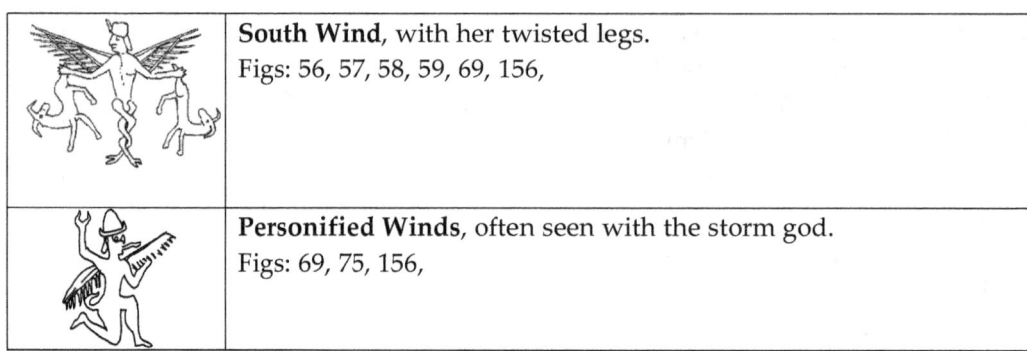	**South Wind**, with her twisted legs. Figs: 56, 57, 58, 59, 69, 156,
	Personified Winds, often seen with the storm god. Figs: 69, 75, 156,

Animals

	Lion, symbol of heavenly light and the birth goddess. Figs: 31, 32, 34, 52, 83, 84, 86, 111, 142, 149, 167, 174, 176,
	Dog, symbol of the birth goddess Gula. Figs: 44, 156, 159, 160,
	Flying bird, symbol of the sky goddess, carries the child-calf down from heaven; broadly equivalent to **Anzu**. Figs: 7, 8, 36, 50, 60, 64, 68, 76, 77, 83, 84, 92, 145, 146, 148, 149,
	Mother Bird, with long legs. Figs: 12, 24, 42, see also 143 for the fate bird of Enlil.
	Chick, symbol of the child. Figs: 7, 13, 14, 15, 24,
	Cow & Calf, symbol of mother goddess & her calf-child. Figs: 5, 29, 36, 79, 93, 94, 95, 96, 97, 98, 130,
	Mother Beast & Star, symbol of a pregnant mother. Figs: 50, 99, 100, 101, 102, 105, 107,

Symbol Index

	Standing Goat, the potent male, often seen eating from a tree. Figs: 10, 12, 25, 27, 28, 29, 30, 31, 32, 34, 40, 44, 85, 131, 163,
	Stag, its radiant horns are a symbol of potency. Figs: 34, 51, 123,
	Descending Calf, symbol of the child descending from heaven, usually carried by a **Winged Goddess** or a **Flying Bird**. Figs: 3, 6, 21, 36, 48, 49, 56, 61, 66, 77, 92, 132, 135, 177,
	Calf, symbol of the foetal child. Figs: 31, 32, 33, 34, 39, 41, 43, 76, 83, 84, 131, 136, 156, 164,
	Bull head abbreviation for parental cattle. Also the heads of goats and wild rams. Figs: 34, 65, 124, 125,
	Calf head, symbol of the child, equivalent to the **Child's Head**. Figs: 4, 32, 35, 65, 133, 170,
	Horns, ancient symbols of fertility and procreative power. Figs: 27, 32, 34, 87, 98, 100, 123, 124, 125, 152, 154, 163,
	Bull Sacrifice, brings on the winter rains. Figs: 73, 74,
	Kid Sacrifice, offered to the gods to gain a child. Figs: 133, 137, 154,
	Pig or **Boar**, Figs: 159, 160,

Symbol Index

	Scorpion, symbol of impregnation. Figs: 36, 37, 42, 43, 98, 116, 121,
	Serpent, symbol of sexual potency & ancestral inheritance. Figs: 52, 159, 160,
	Fish, symbol of the early stages of the foetal child. Figs: 9, 10, 11, 19, 20, 34, 36, 43, 47, 84, 123, 147, 172,
	Frog, symbol of the foetal child in the celestial waters. Figs: 17, 18,
	Monkey, symbol of the later stages of the human foetus. Figs: 19, 20, 21, 33, 41, 42, 46,

Plants

	Tree, their seed is a metaphor for the seed of mankind & they are the source of potency for man & beast. Figs: 5, 8, 10, 25, 26, 27, 28, 29, 30, 33, 34, 44, 45, 77, 84, 93, 94, 96, 99, 105, 113, 145, 152, 157, 178,
	Plant of Life, contains the power of fertility. Figs: 36, 40, 78, 133, 171,
	Palm Tree, the fruit-producing palm is the only recognisable tree in Mesopotamian art. Figs: 48, 130, 146, 149,
	Falling Seeds, symbol of procreation & the birth of offspring. Often seen falling from the skies. Figs: 15, 34, 35, 38, 77, 83, 107, 131, 132, 136, 139, 140, 167, 171, 174,

Symbol Index

	**Flowers**, the seed producing flower, symbol of the fertility goddesses. The clusters of circles are identical to the Date Cluster. Figs: 15, 24, 28, 34, 37, 38, 39, 40, 52, 56, 77, 89, 103, 104, 105, 107, 117, 120?, 126, 127, 128, 129, 130, 131, 132, 133, 134, 135, 136, 137, 138, 142, 174,

Geographic

	Mountain, often adorned with trees. Figs: 25, 26, 29, 30, 33, 77, 84, 96, 113, 149, 150, 154, 162,
	Field system, the seeded fields of the barley farmers. Figs: 128, 129, 139,
	Water, often with **Fish**. Figs: 9, 36, 67, 68, 70, 71, 74, 75, 77, 84, 108, 109, 110, 111, 112, 113, 114, 115, 116, 147, 148, 150?, 172, 173,

Geometric & Cultic

	Cross, a solar symbol representing the annual fertility cycle of animals. Figs: 15, 77, 96, 97, 114, 115,
	Rotating Cross or Swastika, a dynamic version of the **Cross**. Figs: 15, 98, 116,
	Circlet, sacred symbol of the sky goddess. Figs: 141, 142, 151,
	Ankh, Egyptian symbol meaning 'eternal life' and 'physical life'. Commonly used as a symbol of the child. Figs: 23, 24, 41,
	Omega, womb symbol of the birth goddess. Figs: 22, 45, 47, 85,
	Womb, set on its side with curved or straight sides. Figs: 10,

Symbol Index

	Spirals & Interlace, perhaps related to the idea of seed. Figs: 24, 31, 41, 42, 52, 80, 83, 167, 171,
	Overflowing Vase, symbol of the celestial waters and the sexual potencies of living beings. Figs: 9, 18, 33, 41, 42, 77, 82, 113, 117, 118, 119, 120, 148, 172,
	Crook, symbol of Gula in her aspect as shepherdess of mankind. Figs: 42, 44, 45, 47,
	Comb, symbol of baby girls. Figs: 160, 161,
	Spindle, symbol of baby girls. Figs: 161,
	Belt, symbol of a familial bond. Figs: 30, 43, 52, 63, 135, 164, 166, 169, 173, 174,
	Gatepost, often held by attendant figures, may be a form of the **Ring-post**. Figs: 89, 172,
	Tom's Stick, of uncertain derivation but may be related to the **Ring-posts** or the drinking straws seen in **Drinking Scenes**. Figs: 164, 171,
	Ring-posts, symbols of the goddess Inanna commonly seen on cattle-pens and shrines, & used in writing her name. Figs: 74,
	House or **Temple** or **Shrine**, Figs: 85, 89, 141, 157,

Sumerian Signs

Many of the written signs of the cuneiform script are very helpful when trying to establish the meanings of various symbols used in ancient art. Indeed it is fair to say that some of the signs with multiple meanings function as symbols in their own right. There is every reason to suppose that the inventors of the cuneiform script drew extensively upon the older artistic traditions when creating the signs of the world's first writing system (*see pages 112-113*).

SIGN	MEANING	PAGE
	Sumerian A; Akkadian *mû*. 'Water, semen, human progeny'. The Akkadian term refers to 'body fluids' in general and 'amniotic fluids'. The sign depicts the banks of a river or the wave-like motion of flowing water.	22-23, 50
	Sumerian A₂; Akkadian *idu*. 'Arm, labour, wing, horn, side, strength, wage, power'. The sign depicts a human hand and forearm.	58
	Sumerian ADDA; Akkadian *pagru*. 'Corpse, wreck of a boat'. This sign depicts the figure of a man (**LU₂**) with the sign for 'to die' (**UŠ₂**) added.	163
	Sumerian AMA; Akkadian *ummu*. 'Mother'. The sign is a container enclosing a star.	103
	Sumerian AMAR; Akkadian *būru*. 'Calf, young, youngster, chick, son, descendant'. The sign depicts the face of a calf.	18-19, 28, 50
	Sumerian AN; Akkadian *šamû*. 'Sky, heaven, upper, crown (of a tree).' Also refers to An, the god of Heaven, and is used a classifier written before the name of 'divine beings'. Usually described as a star, this sign is probably a glyph of the sunlit heavens.	14, 83, 98, 102, 118
	Sumerian AŠ; Akkadian *išten*. 'One, Single One' A single stroke, the most basic sign.	99
	Sumerian AŠME; Akkadian *šamšatu*. 'Radiance & sun-disk ornament'. A combination of two signs making up a cross.	93-94, 99
	Sumerian DIM₃ 'Corpse', also used in the name of various 'demons' like Lamaštu. Probably a winged figure based on the form of man (**LU₂**).	163

	Sumerian GIDIM; Akkadian *eṭemmu*. 'Ghost'. Loosely based on the figure of a man (**LU₂**).	163
	Sumerian GUD; Akkadian *alpu*. 'Bull, ox, cattle, calf, lion' and in later times occasionally 'ghost'. Depicts the face of a horned bull.	103
	Sumerian GURUN; Akkadian *inbu*. 'Flower, fruit, flower shaped object and sexual appeal' Probably depicts a simplified version of the radiant flower.	119-120
	Sumerian LIL₂; Akkadian *zīqīqu*. 'Wind, breeze, & ghost'. The sign apparently depicts a reed mat.	141
	Sumerian LU₂; Akkadian *amēlu*. 'Man & person'. The simplified figure of a man.	162
	Sumerian ME; Akkadian *parṣu*. 'Being, divine properties enabling cosmic activity, office, cultic ordinance'. The sign is of unknown origin.	99
	Sumerian MUL; Akkadian *kakkabu*. 'Star, constellation, planet, comets and meteors'. Three stars.	125-126
	Sumerian MUNUS; Akkadian *sinništu*. 'Woman or Female'. Read as **GALA** it refers to the 'vulva or female genitals'. An image of the female genitals.	83
	Sumerian MUŠ₃; Divine Standard made of reeds. Used in the name of Inanna.	79
	Sumerian NAM₂. 'Noble, lord'. Perhaps depicts a seat of some sort.	83
	Sumerian NIN; Akkadian *bēltu*. 'Lady or queen, mistress, owner, lord'. The sign for 'woman' set upon the sign for 'noble'.	83

Sumerian Signs

	Sumerian NUMUN; Akkadian *zēru*. 'Seed' of plants and cereals.; in Akkadian it also means 'sown land, human semen, offspring & descendants' Presumably depicts a sprouting seed.	40-41, 50
	Sumerian U₈; Akkadian *immertu, lahru*. 'Sheep & Ewe'. Two bull's heads (**GUD**) within a container.	103
	Sumerian UD; Akkadian *ūmu*. 'Day & sun, heat, fever & summer'. Depicts the sun rising between two mountains.	144
	Sumerian UDUG; Akkadian *utukku*. 'Evil Demon & figurine of a demon' Closely related to the sign for 'ghost' (**GIDIM**) with the addition of a **Tar**-sign meaning 'to cut', as in cutting fate.	163
	Sumerian UŠ₂; Akkadian *mâtu*. A sign of multiple meanings and readings. It is often used to write the verb 'to die'. The sign is of unknown origin.	163

Word Index

Because I have taken a visual approach to indexing, the following word index is largely limited to referencing the principal discussions of the symbols and various proper names.

Ages, Three 132, 154
An 63, 94
Ancestors – see Fathers
Ankh 33-34
Anzu 61-63, 66, 69, 72, 79, 108, 134
Asherah 134
Aštar 86
Battle of Mu (Chinese) 133
Battle of the Gods 85-86, 131-139
Belt 122, 149-150
Bird
    Bird of Death 68-70
    Bird-man 132, 134, 139
    Chick 27-28
    Flying Bird 20-21
    Storm Bird 72-73, 80
Bison 136, 147
Bison-man 54, 57, 132, 136-138
Calf 17-19
    Descending Calf 18
    Cow & Calf 19
Catal Huyuk 69-70
Cave 152
Celestial Waters – see Waters of Heaven
Child 14-15
    Descending Child 30
    Child's Head 18, 150
Circlet 137
Clay (in creation of man) 158-160
Comb 143
Courtesan 54, 57, 82-83, 88-89
Cow of Heaven 19, 94 (see also Calf)
Cross 99, 109,
    Rotating Cross 109, 114, 115
Cyclopes 156-157
Date Cluster 116, 117-118
Dead, Cult of 160-161
Death of Man & Birds 68-70, 71
Demons 43, 141-143, 156, 163-164
Eagle 147
E-Anna 91

Eclipse (of the sun) 94
Enheduana 139
Enki-Ea 85, 134-135, 158, 159
Enkidu 67, 69, 160-161
Enlil 77, 131, 141, 158
Eriškigal 145
Excarnation 69, 142, 162
Eye Idols 95
Eyes 94-96, 147
Fathers 37, 54, 82, 154-155
Fields as Chequer-boards 117
Fish 22-25
Flower 42-43, 101-102, 104, 116-127, 150 (see also Date Cluster)
Freya 93
Frog 29-30
Geštue 158
Ghost 141, 145-146, 156, 158, 160, 162-164
Gilgamesh 67, 98, 141, 150, 151-152, 160-161
Goatfish 25
God
    Moon God 145
    Mountain God 80
    Storm God 74-78
    Sun God 137-138 (see also Utu & Šamaš)
    Sun God & gaze 94, 95, 97, 144, 147
Goddess
    Bird Goddess 60-71
    Celestial Goddess 85-96
    Goddess of Life 53-59
    Mother Goddess 32, 65
    Naked Goddess 31
    Storm Goddess 74-84
    Syrian Goddess 20, 34
    Womb Goddesses 159, 161
Gorgon Goddess 28, 64
Griffin 75-78, 107-108
Gudea Inscriptions 93-94, 138
Gula 55-56, 57
Hair 112, 114
Hand symbol 58-59, 115

Word Index

Harpies 68-69
Hat 149
Hierodule 86, 88
Horns 100, 101, 114, 138
Humbaba 149-156
Inanna 76, 77, 78-79, 83, 85-89, 90-93, 96, 124-127, 139-139, 146, 147-148, 156, 161
Išhara 54-55
Iškur 76
Ištar 85-87, 139
Juno Lucina 121-122
Knots & Bindings 122
Lama Goddess 14, 15, 135
Lamaštu 141-143
Light 89-90, 91, 92-96, 97, 124-127
Lilu 140-141
Lineage Figure 37, 149, 151, 153-155
Lion 92, 107-108, 147
   Lion-headed Demon 43, 156
   Lion-headed Fountain 108
Lord 13, 15
Lucina 121-122
Mami 159, 161
Marriage Bed 54-55
Me 86, 88, 99
Mermaid, Merman 22
Monkey 30-32
Nanše 148
Navel of the Sky 24, 112
Necromancy 146, 161
Nergal 145
Ninhursag 62-63
Ninlil 141
Ninsun 98
Nintur 63, 158, 159
Ninurta 131-132, 135-136
Omega symbol 59, 114
Orphans 148, 152
Planets 125-126
Plants & their powers 35-37
Pleiades 92
Sacrifice
   Bull Sacrifice 77-78
   Human Sacrifice 164-165
   Sacrifice of a god 158

Šakkan 126
Šamaš 85, 90, 91, 139, 144-146, 151, 152, 156
Šapaš 90-91, 144, 145, 146
Sargon 139
Saw (of sun god) 144-145
Scorpion 54-55, 109, 140
Seed of Mankind 22, 40-41, 42-43
Shawl (of Courtesan) 83
Slain Heroes 132, 138
Spindle 143
Standing Goat 38-39
Stars 125-127
   Star & Mother 100-104
   Shooting Stars 67
Šumma Izbu 33
Sun-disk 105-106, 017, 109, 124-127
Swastika – see Cross
Tell Brak 95
Torch 89-90, 91, 147
Touch of Goddess 21, 61, 143
Tree of Life 39-42
Ugarit, City of 90
Underworld & the Dead 145-146, 160-165
Ur, City of 164
Utu 85, 91, 94, 96, 144, 146-148, 152, 156, 157
Vase
   Over-flowing 22
   Vase Goddess 103-104, 111-112
Vedas
   Vedic quotes 24, 71
   Vedic Sun God 114
Venus 85, 86, 87, 89
Vesica Pisces 112
Waters of Heaven 22-25, 53, 79-80, 105-115
   Water Cycle 105-107
Weather Patterns 66, 79
Widows 148
Wild Sheep (planets) 126
Winds 65-67, 74, 78, 140, 142
   South Wind 65-66, 140
Winged Disk 30, 81
Winged Genie 31-32
Yama 71

Prehistoric Eras

The following tables map out the principal periods of Mesopotamian history. The first table (*below*) concentrates on the Pre-historic periods and the second table on the Historic Era.

DATE BCE	SOUTH IRAQ	NORTH IRAQ	PERIODS	MY AGES
7000	[*largely uninhabited*]		NEOLITHIC [*rainfall farming, livestock domestication & villages*]	FIRST AGE
		PROTO HASSUNA		
6000		HASSUNA SAMARRA		
	EARLY UBAID	HALAF	CHALCOLITHIC PERIOD [*irrigation farming*] [*stamp seals*]	
5000				
	LATE UBAID	NORTHERN UBAID		
4000	EARLY URUK		[*first large cities*] [*cylinder seals*]	
	LATE URUK	URUK	[*invention of notation writing*]	SECOND AGE
3000	JEMDET NASR	NINEVITE 5		
	EARLY DYNASTIC [*Gilgamesh*]		EARLY BRONZE AGE [*palaces, city-states & full writing*]	
	AKKADIAN	AKKADIAN		THIRD AGE
	NEO-SUMERIAN			
2000	UR III	UR III		

DATE BCE	SOUTH IRAQ	NORTH IRAQ	PERIODS	MY AGES
3000	JEMDET NASR	NINEVITE 5		SECOND AGE
	EARLY DYNASTIC		EARLY BRONZE AGE	
	AKKADIAN	AKKADIAN		THIRD AGE
	NEO-SUMERIAN			
2000	UR III	UR III	MIDDLE BRONZE AGE	
	OLD BABYLONIAN	OLD ASSYRIAN		
1500	KASSITE OR MIDDLE BABYLONIAN	MITANNIAN	LATE BRONZE AGE	
		MIDDLE ASSYRIAN		
			EARLY IRON AGE	
	Period of disruption			
1000		Period of disruption		
	ASSYRIAN DOMINANCE	NEO-ASSYRIAN EMPIRE		
	NEO-BABYLONIAN			
500	PERSIAN EMPIRE		MIDDLE IRON AGE	
	Alexander 331-323 BCE			
	HELLENISTIC			
	PARTHIAN			
000				
	SASANIAN		LATE IRON AGE	
500 CE				
			MIDDLE AGES	
	Advent of Islam 636 CE			

www.ingramcontent.com/pod-product-compliance
Lightning Source LLC
Chambersburg PA
CBHW080959170526

45158CB00010B/2839